Innocent Victims In The Global War On Terror

Dr. M.A. Salloomi

authorHOUSE®

AuthorHouse™ UK Ltd.
500 Avebury Boulevard
Central Milton Keynes, MK9 2BE
www.authorhouse.co.uk
Phone: 08001974150

First published by AuthorHouse 7/22/2011

ISBN: 978-1-4490-8526-1 (sc)

<u>*Dedication*</u>

To the victims of the global campaign against charities from among the recipients: poor, orphans, widows, and sick people whom the relief organizations were prevented to reach and the donors, the workers and the defenders of humanitarian work around the world who are struggling to bring out the truth.

AND THE TRAGEDY CONTINUES

2 billions: The number of people affected by natural disasters in last ten years.

80 millions, The estimated number of people affected by natural disasters in 2007

629$ billion: The value of property destroyed by natural disasters

(Http:/ olom.info/ib3/ikonboard.)

CONTENTS

Foreword

By Former U.S. Congressman Paul Findley

Very few people in the private sector and very few –unfortunately-in the public sector understand the vital importance of charitable organizations in meeting human tragedy, especially the tragedy spawned by the war on terror. I believe the book "Innocent Victims in the War on Terror" is a timely and effective call for action by government leaders and I hope they will respond to it quickly and thoroughly. It is obvious that what has been done already has undercut the priceless contributions of charitable organizations, and unless changes are made in the work of the government and its endeavor for the war on terror, there will be many more millions of people who will suffer needlessly. The organizational structure of charities is already one of the victims of the war, which resulted in unmentioned and untold calamities that are intensifying the toll of war in human terms. The book has done a splendid job in presenting these calamities and pointing to the steps taken to restore some semblance of order and goodwill and effective service by Non- Governmental Organizations.

NGOs have been a part of international life for a long time and I am sure that the people who have been framing the war on terror took steps without any historical knowledge of the past, without any appreciation of what has been done before. They need to do that even this late, and this book provides the historical foundation upon which the corrective action, the remedy, the repair can be accomplished. NGOs have been historically and vitally important to our nation and to all nations and that fact I am afraid has been almost overlooked totally by those who put together the voice on the war on terrorism. This war on terrorism has been misdirected

1

from the start. This is only one aspect of the war on terror that has brought more damage than gain to our human brethren.

The book depicts an underreported story of human tragedy and the author demonstrates in a unique skill and impartiality the human impact along with the statistical information that, taken together, is a very telling story which deserves urgent attention by our current power structure and those who can influence that structure. As far as I can tell, the mass media has totally missed this compelling story and the author has done a great service in presenting it so well that any editor, any reporter, and any student will find it compelling and highly important. I think the author has done, as far as I know and can tell, an absolutely comprehensive study of the problem, has condensed it to a very brief document, and has done it with the lucidity that the human tragedy deserves. The book is brief enough that it should have the attention of the opinion-makers, the power structure in our government, and the private sector.

Very few people outside the non-governmental arena appreciate the extent of the services of human character rendered by the charities. This book along with its other attributes is an introduction, a resource, and a reference document that can help step by step those who are determined to rebuild the structure of the affected charities as quickly as can be done.

Moreover, a war on terror is something new in human experience. I am not sure there is a good rationale or a plan for a war on terror, this war has been put together in a haphazard way, without much fore-thought, our law-makers jumped in the challenge and made rules that were not carefully thought. So we have to eradicate the bad deeds of yesterday and have as our goal the resurrection and the strengthening of the non-governmental organizations. That needs to be our goal and this book speaks perfectly through it.

Paul Findley
May 24, 2006

Introduction

A new century has heralded a new world with new opponents, new wars and the anguished cries of new victims: the innocent victims of the "War on Terror", that still to be defined enemy.

What distinguishes the victims of this new global war, the "War on Terror," is the fact that they are as much from among the wealthy as they are from the poor. They represent nations, organizations, and individuals and the victims come from countries of both the North and the South, the East and the West.

There are also the victims of the victims, and they are the most innocent of all. The most poignant of human emotions are inflamed when one witnesses the crises and disasters that have so stricken people around the world. The consequences are poverty, starvation, fear, sickness, ignorance, death. Above all that, the millions of refugees pouring into camps unfit to house even cattle, let alone humans. It is a world where the rights of humans and those of animals are slighted with the same casual ease. Former US Secretary of State Colin Powell noted that: "Half the people on this planet, about 3 billion human beings, live in destitute poverty. More than a billion people lack clean water. Two billion lack adequate sanitation and electrical power."[1]

The last few years have seen devastating human crises occurring all over the world: in Afghanistan, Bosnia, Chechnya, the Congo, Iraq, Kashmir, Kosovo, Pakistan, Palestine, Rwanda, and Sudan. On December 2005, the UN Food and Agriculture Organization (FAO) warned that "an estimated two million people in Somalia are facing an imminent humanitarian emergency and acute livelihood crisis over the next six months"[2] In January 2006, the FAO released statistics to the effect that 3 million people in Niger[3] and 11 million in the Horn of Africa are facing starvation[4]. The Tsunami of 2004/2005 is sufficient a tragedy to render the world speechless. Half a million people, roughly 250 thousand from Indonesia alone, have either been killed or declared missing. Over a million displaced people have been struggling against death on a daily basis. The magnitude of this crisis far exceeds the capacity of the world's relief organizations. The states themselves have been unable to cope with the demands placed upon them.

The impact of these disasters is compounded by the attempt to focus people's attention on the singular threat of terrorism, diverting it from other, perhaps more important, dangers. In the findings and recommendations of the UN High level Panel on Threats, Challenges and Change, the most serious threats listed were poverty, sickness, and environmental pollution, and thereafter warfare among nations. While listed as a threat, the Panel reported that "terrorism flourishes in environments of despair, humiliation, poverty, political oppression, extremism and human rights abuse; it also flourishes in contexts of regional conflict and foreign occupation; and it profits from weak State capacity to maintain law and order."[5] The Panel chairman added in the report:

> *"The United Nations must be able to articulate an effective and principled counter-terrorism strategy that is respectful of the rule of law and the universal observance of human rights. One of the obstacles hitherto, I believe, has been the inability of the membership to agree on a definition of terrorism."[6]*

These circumstances reflect the contradictions of the new world in which we live, where billions of dollars are wasted on wars waged on false pretenses instead of being used to alleviate poverty and improve the standard of living of the destitute. The effects of humanitarian crises are compounded by what some critics have characterized as the U.S. administration's deliberate isolation of many relief organizations on account of their religious affiliation and their political independence. The history of this new century's beginning records that the most conspicuous of these innocent victims are Islamic charities, relief organizations, and educational institutions, as well as other organizations that promote justice. Since September 11, 2001, many Islamic charities have been closed down and subjected to sweeping allegations of terror financing, allegations not backed by any evidence. Such charities often get suffocated by crippling administrative or financial regulations, which prevent them from working along with other international relief efforts on a global level, where more - not less - participation is needed and the void thus created becomes deeply felt.[7]

Alvin Toffler, in his 1990 book *Powershift*, discusses the "Global Gladiators" and the "new competitors" and mentions among them the rapidly spreading global non-governmental organizations whose strength has started to rival that of nations and governments. "A new group of power-seekers are leaping onto the world stage and seizing sizable chunks of the clout once controlled by nations alone"[8] wrote Toffler.

Many governments are looking at these international organizations, including Islamic charities as elements of instability, as parties that do not fall under the framework of nations, are considered obstacles to the Capitalist control of the global marketplace. It seems that non-governmental organizations which had been instrumental in bringing the Communist threat down have come to the end of their usefulness at the end of the Cold War, because the new competitors around the world would benefit from them. Thus any organization whose programs and policies do not coincide with Western political, military, economic, and cultural concepts can be perceived as threatening.

This book aims at uncovering the truth concerning the declared objectives of the campaign against Islamic charities and its real motives. It depicts the magnitude of the problem that besets Islamic charities around the world, on account of which the governments and people the world over are experiencing political pressure. The book also documents the suffering of the charities' recipients as a consequence of the disruption of the charities.

Sound humanitarian values, regardless of differences in religion, culture, and political views, affirm the need to combat international terrorism. However, the enemy must first be properly defined, and then the fight must be conducted on the basis of moral principles, the rule of law, respect for the sovereignty of nations, and the human rights of all. Likewise, our common humanity confirms the need for the truth to be freely told and to stand by the oppressed and to expose the oppressor.

This book has been written following consultation with more than 150 Islamic organizations in seventeen countries around the world after September 11, in sincere efforts to verify the American allegations. Whenever possible, news reports, opinions, and analytical observations, and commentary have been sought from their original sources. I have endeavored to take most of the statements from American and Western sources. In addition, personal interviews and field research was conducted to ensure that the book will be factual and accurate.

I wish to thank and acknowledge all those who helped me complete this work. I wish to particularly thank Dr. Wendell Belew, member of the Friends of Charities Association (FOCA), and other lawyers for their constructive advice. I would like to especially thank Professor Ralph Salmi of California State University, San Bernardino, Department of Political Science, for his meticulous revision of the book. Finally, I would like to thank all those who contributed their advice, opinions, and corrections in the final stages towards preparing the manuscript for publication.

Dr. M. A. Salloomi
May/01/2011
Email: info@3rdsector.org

Chapter I

The New Competitors and
the Shift of Power

The rise of Non-Governmental Organizations (NGOs)

During the latter part of the twentieth century, non-governmental organizations – both Islamic and non-Islamic - worked to create a peaceful power that was a true social expression of solidarity among mankind. The role played by these organizations in disaster relief and development– as well as in international relations – kept increasing both in magnitude and importance.

Newsweek discussed the importance of this power on the occasion of the 2004/2005 Tsunami: "The concerns have been prompted in part by the growth of the nonprofit sector, a $1 trillion industry that is far less regulated than the corporate world."[9]

It also said:

"According to Johns Hopkins, employment within NGOs grew 3 times faster than overall employment in nine major developed countries over the course of the 1990s. Even global recession hasn't slowed the growth - American nonprofit organizations have

increased employment by about four percent a year since 2000,
even though as many other industries are cutting back. The result
is that NGOs are now operating in an environment, which is just
as competitive - if not more so - than any other global industry."[10]

The Internet allowed these organizations to form new alliances. Alliances between environmental and peoples' organizations were established in this way in publishing a declaration against the World Trade Organization that was signed by around 1500 organizations, running the gamut from citizens groups, consumer rights groups, environmental protection groups, and other types of organizations.

Some governments consider the unwillingness of these alliances to distinguish between wealthy and poor nations a severe issue. This solidarity over the Internet enabled the free exchange of information concerning regional misconduct towards workers and their rights, consumer rights, environmental decline, and other matters usually concealed by governments and other agencies. These NGOs were able to make such things public.

These NGOs were able to confront government and corporate giants with documentation and hard evidence. The governments and corporations were unable to make light of the evidence or discredit it. *The Economist* repeatedly posed the troublesome question: Are they "the first steps toward an 'international civil society' (whatever that might be)? Or do they represent a dangerous shift of power to unelected and unaccountable special-interest groups?" [11] This last question conceals a veiled accusation: Since, according to *The Economist*, these organizations are unelected, then they are lawless and illegitimate and need to be combated and regarded as criminal.

This is the attitude of some governments and corporations towards these international organizations that come to the defense of the rights of citizens groups and that have achieved important victories by presenting free scientific, health, and social services to humanity through their independent and effective efforts. This strong competition with the governments has reached a vast global extent, which has caused some of the world's peoples to give some of those organizations more credence than they give their own governments.

Non-governmental relief organizations have been the ones working to realize the aspirations of the people for a better life, trying to save the lives of numerous victims of war, famine, and economic exploitation. The people have been aware of the importance of the role played by these NGOs which have become the common denominator among the nations of the world. They have strengthened the role of societies and individuals and have brought about a continuous human interaction and cooperation in the general lives of the people on both the domestic and the international levels. Various governments, political organizations, and economic blocks have tried to influence this phenomenon to use or exploit it for their own political, economic, or cultural ends – to bring it within their own geo-political framework.

The governmental control, or political exploitation, which some non-governmental humanitarian and relief organizations suffer from has, without doubt, weakened their positive role. Rather it has planted doubts in the worldwide public opinion sectors whenever it becomes a distinctive feature of the policies of some countries. By contrast, genuine humanitarian and relief organizations strive to keep their work free and independent and for the sake of mercy and humanitarian ends only.

Aspects of NGOs Strength

These NGOs constitute a non-governmental power for realizing political and humanitarian aims and for protecting the environment. The independent organizations among them play a forceful role in opposing greedy corporations' interests. In this context, Professor Adeeb Dimitry said that non-governmental organizations have become an obstacle to the programs of capitalist nations after having been a useful means for them during the Cold War. [12]

Professor Dimitry writes: "Called 'citizens groups' by some, these NGOs have played an important role on the global level, which was apparent in the Seattle confrontations. Their role is at times more important than political and labor parties, and they have proven very capable in mobilizing a great number of people through the internet for resistance and confrontations at a time when the peoples of both developing and developed countries, and equally from the South and the North, have been excluded from participation."[13]

The same author mentions the question put forward by *The Economist* which provided a description and a thorough survey of these organizations around the globe on the occasion of their prominent role at the Seattle confrontation. The question was about the role that these organizations play in today's world. The question was not free from a tinge of worry: Will these organizations bring about a greater degree of democracy, or more correctly, widespread justice around the world? Or will they lead to anarchy and bring instability for the established political authority?

This line of questioning, in and of itself, shows the extent to which the possessors of economic power are fearful and worried by the extent and influence of these developments. This is what has and continues to spur governments, particularly non-democratic ones, to restrict and contain these organizations and to enact measures to curtail their activities.

The Economist further comments on the activities of these organizations before and during the Seattle Summit, when these organizations had a clear and unified aim: "They were well organized. They built unusual coalitions...They had a clear agenda - to derail the talks. And they were masterly users of the media." [14]

During the 1992 Earth Summit in Rio de Janeiro, these organizations stirred up public opinion about greenhouse gasses. Likewise, in 1994, they were able to dominate the celebrations on the anniversary of the global banking system where they raised the banner of "fifty years is enough". They campaigned for a review of the objectives of banks, their system of loans, and their business approaches. They also brought up the waiving of third-world debt, and they were able to bring about a similar alliance to campaign for debt relief for the poorest of nations.

The activities of the NGOs are not limited to confronting governments, but also to confronting major multinational corporations. The Nike Corporation was faced with a campaign from these organizations on account of bad working conditions in its overseas factories. Nestlé was likewise confronted for selling powdered milk for use by infants in poor countries. Monsanto was confronted for its genetically modified foods. Shell also faced a campaign. Organizations representing societies, ethnic groups, and nationalities have become more powerful, have more influence and effects, and have become the focus of serious study.

Global Spread and Future Threat:

The Economist followed this detailed examination by saying: "Over the past decade, NGOs and their memberships have grown hugely... [T]he social and economic shifts of this decade have given them new life. The end of communism, the spread of democracy in poor countries, technological change, and economic integration - globalization in short - have created fertile soil for the rise of NGOs. Globalization itself has exacerbated a host of worries: over the environment, labor rights, human rights, consumer rights and so on. Democratization and technological progress have revolutionized the way in which citizens can unite to express their disquiet."[15]

The same publication estimates the number of these organizations worldwide to presently be around 26,000 – though it seems that they only considered the influential ones – after having numbered only around six thousand in 1960. They give the Global Fund for Defending the Environment (Greenpeace) as an example of this growth. Presently, the organization boasts around five million members, though in 1985 their membership was a mere 75,000. The danger of these organizations is aggravated by the lightening fast exchange of communication, thanks to the internet. Relationships are maintained, and alliances are quickly formed, which used to be slow and costly.

The New Competitors and the Shift of Power

A major battle broke out just as the dust of the September 11 bombings began to settle, a battle with American actions to combat terrorism on one side and the forces of moderation, freedom, democracy, and peace on the other. This battle is being waged both within the United States and abroad. This other side is represented by nations, independent international organizations, regional NGOs, and downtrodden peoples throughout the world.

A large cross-section of the American people from all walks of life yearns for a return of civil liberties and popular democracy which have been reduced greatly in the aftermath of the attack on the World Trade Center. This yearning for civil liberties and peace exists globally on the level of peoples and governments, who fear that this unjust despotism will classify some broadcast and print media, independent websites, educational centers, intellectual movements, and even some independent international organizations among the "new competitors", for fear of a transfer of power or authority, and because they are in conflict with the policy of the new era, the era of American hegemony and warfare under the cover of "the War on Terror".

Many factors have begun to present a challenge to American hegemony: civil liberties, activities of non-governmental political, humanitarian, and rights organizations, especially the independent and powerful ones, possession of information and the means to attain it, freedom of the press, power of knowledge and technological capabilities. All of these factors have become competing powers and obstacles to global hegemony. The ways of the old world are to come to an end by the marginalization of the role of nations and peoples' organizations and the return of imperialism. Likewise, among the many features of this new world are the programs of the new American century, the greater Middle East plans, and the exclusion of the Palestinian issue.

The New Competitors (*The Global Gladiators*)

Alvin Toffler's viewpoint along with other authors, explain why international NGOs, whom he called "Global Gladiators", are considered a danger to governments and especially to the American hegemony.

Alvin Toffler sees that along with the spread of globalization on many levels, new problems have appeared that cannot be addressed by nations working within their own borders. Nations are faced with increasing difficulties in controlling the outflow of money, people, information, disease, and pollution. On account of this, some countries appear weak and ineffective.

Toffler mentions the role of NGOs, according to what he sees as their future dangers. With the spread of globalization at many levels, "nations are having a harder time controlling their own borders, currencies, ecological conditions and information flows," Toffler wrote.

> *"So there are many signs that the power of the nation-state is diminishing in today's world, while new political entities (or old revived ones) grow in relative clout. I believe we'll see all kinds of new political units spring up –many made possible by the internet. We may see a league of city-states allied with a group of NGOs - all electronically connected, 'Internetted' and perhaps with weapons of mass destruction available to them."[16]*

This danger is most felt in developed countries: "Wherever you have advanced economies," Toffler said, "centralized governments will have to give up power to maintain power. And when you add regions to transnational NGOs, religions, and corporations, plus financial markets that now dwarf central banks, it becomes clear that nation-states will have to come to terms with the non-national Global Gladiators."[17] The "global gladiators" have become even more important contenders for power in the global arena, and Islam is one among them, says Toffler, "Islam is clearly a major player whose interests reach far beyond any individual nation."

Additionally, he says: "There are the fast-multiplying NGOs ranging from Green Peace to thousands of lesser known but very active groups. They are internet –savvy and gaining power."[18] And these NGOs are going to be demanding more say in the global scene. "The United Nations, which until now has been little more than a trade association of nation-states, may eventually be compelled to provide representation for non-states too."

Indeed, Toffler sees it as imperative to confront these new competitors when he says: "But whatever form the global organizations of tomorrow assume, they will have to pay more attention, both positive and negative, to the Global Gladiators."[19] These NGOs are at times allied with the nations and at others form alliances to abort the nations' plans (such as Green Peace against France's nuclear tests). In either case, says Toffler, nation-states and other "competitors" should take these NGOs into account in their decision making, more than at any time before.[20] Toffler even went further to say that nation-states will inevitably attempt to control or diminish the role of these NGOs; the new harsh measures introduced to fight terrorism may be used against the "global gladiators".[21]

The Reactions of Nations

Toffler makes clear that some countries are ready and willing. The War on Terror has brought about a wave of changes among nations. One nation after another has started to intensify its national security regulations, often at the expense of the very civil liberties that had been the defining principles of those nations. These regulations give many countries increased capabilities to monitor local NGOs, including legitimate opposition groups that do not resort to violence or terror tactics. The events of September 11 have facilitated the introduction of broader restrictions on NGOs.

Even in the more democratic Western countries, like the United States, France, Germany, and Britain, the authorities are increasing their supervisory powers and broadening their authority to eavesdrop on telephone conversations and e-mails. They are tightening immigration laws and intensifying the surveillance of their borders. They are also weakening the restrictions against monitoring bank accounts. For instance, the German Government has began banning any religious organization it deems harmful to the democratic process or that advocates violence.

Beyond that, countries are also taking precautionary steps and tending towards the exchange of intelligence among the various national security agencies within them and with other countries. Despite the protests of civil liberties organizations in many countries, it has become clear that some of the tough measures necessary to fight transnational terrorism threats may be used not only against terrorists, but also against other "global gladiators", says Toffler.[22] At the same time, he says, they may be used against NGOs for political purposes, and in reality there are specific cases where the pursuit of some of these organizations is necessary, because, Toffler says, some organizations which appear innocent, providing education and help for the poor, but are secretly financing terrorism. It is difficult for some nations to penetrate or monitor these organizations without expanding the jurisdictions of its security apparatus, he says.[23]

Illegitimate Powers and their Global Extent

Toffler identifies the threat of NGOs on governments, explaining that states' degree of weakness varies from state to state according to certain factors and situations, but in general, the state becomes weak when it loses its citizens' trust. Today, most politicians - almost globally - are seen as selfish, corrupt, and lacking competence. Therefore, the legitimacy of the representatives and rulers are put into question. Such is the case of the United States during the Bush-Gore elections in 2000 and thereafter, where the election results were settled by the Supreme Court. If in this case the nations are losing their legitimacy, the NGOs have none to lose, says Toffler.[24]

International organizations may be considered illegitimate, Toffler says, thrusting their nose into the internal affairs of governments, that they are an obstacle to the economic development of nations. He sees that the NGOs are accountable to nobody but their members, and cannot claim that they represent popular circles bigger than the number of their members. For example: there is nobody who elected Green Peace and empowered it for the defense of environmental issues, and nobody elected Oxfam and empowered it for the defense of famine victims. Until there is a system to grant legitimacy to these NGOs and until they acquire some jurisdictions, they will remain in the service of a small section of people who are often far removed from the NGOs' field of action.[25]

Capitalist countries in particular those who are experiencing the growth of NGOs, which Toffler describes as "illegitimate powers" give us a clear understanding of the new manner in which these NGOs are being dealt with. It is not merely a counterattack that these nations are launching against possible sources of terrorism and violence as was the case with the large number of police forces that had been mobilized to contain the protests against globalizations in various parts of the world, but, as Toffler explains, this is the implementation of new tools that nations can employ on the domestic, regional, and international levels to curb the growing power of NGOs.

One international policy analyst, Dominique Moïsi of the Institute for International Relations located in Paris, France made a study of these changes. He writes in the *Financial Times*: "In the post-cold-war global age, the state's legitimacy and competence appeared to be waning. Caught between the emergence of civil society and the growing power of transnational corporations, the state appeared to be fighting a rearguard battle. With security a priority the state is back with a vengeance."[26] In any case, it is not clear up to now whether the state's clinging to power will continue for long or whether the state is capable to contain the spread of the NGOs that seek to get seats at the green tables which were previously restricted to diplomats and where global decisions are taken. Should we expect then a violent and revengeful return?[27]

After the fall of the Soviet Union, which held it in check as its main competitor, America worked to marginalize or weaken those international organizations by refusing to comply with any international treaty that restrains its ambitions and its global hegemony. Among these - by way of example and by no means an exhaustive list - are the following:

1. America refused to sign the resolutions to limit environmental pollution and preserve the Earth that conflict with the interests of major American corporations, like those issued at the Earth Summit. Another example is America's pulling out from the Kyoto accords in 2001.[28]

2. America refused the most important of the Durban resolutions, in South Africa, 2002, concerning racism and the environment.

3. America refused to join or participate in the new World Court against war crimes that was ratified by approximately 160 nations. America was joined in its refusal by India and Israel.

4. America pulled out of its second mutual agreement on arms proliferation with the Soviet Union.

5. America used its veto power more than any other country. America works more than any other country to dissolve the United Nations under various pretexts, among them "reform". Former American senator Paul Findley expressed this when he said late in the year 2003: "Most Americans are not even aware that President Bush has decided that the United States must police the world and that Congress, at his request, has authorized him to undertake preemptive military assaults anywhere he deems it necessary and to impose severe restrictions on the liberty of U.S. citizens and others living in our country."[29]

Has America after the fall of the Soviet Union become above the law? Or are the moves to marginalize, weaken, attack, and immobilize non-governmental organizations a preparation for future wars and for overt hegemony, as some analysts claim?

The growth of international organizations is being carefully monitored by imperialist circles. It may be true that non-profit international organizations, Islamic charities among them, used to be regarded as something positive in the previous era for their contribution to the fall of the Soviet Union, politically, ideologically, and even militarily. It seems that the blossoming of these non-governmental organizations was a requirement of the Cold War to defeat the Communist adversary that did not recognize civil organizations. In fact, many of them were used to help bring down the Soviet Union.

This idea is confirmed by the fact that the Soviet Union's imperialism and its communist ideology were opposed to the very idea of civil organizations, as mentioned by Benthall and Jourdan: "Hard-line state socialists opposed charity...To push this line of argument to its logical conclusion and outlaw all charity is however to place all power in the hands of the state. This was the policy of the former Soviet bloc, since the earliest days of the Bolshevik revolution. The network of the Russian charitable organizations was as far as possible abolished by the Soviet as inimical to the principles governing human relationships in socialist state."[30]

After the defeat of Communism, these international organizations, and Islamic charities in particular, which are an expression of freedom and democracy for the world's people have become a danger to the new global imperialism, and especially to American imperialism. Indeed, they have become a powerful competitor entailing a new era, that of a "War on Terror" and unilateral politics to neutralize their power. This is being carried out on a global level, differing in approach from one type of organization to another.

Dr. Haytham Manna, President of the International Bureau for Humanitarian NGOs (IBH) in Paris, says:

> *"The phenomenon of non-governmental organizations is the peaceful revolution involving, in terms of secularization, the most threats for the centers of power. Because it establishes the biggest gathering of the organized society that considers the decentralization as one of its progress factors it becomes difficult to control it by any dictatorship of money, weapons, oil, or ideology. It also establishes the only field where the abduction of the private initiative is useless; whatever are the repressive politics and the offenses against the liberties."[31]*

Could it be that the War on Terror, coming after the Cold War and the emergence of unilateral power, has among its objectives the eradication of the opposition or the "new competitors," demoting them to the ranks of illegitimate powers, as Dominique Moïsi mentioned? Among the "illegitimate powers" are the United Nations, NGOs, and other powerful organizations with a global reach. Indeed, among them is every sort of NGO, each of which is a competitor in one way or another.

Finally, perhaps what we mentioned here reveals something of the truth behind America's campaign against NGOs in general, and against Islamic charities in particular - the truth being simply that the work of those organizations is incompatible with American global hegemony and the program of globalization and Westernization.

Bringing Relief Organizations under Control

Newsweek, in an article entitled "Wary of Aid" published on the occasion of the tsunami disaster, mentioned that: "Indonesian Vice-President Jusuf Kalla made waves last week when he declared that American and other foreign troops helping out with the relief effort would have to clear out of Indonesia by March 26"[32] *Newsweek* goes on to say: "More and more often, the neutrality and independence of aid groups is coming into question."[33]

Newsweek adds: "In some cases, groups are taking money from government agencies like the US Agency for International Development. In others, they're simply tainted by association with the rise of the so-called humanitarian wars like those in Kosovo and Afghanistan, NGO relief and reconstruction work has become part and parcel of military missions."[34]

Newsweek also says: "In Sudan's Darfur region, numerous aid workers have been expelled or killed for speaking out against the government. Later last year, the Afghan Planning Minister, Ramazan Bashardost, proposed throwing out hundreds of foreign NGOs, which he believed were corrupt and inefficient. The proposal was denied, and Bashardost was forced to resign. But Afghans are still wary of relief workers, partly because of leaflets like those passed out by the U.S. military, offering aid only in return for intelligence on Taliban insurgents. Many do-gooders are already leaving willingly: seen as easier targets than U.S. troops, some 24 aid workers have been killed in the past year in Afghanistan compared with 13 in 2003."[35]

In 2003, USAID head Andrew Natsios raised the hackles of a number of American NGOs by publicly telling them they must do a better job of highlighting their links to the United States Government if they wanted to receive more funding in the future.[36]

Newsweek quotes findings published by Britain's *Guardian* that reveal how America has increased pressure on NGOs working in Iraq, particularly American NGOs.

The American branches of both Save the Children and CARE say that they have been pushed to inform US officials before they could speak to the media and "to highlight 'Brand America' with labels on equipment and property - a policy that can raise security issues in places like Aceh, which is devoutly Muslim and suspicious of outsiders."[37]

CARE's vice president, Michael Rewald, says: "Increasingly, any money we get from USAID has to be linked with logos"[38]

While USAID denies that it seeks to silence the NGOs that are critical of its policies, it admits to "strong-arming on other fronts" Bill Garvelink, USAID deputy assistant administrator says: "We are putting more pressure on groups to let people know where supplies and equipment come from"[39]

On the question of pressure from US military, Newsweek reports:

> *"At the same time, some of the bigger groups are uniting to fight pressure - in Iraq for example; a group of NGOs including Save the Children refused to sign project contracts unless a clause requiring workers to notify the U.S. military before speaking to the media was taken out. NGOs have also successfully united to fight U.S. demands for increased vetting of workers."[40]*

This report from *Newsweek* reveals the extent of the crisis' exploitation, and the effect of the war on terror on the increase in the number of innocent victims. The report quotes Niranjan De Soyso, media coordinator for the Center of National Operations, which is overseeing tsunami relief efforts: "We will want to take back control. We can't let foreigners hijack the process"[41] Even when the need is great, the fear can sometimes be greater remarked the report.

The State Department journal published an article by Senator Jesse Helms, President of the Congressional Committee on Foreign Relations that basically says that the President of the United States George Bush Jr. is personally interested —in a manner unprecedented for an American president- in empowering Christian charities both domestically and abroad, charities which George Bush Jr. refers to as "armies of mercy". George Bush Jr. sees these organizations to be of greater importance than other charities and social security organizations. During a large White House reception, the President presented a check for ten million dollars to Pat Robertson. This White House reception counts as practically unlimited support for the church and its affiliated "charities" both within the United States and abroad. It appears that the churches in the United States are wealthier than the Federal Government.[42]

During the Bosnian War, some European churches expatriated thousands of Muslim children from Bosnia and Herzegovina to various European countries to be hosted by European families under the care and supervision of the churches, according to what the global press agencies reported at that time and what was reported by the Islamic organizations operating in the region.

If humanitarian relief work is seen as a legal right of American organizations, this type of work is viewed in Muslim regions as a threat to those countries and to Muslim minorities. It is seen as an opportunistic exploitation of the deliberate eradication of Muslim relief organizations, thus victimizing Muslims. This is expressed in the conclusions of the report of the Center for Asian Studies in Islamabad in its comments on the occasion of the closure of Qatar Charities, the last Arab Islamic charity operating in Pakistan a the end of 2004. The organization had been providing for no less then 10,000 orphans and needy people throughout Pakistan and Kashmir and for Afghan refugees. It also had played a role in building thousands of mosques and dozens of orphanages and clinics. Likewise, it provided reliable sources of potable water to thousands of people.

Pakistani sources point out that the attack on Arab charities in Pakistan led to half a million Afghan and 200,000 Kashmiri refugees cut off from humanitarian assistance. It also led to the loss of support for over 100,000 orphans and widows and the cessation of the construction of relief projects like orphanages, hospitals, and mosques[43].

These sources also say that: "At the very time that all of the Arab charities have been prevented from working in Pakistan, around 3000 new Western NGOs started operations, since they were permitted to engage in relief work to replace the Arab Islamic charities."[44]

In Sudan, according to the former governor of Southern Darfur, Ata al-Mannan, the real danger during the Darfur crisis that flared up with frightening suddenness was not from foreign armed intervention, but from the virtual absence of Islamic organizations. The greatest danger lied in the Christian proselytization of the people of Darfur who are known for their love of the Qur'an and their activity of writing copies of it.

The Sudanese Interior Minister revealed that there are more than thirty European and American Christian organizations operating in Darfur who engage in extremely dangerous roles and use relief work as a means of Christianization in that Muslim majority region that does not possess a single church.[45]

There is clearly a double standard concerning the treatment of Islamic and Christian relief organizations. Why did the US Government cast a wide net of baseless suspicions over Islamic relief organizations, preventing them to provide relief for their desperate co-religionists? Why does it facilitate and even financially support Charities who are eager to Christianize Muslims in areas where they are not welcome?

The United Nations and the Fourth World War

The fundamental objectives of the United Nations represent a symbol of the political, religious, cultural, and social rights and freedoms that the peoples of the world should enjoy, away from the governmental domination policies. Because of the policies of its affiliated organizations and committees, which are an authority for independent, non-governmental work, the United Nations is seen as a competitor against imperialist hegemony.

In their book, *An End to Evil,* David Frum and Richard Perle reveal America's new policies towards the United Nations and its shift from a policy of containment to one of military domination of its opponents[46]. The book is like an official declaration of the neo-conservatives regarding what the future of American foreign policy should be. It proposes that American hegemony should be secured through means similar to those employed in Afghanistan and Iraq.

The book's two authors are among the most influential people in the Bush administration. Their views represent the prevailing opinions of the neo-conservatives. Among the general measures that they propose for future policy is to amend the UN charter: "The UN must endorse our 'inherent' right to defend ourselves against new threats just as forcefully as we are entitled to defend ourselves against old threats," they explain. "If not, we should formally reject the UN's authority over our war on terror."[47]

The United Nations was moderately successful in maintaining world peace and international stability after the Second World War and during the Third (Cold) War, in spite of the many drawbacks, one of which being that the number of people killed directly and indirectly in regional military conflicts during that time exceeded the total number of people killed during the Second World War. Another negative aspect is that the United Nations was never independent of American pressure and American foreign policy aspirations.

The events following September 11, 2001 are an indication that the United Nations, in spite of its past achievements, is not safe from becoming a victim at this turning point in history. It is seen as an obstacle to American hegemony. This, more specifically, is the neo-conservative program. From the perspective of the "new competitors", Western capitalism in general, and American capitalism in particular, have entered into a deep crisis with itself. It is beginning to attack the very institution that it created, in spite of the fact that it had given itself the veto power in that institution. However, today it regards that institution as a forum for smaller states.

In spite of its weakness, the United Nations might be an obstacle. It might expose and criticize the specious justifications for the new ambiguous "War on Terror." International alliances woke up after the September 11 attacks to discover little by little that the consequences of that war do not serve the interests of the peoples of the world, nor the United Nations, nor even of nations themselves.

From this perspective, the United Nations is targeted to be tamed or even eliminated. Its lofty purpose, which needs to be strengthened more than ever before to provide security for the world's competitive nations and peoples when the world has become smaller, and interactions among civilizations are more acute, is seen as a hindrance. It stands in the way of illegitimate wars for preeminence that threaten world peace.

There are indications that the United Nations and its General Secretary are to be targeted as renegades. The United Nations may have to pay the price for declaring on September 14, 2004 that the war in Iraq was illegal and for refuting America's false claims for starting the war.

The coming months or years might be witnessing smearing campaigns against the United Nations, especially accusations of corruption in its financial and administrative dealings as well as those of its officials and of countries that have close dealings with it, even with respect to events of long ago.

Here are some indications of the expected aggression:

1. Iraqi "Weapons of Mass Destruction"

During the roughly thirteen years of political and economic sanctions against Iraq since 1990, the United Nations and the International Commission for Nuclear Energy - in its capacity of being responsible for the matter - issued reports that clearly stated that Iraq did not possess weapons of mass destruction. This is the result arrived at by its special committees whose participants numbered over 1300 people. The chief international inspector, Hans Blix accused the British Government of falsifying the documents that invoked the controversy. This was before the American occupation of Iraq. This was confirmed by the president of the organization, Muhammad Baradei.[48]

2. The Oil-For-Food Program

The General Secretary of the United Nations, in a statement he gave before the Security Council on November 20, 2003, said that the program which was to end on November 21, 2003 was the only humanitarian assistance program that was fully funded by the resources of the country that it was intended to help, in this case Iraq.

He also said that: "In nearly seven years of operation, the Oil-for-Food Program has been required to meet an almost impossible series of challenges, using some 46 billion dollars of Iraqi export earnings on behalf of the Iraqi people. Under it, nine different United Nations agencies, programs and funds developed and managed humanitarian operations in Iraq, meeting the needs of the civilian population across some 24 economic and social sectors."[49] According to *al-Majallah* magazine, this program was initiated by members of the United States Congress in conjunction with former UN General Secretary Boutros-Ghali in 1996 with the overt purpose of relieving the suffering of the Iraqi people that resulted from the sanctions imposed upon Iraq. However, its ultimate effect was the humiliation and subversion of Iraq, rendering it open to the policy suggestions of Washington.[50] It can be observed that a number of the United Nations personnel working for this program, Dennis Haliday among them, tendered their resignations due to their disapproval of the unjust sanctions that were against the Iraqi people instead of against its rulers who were living in comfort.

On the other hand, Senator Norm Coleman who was chairman of the United Nations Oversight Committee for the Food for Oil program, called for the resignation of UN general Secretary Kofi Annan by accusing him of corruption in handling the program. He alleged Kofi Annan was ultimately responsible for the fact that Iraqi President Saddam Hussein received billions of dollars. Senator Coleman said that he hesitated to call for Kofi Annan's resignation, but the United Nations would not be able to uproot the corruption as long as he remained at its head.

The *BBC* correspondent in Washington DC reported that the Republican Party in the United States is displeased with the way Kofi Annan is handling things and that the White House shares this dissatisfaction. Kofi Annan expressed his disappointment with the news about his son Kojo Annan's inculpation in the Food for Oil scandal.

It should be mentioned that Kojo Annan for four years received a monthly salary of only 2,500 dollars from Swiss-based COTECNA, and was a consultant for one of its subsidiary. This company obtained a contract with the United Nations within the framework of the Food-for-Oil program which is currently under investigation.[51]

3. Neo-Conservative Renewed Effort to Marginalize the United Nations

London-based newspaper a*l-Hayat*, under this headline, reported that the American administration returned to warning UN General Secretary Kofi Annan that his positions regarding Iraq expose him to the threat of being dismissed and the United Nations to becoming a worthless organization. It appears that what instigated this attack against Annan was his letter addressed to U.S. President George Bush, Britain's Prime Minister Tony Blair, and provisional Iraqi President Iyad Allawi concerning Fallujah.

The timing of the letter was regarded by extreme elements in the American administration as being akin to treason, since it came right before a serious attack on Fallujah in November 2004. An American official speaking under conditions of anonymity said that the positions taken by Annan did not surprise him since Annan was trying to appease those who were criticizing him and because he was against the Iraq war. This official also pointed out that the United States is the largest contributor to the United Nations and said: "We do not want it to be seen that we are merely a source of funding." He also said: "We deserve to have the greatest say since we provide the most money. It is not right that France and Germany have a greater say while we are spending the most money."[52]

The newspaper also articulated the view that there were many factors behind America's campaign against Kofi Annan, among them the disagreement on how to assess situations and the fact that the neo-conservatives and hawks in the Bush administration are essentially opposed to the United Nations, and do not accept Bush having to ask the UN for help while they are trying to do away with it.

4. The United Nations between Interests and Rights

A campaign in New York was created that presented itself as a being concerned about Israeli interests. Its real purpose was to bring down the United Nations. The Committee for Accuracy in Middle East Reporting in America (CAMERA) ran a full page advertisement in *New York Times* under the headline "UN Corruption Includes Bias against Israel" where it wrote: "for more than 30 years, Arab states have used their oil wealth and the threat of withholding oil to guarantee an automatic anti-Israel majority"

Some people believe that the ideological bias against the United Nations shown by a number of neo-conservatives like former Defense Department official Richard Perle and Assistant Defense Secretary Paul Wolfowitz, both of whom are staunch supporters of Israel, may have nothing behind it other than Israel's interests and the achievement of the new political goal of eliminating the "new competitors". In this manner, the United Nations is being pushed to take the side of certain interest groups at the expense of others' rights. International and regional laws have become victims of the War on Terror.

5. Spying on the United Nations

Reuters reported that the United Nations headquarters in Geneva has become like "Swiss cheese" in the number of holes that it has. UN spokesperson in Geneva, Marie Heuzé confirmed the accuracy of the report broadcast by Swiss Television (TSR) regarding spying on the United Nations. A security source of the United Nations announced that the international headquarters in Europe is packed full of hidden surveillance equipment after an audio surveillance device was found in the ministerial assembly hall.[53] Marie Heuzé told a news briefing: "UN technical workmen found what is considered to be a sophisticated listening device."[54]

The United Nations (with its affiliated organizations, councils, and committees that make up around 40 bodies) will be in a truly dangerous situation if it changes from being a representative of the world's nations and peoples – as its namesake suggests – and becomes a representative of a single nation or becomes "the United Governments". This would mean a complete departure from the purposes for which it was originally established to be co-opted for a new agenda under the name of "reform". The U.N. purposes would be yet another victim of the War on Terror.

Yet, the biggest question remains: excluding those whose national interests are seen by some as opposed to the U.N. and NGOs, is the majority of the free world going to accept the marginalization of those organizations? To what extent is the world going to respond favorably to this and for how long? Is this really the forced death and burial of international representation and liberty being ushered in by the success of a small, bigoted group that does not represent the people of the world and their liberties in any way?

It appears that a precise answer to this question is going to be difficult, since the time factor is so critical to our seeing this new tendency. It also appears that the 2004 elections in the United States that were won by Bush by a mere 3% margin against Kerry shows that America - A nation best represented by its affiliation with the fourteen principles of human freedom outlined by former President Wilson - has begun to develop a political and psychological rift and is becoming divided on account of the new directions being taken by the neo-conservatives who have forgotten or simply chose to ignore what Harry Truman said in front of 3500 representatives of various nations at the inauguration of the UN: "No single nation can always have its own way, for these are human problems, and the solution of human problems is to be found in negotiation and mutual adjustment."[55]

However, the election results show how much the American people long for a return of their civil liberties. But these liberties disagree with the policies of American hegemony and the principles of a new imperialism commandeered by the hawks and exploited to further their goals, and interests. The hawks assumed that it was going to be easy to mislead the people about the truth of the matter, they are demanding the elimination or marginalization of all NGOs, particularly those that object to preemptive wars that aim to eliminate the chance of possible future competitors, though all such wars lack legitimacy. So, who is going to win out in the end - the neo-conservatives or the new competitors? The answer could be provided by the outcome of the war in Iraq - as a case study - It could provide an example of the success of the elimination of new competitors and of their influence. Or it could be a cause of its failure. The world awaits the outcome of the war against Iraq, a war that may go on for a long time, because success or failure in Iraq brings with it many significant implications for the direction the world will take in the future.

Alvin Toffler has written about some of the justifications for the War on terror. I shall be discussing some of what he and others have written on the topic, since their viewpoints taken together show with certainty that this new war that is being called the War on Terror or the War on terror Financing is a necessity for this new historical era after the end of the Cold War. According to the view of some, this new war requires bringing about an incident or incidents of great historical magnitude to justify the pressing need for such wars.[56]

Another view holds that this new war is a capitalization on the incident, by using it to lend legitimacy to the program of world domination. This program requires the elimination of some of the new powers, as will be discussed. Indeed, Toffler considers such struggles to be hidden wars for global domination. On this basis, we can say that this perspective exposes an important side of the propaganda war on terror being waged against NGOs and more specifically Islamic charities. This is because the American administration considers those organizations to be among its most serious competition.

Future Outlook for the Third Sector

In addition to the fact asserted by Alvin Toffler that the non-governmental, non-profit sector has reached a stage where it is considered an opponent or competitor to the government, this third sector, as the United Nations calls it, represents all activities with an independent administration from the first (governmental) and second (private, business) sectors. However, this sector is important and fundamental because it supports and complements the two others, and participates with them in comprehensive and continuous development projects encompassing the education, information, health, and economics. This is especially true for countries that refute totalitarianism.

It is the opinion of this author that in addition to the fact that the NGOs have acquired a prominent position during the cold war, the future is for the third sector, both organizations and individuals, as a moving force of change. The development of events after World War II reveals that the military power, the political power, and the economic power strongly supported by the media were used to realize international hegemony; and all these powers subjugated human beings at the expense of their spiritual, human, and social needs.

Most governments and political forces have given priority to their economic greed and political interests over human rights, and have negatively used the media against the rights of humankind, and used them in a war against truth, to the point that they have lost the trust of the people, the nations, and especially the NGOs. Political powers are not trusted by the peoples to lead humanity and to fulfill its needs and rights. The basic freedoms and rights of the people are gradually eroded after the 9/11 where new security laws have curtailed freedoms even more.

Arguments in favor of the vision that the future holds much power for the NGOs are as follows:

- The loss of trust in the governmental sectors where special interests are given priority over human rights, where moral principles are ignored, and where international laws are equally ignored by the governments of the North and the South. The pretended great model of freedom and justice has collapsed when the United States has enacted the new Anti-Terrorism laws, among them the PATRIOT Act, the domestic surveillance program, the guilty by association laws[57], and has erected prisons where basic human rights are violated, such as the Abu Ghraib in Iraq, Guantanamo Bay in Cuba, and Bagram Base in Afghanistan, not to mention prisons throughout Europe, where alleged acts of torture occurred. The wars in Afghanistan and Iraq are both examples of denying freedom, justice, and democracy to the peoples of those countries where poverty and sickness are on the rise! According to statistics released by Amnesty International, 150 governments resort to torture, and until 2004, there are at least 300,000 prisoners of conscience around the world without any accusation or due legal process. Donors, states and organizations alike, do not have confidence in the capability of the governments' administration in executing relief and development projects, as much as they have confidence in the citizens groups and NGOs to do so.

- The proliferation of various social diseases and ills afflicting governments and societies. For example, The Americans spend around $10 billion every year on pornographic movies and prints and there are more than 300,000 pornographic websites[58]. The European Union spends $2.5 every day on each cow European farmers own, almost twice what an African human being spends for his daily subsistence[59]. The failure and contradictions of the governments are highlighted by the statistics released by the United Nations, which estimated the trade in illegal drugs at about $400 billion a year, meaning that the trade in illegal drugs equals that of pharmaceutical drugs, and is 8% of the global trade.[60] These political diseases compounded by the greed of the economic powers are a sign of the lack of allegiance and respect toward the governments. States' national sovereignty has been further weakened in the wake of global trade built on a culture of consumerism and on privatization of essential services of the population for the benefit of the corporations, to the point that a quarter of the world's assets is in the hands of just 0.13% of world population[61].

- Signs of failure of the capitalist system in fulfilling the well-being of the people of developed countries (or the North) or satisfying the minimum needs of the other populations. The mergers of large corporations and the negative economic competition between giant corporations, especially the ones that are rising from the East in opposition to their counterparts in the West will cause the disappearance of the middle size companies and the shrinkage of the middle class resulting in an increase in the rank of the poor, thus increasing the feeling of anger, and therefore an increase in violence in an attempt to get their rights back.

The industrial revolution followed by the information revolution have produced great wealth and prosperity but are void of spiritual enrichment, that in turn has created a deep psychological schism in societies, especially among the well to do. This is compounded by the new wars of the twenty first century, which benefit neither party. In the absence of a spiritual or religious strength that instills a belief in the Hereafter and acceptance of God's decrees, we are witnessing an increase in depression and in individual and collective suicides equally in the East and the West[62]. Spiritual happiness is the pursuit of all people, and it is most often realized by turning to the religions and worship no matter what religion it is. In Islam, for example, this spiritual peace and satisfaction are fulfilled to a great extent through humanitarian charitable work where altruism and compassion toward both Muslims and non-Muslims are expressed, and where bringing relief to mankind is its hallmark. These are factors that engender happiness and spiritual well-being in the recipients, the donors, and the intermediaries in the charitable process, a feeling which only those who work in charity experience.

- The powers of freedom of information, communication, and knowledge, are not the exclusive right of governments and corporations any more. They are effective powers that are common to all. NGOs, individuals and populations are benefiting from them in a way that surpasses in many aspects the way government administrations do. The proliferation of these powers is a reaction to the militaristic policies of the international powers that are led by the US administration, and whose aim is to legislate extreme international laws that would lead to the plundering of cultures, deprivation of the others of their rights and their interests, the confiscation of their patrimony, their moral principles, and the attempt to deprive them from their freedoms, especially that political awakening in the East happened after the awakening in the West, and in the South after the North, in other words in the poor countries after the rich ones, and thus the later saw their monopoly of power disappear.

- A widespread increase in religious awakening (Jewish, Christian, and Muslim), which is a major incentive in humanitarian and charitable work, and charitable giving. In the case of Judaism, religious motives played a major factor in the establishment of Israel, a state built on religious foundation (a Jewish state) and with the financial support of international organizations before and after the establishment of Israel. Christian religious fervor is also on the rise, and is apparent in the religious charitable giving which is increasing every year: statistics released by the Center of Philanthropy at Indiana University indicate that religious organizations received about $74.31 billion in 2000, $80.96 billion in 2001, $84.28 billion in 2002, and $86.39 billion in 2003[63]. In Islam, religious motives are even more important in charitable work, because charity is an integral part of the faith. By opposition to other religions, religious incentives form 100% in giving, a person is rewarded if he gives Zakat and punished if he withholds it. As emphasized by Jonathan Benthall: "It is a fair claim that among sacred books, the Qur'an seems to be the only one in the world which sets out precisely [in 9:60] the basic principles of the budget and expenses of the state. It is doubtful too whether any other religion has an equivalent to the Islamic principle that hungry people have the right to share in the meal of those who are well fed."[64] In reality there is no religion like Islam that is capable to employ and mobilize its followers as human resources, young and old, men and women, and people with different capabilities, all are either employees, or volunteers seeking to fulfill their religious obligations and reap rewards, and avoid punishment which would be incurred on those who withhold the human rights of the poor and the orphans.

A financial principle in Islam stipulates that wealth belongs to God as stated in many verses of the Qur'an and also in the Sunnah (sayings and actions of the Prophet) and man is merely the inheritor of this wealth, as he is God's vicegerent. The poor and needy have a right to it before the rich, and Zakat (obligatory giving) was established as part of the Islamic faith to fulfill this right of the poor. It is well documented that Abu Bakr, the first Khalifa after the Prophet, waged a war on those who refused to give Zakat. Money is also given voluntarily to seek reward from God and wash one's sins.

Islam has legislated the establishment of *waqf* (charitable trust or foundation) as a lasting financial resource, which has permitted a continuous development of the charitable work, and it is an uncontested fact in the history of Islam that all aspects of the Islamic culture were a fruit of the establishment of *waqf*: the schools, mosques, libraries. There are *waqf* to fulfill animal rights: there were *waqf* for injured birds, stray dogs, etc.. *Waqf* was a supporting power for the successive Islamic states. The concept of *waqf* has then spread to Europe through Spain (then known as Andalousia) in the West, and Turkey in the East. With respect to its considerable size, its vital participation in the development and its human and permanent financial resources, the charitable sector was the first or second sector in the Islamic history.

- Many governments consider independent, successful NGOs to be new competitors (opponents). This has become especially clear after the events of September 11, when the new global policy is seeking to diminish and weaken the goals for which these NGOs were established since the cold war. This has affected international and local NGOs of all sizes. This in turn will lead to an attitude of defiance. Trends opposed to these new policies will invariably develop to uncover the defects of the new world order and its proponents among the governments. Perhaps a sign of the rise of the third sector to be the moving power in local and global policies is that its successful management has fulfilled the economic goals and moral values because the humanitarian and religious motives are reflected in the quality of their work and the strength of their production and creativity, things that are not present in this manner in the governmental and business sector. There are lessons that the for-profit sector needs to learn from the non-profit sector Peter Drucker said. While still dedicated to doing good, the nonprofits also "realize that good intentions are no substitute for organization and leadership, for accountability, performance, and results. Those require management and that, in turn, begins with the organization's mission."[65] To illustrate the success of the third sector in the USA Drucker wrote, "Few people are aware that the non-profit sector is by far America's largest employer. Every other adult - a total of 80 million-plus people - works as a volunteer, giving on average nearly five hours each week to one or several nonprofit organizations. This is equal to 10 million full-time jobs. Were volunteers paid, their average, even at minimum rate, would amount to some $150 billion, or 5 percent of GNP. And volunteer work is changing fast."[66] This success has been realized in spite of the attempt to marginalize and weaken certain organizations which are independent of the government's programs, such as the OMB WATCH[67] which monitors the US Office of Management and Budget, or the environmental organizations which oppose unchecked capitalism, the spread of wars, and arms races, and those that work to limit racism, etc[68].

- The last third of the twentieth century and the beginning of the twenty first have witnessed a considerable increase in the wealth of certain individuals and corporations, which has surpassed tens of billions of dollars. In India, a country with a high poverty rate, a number of super rich billionaires has sprung, such as the multi-billionaire Mittal who now resides in United Kingdom. Worth $24.8 billion, Mittal's fortune permitted him to indulge in buying a $96 million villa in London, and *Paris-Match* estimated his daughter's wedding ceremony at $55 million, more than Lithuania's budget. But these expenses did not even diminish the compounded profits he earned from his fortune. Despite these extravagances, Mittal has donated $85 million to rebuild the entire town of Long Beach after Hurricane Katrina, and he also donated to the Tsunami victims and the Pakistan earthquake victims[69]. These are just few examples which illustrate that the outlet most capable to absorb the surplus of wealth is the charity sector through endowments, relief work, and development, no matter what the religious or humanitarian motives are. A number of the super-rich have established charitable foundations committed to spend their wealth surplus. In Saudi Arabia, the Suleiman al-Rajhi Charitable Foundation and al-Walid Ibn Talal Charitable Foundation, and in Lebanon the Rafik Hariri charitable foundation, are examples of such foundations. In the US, Bill Gates and his wife have endowed $28 billion in the Bill and Melinda Gates Foundation, 40% of his fortune, in addition to his yearly $2 billion to $5 billion donations[70], and Tom Monaghan the owner of Domino's Pizza has donated almost all of his fortune to the Catholic Church[71]. The Soros Foundation is another example[72]. All these examples illustrate the global trend to support the development and goals of the third sector.

- The new century has been characterized by wrong government policies and practices that have increased the extent of poverty, sickness and illiteracy, and have increased international terrorism, and discrimination against certain religions. New phenomena have appeared which along with what has been mentioned form the factors of a power shift, we mention for example:

- New global wars where weapons of mass destruction have been used such as in Iraq and Afghanistan. Other areas in the world are candidates for more wars as neo-conservatives seek to expand the US administration's sphere of influence, perhaps violating international laws and infringing upon the rights of people, of the environment, and increasing poverty and sicknesses, and thus the intensity of the clash.

- Failure of governments to fulfill their pledges of relief and financial help as stated by the United Nations, which has led to the multiplication of the negative effects of earthquakes, floods, and other natural disasters, as in the cases of the Tsunami, the Pakistan-Kashmir and Iran earthquakes, and the hunger crises in Africa. The failure of fulfilling their pledges has become a habit of most governments toward the UN whose annual budget is around $10 billion, the equivalent of five days expenses of the armies of the world. As of March 31, 2003, the financial obligations due to the UN have reached $2.77 billion, and the biggest debtor was the United States with $1.3 billion[73]. In that same year the US has spent $396 billion on defense and in 2004 it spent $399 billion[74].

- Global population increase accompanied by a global increase in unemployment and poverty, as statistics about famine around the world demonstrate: 3 million in Niger[75] and 11 million in the Horn of Africa are facing starvation according to the January 2006 FAO statistics[76]. The former World Bank Director has warned about the danger of poverty saying: "Over the next three decades, more than two billion people will be added to the planet's population, 97 percent of them in the poorer nations," he said. "Instability is often bred in places where a rapidly increasing youth population sees hope as more of a taunt than a promise."[77]"

- Global increase in sickness cases and the appearance of new diseases such as AIDS requiring large funds in countries unable to provide treatments. AIDS victims are estimated to be 30 million to 40 million[78], partial or total handicap cases due to wars and natural disasters have increased, as have the number of blind people in the world which has reached 50 million in 2005. Forty million persons in Africa alone suffer from treatable diseases which lead to blindness. It is estimated that 100 million will join the rank of the blind, 80% of them could have been treated[79].

- Widening gap between the rich and the poor in both countries of the North and the South, with an increasing discrepancy in the individual income. The World Development Report 2006 has confirmed that the number of people living on $1 a day exceeds one billion, or 15% of the world population, and that the average individual wealth in the Western countries is 15 to 58 times the average individual wealth in developing countries[80]. This is accompanied by a discrepancy in local and global justice concerning peoples' rights, states' sovereignty and powers, which negatively affects global stability and security.

To whom does the future belong?

The afore-mentioned facts and considerations regarding the global shift of power point to the conclusion that the future belongs to the non-governmental organizations and to the humanitarian work, because they are neutral, as long as they are kept away from being politicized by the governments, and because, more than at any time before, they have a better feeling and awareness of the local and global problems of the people than the political governmental organizations. The humanitarian sector is stronger because they are committed to their cause and because they are monitored by society and nations. They believe in competition, and not in confrontation and conflict often adopted by most political entities.

The global situation and events indicate that the power of the government sector and private (economic) sector are in retreat in front of the power of the independent citizens groups, supported by the freedoms and nourished by the easy exchange of information, in addition to the power of the readily available and varied mass media. An example of this growing power is the many anti-globalization demonstrations and organizations, the most successful of which was the one held in Seattle, Washington at the 1999 summit of the World Trade Organization and at Durban in 2001. The power of popular monitoring is apparent in the demands to bring the US President George W. Bush and the UK Prime Minister Tony Blair to court as war criminals and the demands that they be tried both in the US and the UK[81]. A symbolic trial of the US President and UK Prime Minister along with Israel's Sharon has taken place in Cairo on February 3-5, 2006, in a large gathering and sponsored by the Arab Lawyers Union[82].

The power of citizens groups was clearly expressed in the worldwide demonstrations against the cartoons published by a Danish newspaper and reprinted by other newspapers in Norway, France, and New Zealand, depicting the Prophet Muhammad in a disgraceful and mocking way. The strong global widespread reactions in the Arab and Muslim streets are a clear example of the power of the people to use their freedoms of expressions and their successful boycott of the Danish products[83]. All this happened outside the governments' control. Aren't these examples a sign of the rising of a power that fulfills the moral and material needs of the people, and which enjoys greater credibility?

Are the powers of citizens groups and non-governmental organizations the powers of the future? I strongly believe so but it is incumbent on all NGOs to protect their gains in the fields of human rights, development and relief, their capabilities in providing relief in crises and emergencies, and to be watchful so that they are not weakened or their goals thwarted; for they were a factor in reining the tyranny of the government and the greed of the corporations.

Islamic Charitable Work: Principles and Means

Charity is an inseparable part of the Islamic faith. It is a basic principle of Islam and an integral aspect of Islamic teachings. It is neither a secondary nor an indistinct element of Islam. In reality, charity is a conspicuous subset of one of the Five Pillars of faith in Islam; and hence it is far from being a wrongdoing. It cannot be considered as an accusation from which one should defend himself. As a Muslim must bow down, prostrate himself and pray, he also must do good in a collective and organized manner, as stated in the Qur'an: "O ye who believe! Bow down, prostrate yourself, and adore your Lord; and do good that ye may prosper."[84] This is God's command. So charity is a sign of success in this world and a hope for salvation in the Hereafter. God Almighty ties worship – which is regarded as His exclusive right – with providing food to the poor, which is regarded as a right of the needy. He says: "And ask of the sinners: 'What led you into Hell-Fire?' They will say: 'We were not of those who prayed; nor were we of those who fed the indigent'."[85] He also says: "Have you seen the one who denies the faith? That is the one who neglects the orphan and who does not encourage the feeding of the poor."[86]

The importance of charity in Islam is that it constitutes an integral part of faith, both in its doctrine and mode of worship. Some aspects of charity work are religious obligations on each and every Muslim. Others are religious obligations of the Muslim community as a whole. Then there is voluntary charity that a Muslim is encouraged to engage in. Indeed, it constitutes part of a Muslim's faith in Divine Decree that views crises, disasters, famine, and disease among the means by which personal reform is achieved. It is not possible for individuals, organizations, or countries – Muslim or otherwise – to marginalize or dispense with this noble work that is a part of Islamic faith and practice.

In spite of the obligation not to differentiate between Muslims and non-Muslims who are in need, most of the people working for Islamic charities give priority to the crises that occur within the Muslim world. One reason for this is geographical proximity. Another is that Muslim regions are often in greater need of charity. Moreover, this work is an expression of sympathy of the Muslims toward those of their faith.

Jamie Wilson wrote in the *Guardian*: "Giving to charity is an integral part of the Islamic faith. The third obligatory pillar of Islam is Zakat, in which a person must give away a percentage of their income to help others. It comprises 2.5% of surplus earnings at the end of the year. Muslims are also encouraged to make irregular payments – Sadaqah - to the needy."[87] And he says about the British Muslims' Zakat: "There are more than 1,000 Islamic charities and trusts in the UK, with a total income of £42m – roughly £21 for every Muslim in the country. Much of the money ends up going abroad to help those facing war, famine and natural disaster."[88]

Jonathan Benthall and Jerome Bellion emphasize the relation between relief work and religious duty says: "Zakat is a major support in the standard Islamic case against the evil of both capitalism and communism... Zakat is a reminder that all the wealth belongs to God."[89]

Sources of Funding for Islamic Charities

There are many principal sources that finance Islamic charity works, and that are allowed by Islamic laws. Without going into details, we briefly mention the most important of them:

Zakah: *Zakah* is the third of the five pillars of Islam, and every Muslim, male or female, is required to observe it. It is required for every Muslim who keeps in his possession a certain minimum amount of wealth beyond his neds for one full year to pay a fixed portion of that wealth in charity. It is called *Zakah* (literally means purification in Arabic), because it purifies, i.e. blesses the wealth from which it is taken as it purifies the donor. *Zakah* is an effective mean to protect the Muslim society from the despotism and greed of the wealthy. It preserves the dignity of the poor as it is their right decreed by God and not a favor from the people. It ensures a social balance, and solidarity. It revives the economy by circulating wealth among all strata of society, away from usury and monopolization.

The Qur'an outlines those who are entitled to receive the *Zakah*: "Alms (*Zakah*) are only for the poor, the destitute, those who employed to administer the funds, those whose hearts are inclined (to Islam), the emancipation of slaves, those who are in debt, in the cause of Allah, and the wayfarer. Thus is it ordained by Allah, and Allah is All-Knowing, All-Wise."[90]

This verse makes it clear that no one has the option of dispensing with this injunction or changing who is entitled to receive the *Zakah* funds. This Islamic legislation is a fulfillment of human rights, especially the rights of those in need of mercy, justice, and dignity. *Zakah* is a primary source of funding for Islamic charities, a fundamental corner and active element in all social and economical developments. It is important to note that at present in many Arab and Muslim countries, the collection and distribution of *Zakah* has been taken over by the government and carried out through government administrations and official or semi-official organizations.

Endowments (Waqf): The Prophet described endowments as: "the setting aside of the source and means of wealth or of the benefits thereof." The evidence for its legitimacy in Islamic Law is the Prophet's statement: "When a person dies, his works come to an end, except for three: charity that continues to yield benefit, knowledge that continues to be useful, and a pious child that prays on one's behalf."[91]

The establishment of endowments is a form of worship. The first endowment in Islam was the Rumah Well. It had been owned by a Jewish man who sold its water to the people of Madinah for drinking purposes. When the Prophet (peace be upon him) arrived in Madinah, the only source of drinking water was the Rumah Well. He announced: "Who will purchase the Rumah Well?" Uthman went ahead and purchased it and made of it an endowment for the people of Madinah.

Endowments play a vital role in social, educational, health, and industrial development. Endowment monies are utilized in all aspects of charity work, including the construction of mosques, shelters, orphanages, refugee camps, and hospitals.

Historically, endowments have represented an effective source of funding for the charity sector and have been a source of protection for society. Endowments have surpassed the experience of the East and West in curbing the excesses of both Capitalism (the excesses of the individual) and Socialism (the excesses of the state), which have marginalized so many people and so many societies. Endowments represent a charity sector independent of individuals as well as of government domination.

Muslim communities enjoyed social solidarity throughout history, unaffected by the falls or rises of the governments or their weakness. History has recorded that endowment was a strong foundation upon which Islamic civilization has been built during its golden era to the point that the whole world and especially Europe has benefited from this unique experience. But the Endowment has become weak in all parts of the Arab and Muslim world when its administration was appropriated by official governmental organizations about 200 years ago.

Voluntary charitable contributions: Voluntary contributions supplement those acts of charity which are religious obligations. Such contributions are occasionally obligatory as well as a means of atonement for certain mistakes.

Voluntary contributions, in general, are not of predetermined amounts. A Muslim makes such contributions when and how and to whom he sees fit according to the dictates of his discretion and moral sense. The Qur'an reads: "But it is righteous to believe in God, the Last Day, the angels, the scripture, and the prophets, and to spend out of your wealth for love of Him to kinfolk, the orphans, the needy, the wayfarer, and to those who ask, and for the ransom of slaves."[92]

The Prophet commanded: "Feed the hungry, visit the sick, and relieve those who are in distress."[93] He also said: "I and the one who takes care of an orphan are like this in Heaven." and he held two of his fingers close together.[94]

Charity work helps protect the individual and the society from crimes and oppression, and ensures for the individual the essential needs to preserve his rights and his dignity. Islamic charity work is considered in Islamic jurisprudence complementary to the government's work. It is not a competitor to other sectors. Rather it was an essential source for the foundation of Islamic civilization and greatly participated in the continuity of its growth throughout history and among different nations Muslim and non-Muslim alike. However, Islamic charities are facing a formidable challenge, due to allegations of terror financing.

Islamic charities and associations:

Charities are regarded in Islam as legal entities in their own right. Likewise, they represent and fulfill the noblest of human rights for those who receive as well as for those who give.

Islamic charities, whether they are in the Muslim world or in Europe, America, or Asia, constitute a part of the community of non-governmental and non-profit organizations. They are not distinct by their religious affiliations from the other organizations in serving humanitarian causes around the globe. Islamic organizations and Islamic centers in Europe, America, Australia, Asia, and elsewhere provide assistance to the Muslim minority communities in their social, religious, and cultural affairs. These are legitimate and legal rights upheld for Muslims as for any religiously affiliated organization in Europe, America, and elsewhere.

Islamic organizations actively participate in relief and development both inside and outside their countries of origin. They are called Islamic because of two reasons:

First: the organizations and their workers believe that the motive and goal of their work is to please God. Their religion impels them to help their brothers in faith. The Prophet Muhammad said: "He does not believe he who does not love for his brother what he loves for himself." And he said: "He is not a believer he who eats his full while his neighbor goes hungry." Giving Zakat is an obligation, not a choice.

Second: most of the areas where these organizations work are primarily in Muslim countries or countries with Muslim minorities, considering that 80 percent of the areas of war, crises, poverty, and illiteracy are predominantly Muslim. 90 percent of the world refugees are Muslim. It is only natural that these organizations fulfill their role of Islamic education and relief according to Islamic teachings.In spite of their limited resources, Islamic charities do not distinguish between Muslims and non-Muslims. But the dire situation of Muslims all over the world requires them to start relief where crises are.

Islamic charities have been at the forefront in warning against violence, and terrorism around the world. Islamic charitable organizations have been and continue to be outspoken against such acts before September 11. The fact that some unprofessional mistakes have been committed by some does not justify their marginalization, because they fill a void and provide a unique service for Muslims in need.

Participation of Islamic Organizations in Global Efforts

There is no place for comparison between the global charities of considerable means and the work of Islamic charities with respect to the tangible success that the latter have achieved, first in the eighties in Afghanistan, then in the nineties in the Balkans, Somalia, Afghanistan and elsewhere. The most important way in which Islamic charities have distinguished themselves is in their lack of discrimination in the field between Muslims and non-Muslims in the assistance they provide. This is despite the fact that 75% of the regions, which suffer from natural disasters and crises are Muslim societies or areas with Muslim minorities, and that Muslim regions are generally in impoverished parts of Africa and Asia.

Testimonials:

In spite of the far greater resources possessed by the larger, global non-Islamic charities, Islamic charities have proven themselves to be equal to the task. Even non-Muslims have attested to this fact. Attorney Martin Mc. Mahon who was in charge of the defense of many Islamic charities said: "The Saudi Government and the people of Saudi Arabia have been globally distinguished by their good conduct in the charitable works. Some Saudi charity names are well known among the refugees and orphans, they are known for their works in digging wells for villages, providing books, scholarships, and for their support of numerous other people."[95]

Dr. Mayke Kaag, a Dutch researcher, affirmed in a field report about Chad the positive role of Islamic organizations in Chad, saying that they have the sincere intention of providing good work. She mentioned some of their positive points, that in general they possess important means, especially the Gulf States organizations, and that they possess international expertise and their workers know what is going on around the world, and have open ideas. Another positive point she mentioned was that Islamic organizations enjoy a good relationship with the Chadian Government."[96]

She also said that it is unreasonable to accuse all Islamic organizations, and that the majority of them present and important help to the African continent and elsewhere. In the Egyptian *al-Ahram* she pointed to the hostile antagonistic treatment of the Islamic organizations by the United States, and that many other countries followed suit. She said that Chad may not get other help if it continues to accept Islamic organizations' help, and the Chadian Government was forced to stop these organizations' activities, yielding to pressure.[97]

Tanya Cariina Hsu[98], senior researcher at the Institute for Research: Middle Eastern Policy (Irmep) said: "I tracked terrorist financing for 3 years, and none was traced to Saudi Arabia." And she also said: "The 'funding' is absurd, charity is charity and there is more corruption in the funding of US charities than anywhere in the world." Outraged by the traumatic decision to removing collection boxes in Saudi mosques, she said: "Would Saudi Arabia demand such of US churches if Christians attacked Muslims?"[99]

These realities are discovered by academic researchers who undertook field studies in Chad and Saudi Arabia looking for the truth. In light of these revealing testimonies, Prince Naif, the Saudi Interior Minister said: "Saudi aid to Palestinians provides for families who lost their sons or guardians." He reiterated the position of Saudi Arabia against terrorism, and said: "These campaigns against Saudi charitable work will not deter the Saudi Government and people from fulfilling our obligations toward our religion, the [Muslim] community, and the world." He refuted the criticism of the Israeli newspaper *Maariv* concerning this issue. And said: "We have nothing to fear. Saudi Arabia offers support to the Palestinian victims of Israeli oppression, especially those who lost their providers." Answering allegations against Islamic charities, he said: "Who can say that this work goes to those who do not deserve it? Is there a single proof?" [100]

Islamic charities' competency during crises prompted some international non-Islamic organizations affiliated with the United Nations to assign some of their work to them, especially when it is requested by the recipients themselves as in the case of the refugees in Bosnia, Kosovo, and Albania. However, the lack of data and statistics gathered by Islamic organizations might be a factor in the world's ignorance about them.

By comparison to other NGOs, the number of Islamic charities in the Gulf Cooperation Council countries working abroad does not exceed 33 organizations with a total yearly budget of approximately 450 to 550 million dollars during the 90s. Compare this to a budget of 60 billion dollars of some other humanitarian organizations[101]. The positive effects and fruits of the Islamic NGOs in spite of their limited funds prove their credibility and effectiveness.

Examples of Relief and Development Programs

The following examples of the work carried out by Islamic charities reflect their positive contributions:

Relief work: Five and a half million people have been helped by Islamic charities during 1997-2001. Relief expenses reached 285 million dollars. International Islamic Relief Organization (IIRO) spent 8.6 million dollars as urgent relief in 2000 alone. Al Muntada al Islami gave relief to 1.5 million people in 2002. World Assembly of Muslim Youth (WAMY) helped more than 2 million persons in Africa, Asia, and the Balkan states in 2001.

Some charities count their relief in tons. Africa's Muslims' committee sent 265000 tons of goods to Africa. IIRO sent 1600 tons of dates in 2002, 200 tons of food, and 20 tons of medical goods in 2005.

Some other Islamic charities have common programs with UN organizations. Qatar charity is member in UNICEF, and WHO. It also participates in UN programs such as AGFUND and ISECO.

Medical camps: A total of 506 medical camps have been set up by Islamic charities in Africa, Asia, and Europe, costing more than 26 million dollars, in addition to field hospitals set up at times of crises and wars. Here are some examples:

* IIRO spent about 5.5 million dollars on more than 3million sick persons in 33 countries during 2000-2001.

* Africa's Muslims Committee built 129 hospitals and health centers directly under its supervision.

* WAMY presented a health program in 2002 that benefited more than 120,000 sick persons, it also provided seasonal programs benefiting more than 530, 000 persons.

Some Islamic organizations are unique in that they specialize in one type of health concern. Vision Charitable Foundation has set up 448 camps to treat eye problems during its 13 years of service, treated more than 1.5 million cases provided 190 beds in different countries where eye surgeries were performed at its expense, financed the implant of 51,441 lenses, set up medical programs called "caravans of light" in 424 camps. It serves 38 countries in Africa and Asia.

Medical expenses far exceed food and education expenses especially during times of wars and crises. Some organizations spent more than 4 million dollars, and remained in areas which most other organizations have fled due to the dangers of wars and crimes (al-Muntada stayed in Somalia when most have fled it).

Wells and potable water:

Water is what sustains life. Islamic charities gave great attention to water projects. 36 million dollars have been spent to dig 7869 wells, more than half of them in Africa:

- Africa's Muslims Committee dug 4250 wells.
- WAMY created 2162 water projects during 1998-2002.
- IIRO dug 1022 wells during 2000-2002.
- Al-Muntada al-Islami dug 750 wells up until 2002.
- Shaikh Al Thani of Qatar dug 395 wells during 2000-2001.

Providing for orphans:

Islamic charities spent more than 49 million dollars to support about 100,000 orphans. This included food, clothing and education. Here are some examples:

- WAMY supported 31,924 orphans between 2001and 2005.
- Qatar Charity supported 16,692 orphans between 1999 and 2000.
- Makkah Charitable Foundation supported 10,903 orphans between 1996 and 2002.
- Africa's Muslims supported 10,000 orphans between 1981 and 2002.
- Kuwait's International Islamic Charity supported 5,289 orphans between 1999 and 2001.

Educational programs, scholarships, and student assistance:

Educational programs constitute a large part of the Islamic humanitarian aid, because Islamic organizations consider education the best tool to fight poverty and ignorance. Here are examples of the projects of some Islamic NGOs:

- International Islamic Relief Organization (IIRO): spent $2,740,209 during 200-2001 on educational institutions in 43 countries.
- African Muslim Committee: established 980 educational projects among them 140 schools, 3 universities licensing school teachers in Zanzibar, Kenya, and Somalia.
- World Assembly of Muslim Youth (WAMY): established 819 educational programs.

- Qatar Charitable Organization and Eid Al Thani Organization: 25 educational programs during 1999-2001.

Nine large organizations had strong presence at different times and created 3,366 educational programs costing more than 133 million dollars, provided 122,489 scholarships costing more than 45 million dollars, and helped more than 562,430 at the expense of 26.6 million dollars.

Additionally, these organizations provide for the maintenance of these establishments (teachers' salaries, books, students health care, etc.). They provided work for 3054 local workers in Africa only.

Also there are charities that are concerned with social and economic welfare as well as those who address women's and children's concerns, providing women's magazines (such as al Osra), teaching Arabic for Muslims (such as "Arabic for All"), building cultural centers (Islamic Endowment built 8 cultural centers, 7 institutes licensing local teachers, has radio and TV programs in Albania, Kosovo, and Kazakhstan, in addition to sewing schools for women).

Ramadan meals:

This project is one that has many positive effects especially on Muslim minorities, and pockets of poverty during Ramadan. More than 45 million meals have been distributed at the cost of more than 46 million dollars.

- Al-Haramain Foundation distributed 25 million meals during 1996-2001.
- WAMY: 3.1 million meals during 1996-2002.

- IIRO spent around 818 thousand dollars to feed more than 1 million fasting Muslims during Ramadan of 2000.

Distribution of sacrificial meat:

- IIRO spent more than 1 million dollars in a project to distribute sacrificial meat benefiting about 850,000 persons.
- WAMY distributed around 104,000 sacrificial sheep during 1998-2001.
- Al-Haramain distributed 100,000 sheep during 1992-2001.
- Kuwait International Islamic Charity distributed 83,180 sheep during 1996-2001.
- Qatar charity: 3,300 sheep.

It is estimated that about 22 million dollars of sacrificial meat/animals have been distributed by the Islamic charities. For most recipients it was one of the rare occasions when they eat meat.

Social services centers:

1,817 social services centers have been built worldwide at the cost of 63.4 million dollars.

- IIRO spent around 23 million dollars on social projects during 2000-2001.
- WAMY helped build 924 centers during 1998-2002.
- Africa's Muslims Committee built 30 centers.
- Qatar Charity 24 centers during 1999-2000.
- Kuwait International Islamic Charity during 1999-2001.

Islamic Organizations are well aware of the danger of preventing them from continuing their humanitarian work. They participated in different conventions of international organizations to discuss the future dangers faced by NGOs and especially the Islamic charities that were a target of a fierce campaign since September 11. The first international convention was in Paris in October 9, 2003, the second was in Geneva, and the third in Kuwait in November 23, 2004. The negative effects of the absence of Islamic charities among humanitarian NGOs were deeply felt in Afghanistan, Palestine, Iraq, Darfur, and the tsunami hit areas as has been mentioned in these conventions[102].

Mosques and places of worship:

Mosques are not only places of worship, but also places for teaching small children, and social gathering places.

- I IRO: built 420 mosques in 2000
- Africa's Muslims Committee: 2150 mosques during 1981-2002.
- WAMY: 1751 mosques during 1998-2002.
- Al-Haramain: 1200 mosques during 1992-2002.
- Qatar Charitable Organization: 282 mosques during 1999-2000.
- International Islamic Charity Committee of Kuwait: 177 mosques during 1999-2001.

The Value of the Islamic Organizations within the International Community

Islamic charities are part of the global network of NGOs. Their importance can be clearly seen in the positive effects of their efforts, a sample of which has been presented above.

Moreover, the endorsement of Islamic charities in America particularly had become a political pawn in elections, as stated by the *Associated Press* on April 24, 2004. Islamic charity work and charitable organizations have become a political concern among nations.

It is possible that September 11 was a date like any other for non-governmental organizations in the North. However, for their counterparts in the South, and especially in the Muslim world, it was a disaster by every meaning of the word. The world would never be the same for them after those tragic events. The transient difficulties they had already been experiencing were transformed into their having to defend themselves against the inquiries of the American administration, a struggle that used exceptional powers, like the Secret Evidence Act, to cover up its transgressions against major, reputable Islamic organizations that had been carrying out their work in an exemplary manner.

It is a merciless war being launched against these organizations with numerous tactics from freezing of accounts to the ease in which they are classified agents of terror, to their being targeted for such ominous perpetual scrutiny that make donors distance themselves from them, preferring to give their donations elsewhere. It is a war in which justice has been removed from the judicial process and from the law, where even the volunteers working for humanitarian organizations in Afghanistan and Pakistan have been harassed, some of them being interned in Guantanamo, others being punished by other means, like the organizations working in Kosovo whose workers were subjected by Italian international forces (Efour) to unprecedented abuses, according to what is reported by the Islamic organizations workers there. These acts are gross violations of the European Treaty on Human Rights and Basic Freedoms.

All of this is taking place right under the eyes and ears of the world and in a way that alienates everyone who works for those organizations or receives benefit from them. Indeed, it discourages them from expressing their faith and their human identity. Keep in mind that these organizations represent more than a billion and a quarter Muslims worldwide who have the same right as anyone else to choose the way in which they wish to work and the humanitarian organizations and programs they wish to contribute to and develop. In accordance with the new outlook on NGOs and what has preceded, and especially after the negative consequences that have been seen since September 11, most of what is taking place against Islamic charities – the accusations, the freezing of accounts, and the restrictions under the pretext of their financing terror – is nothing more than a new strategic cover-up that regards Islamic charities as being among the "new competitors". This is because the element of competition and the element of independence from governments are both very much present in Islamic charities and organizations, and according to this new worldview, they are, as America sees it, out of control. Consequently, these charities with their Islamic, moral agendas, and their financial and ideological independence, are a powerful, competitive element against the extreme fanatical elements in the West.

It seems that the blossoming of these non-governmental organizations was a requirement of the Cold War to defeat the Communist adversary that did not recognize civil organizations. In fact, many of them were used to help bring down the Soviet Union. After the defeat of Communism, these international organizations and Islamic charities that are an expression of freedom and democracy for the world's people have become a danger to the new global imperialism, and especially to American imperialism. Indeed, they have become a powerful competitor necessitating a new era, that of a "War on Terror" and unilateral politics to neutralize their power. This is being carried out on a global level, differing in approach from one type of organization to another.

This idea is confirmed by the fact that the Soviet Union's imperialism and its communist ideology were opposed to the very idea of civil organizations, as mentioned by Benthall and Jourdan: "Hard-line state socialists opposed charity…To push this line of argument to its logical conclusion and outlaw all charity is however to place all power in the hands of the state. This was the policy of former Soviet bloc, since the earliest days of the Bolshevik revolution. The network of the Russian charitable organizations was as far as possible abolished by the Soviet as inimical to the principles governing human relationships in socialist state. "[103]

Imperialism is imperialism, whether it is coming from the East or the West.

On the other hand, emphasizing the inconsistencies of this new world as well as the great extent of its victims,_World Bank President James Wolfensohn, speaking about poverty and terrorism, said: "We thought there were two worlds - the haves and the have-nots - …The wall that many of us imagined as separating the rich countries from the poor countries came down on September 11, 2001. We are linked now in so many ways: by economics and trade, migration, environment, disease, drugs and conflict."[104]

He drew attention to the future threats saying: "In our world of six billion people, one billion have 80 percent of the world's GDP, while the other five billion have the remaining 20 percent. Nearly half this world lives on less than $2 per day. One billion people have no access to clean water; over 100 million children never get the chance to go to school; and more than 40 million people in the developing countries are H.I.V.-positive, with little hope of receiving treatment."[105]

Wolfensohn mentions that: "Recent research suggests that a lack of economic opportunity, and the resulting competition for resources, lies at the root of most conflicts over the last 30 years, more than ethnic, political and ideological issues. This research supports the intuitive idea that if people have jobs, and if they have hope, they are less likely to turn to violence."[106]

Do those who oppose international organizations and charities understand these bitter realities, these frightening numbers, which demand more not less humanitarian organizations – including the Islamic ones – to shoulder a great share of the burden of relief? However, in reality, the campaigns and measures being implemented against humanitarian and relief organizations have the purpose of worsening these tragic statistics, and are unfortunately achieving that purpose.

The free press and those who work for it have also become victims. Fifty-six journalists were killed in 2004 alone, according to a report of the American Council to Protect Journalists on 14 March 2005. As a consequence, less information is available concerning the painful situation of innocent victims of violence, hunger, and disease.. An example that illustrates the drastic change in freedom of press is what happened to the Qatar-based *al-Jazeera* TV. *Al-Jazeera* has exercised its freedom of press and was a shining example of freedom and democracy in the Arab world during the mid 1990's; but it became undesirable to the American administration after the events of September 11, when freedoms were curtailed and democracies stifled. *Al-Jazeera* has caused a change in the quality of media in the Arab world in particular, and has become an active partner in bringing world news to TV viewers, and is no more dependent on the international media corporations; it formulates news from its own viewpoints. This seems to be in conflict with the US administration's new attitude toward freedoms. *Al-Jazeera*'s quarters in Afghanistan and Iraq have both been bombarded by the US army and there have been attempts to corner them at other places, in addition to the killing of some of their correspondents, and the arrest of others such as Taysir Alluni[107] in Spain and the cameraman Sami al-Haj in Guantanamo[108].

In defense of humanitarian work, those who work in this field see that the first step towards resisting such long-term, precisely planned, and forcefully carried out campaign requires exposing the voices of bigotry, the promoters of a clash of religions, a clash of civilizations, who are relentless in provoking and instigating the political and civil powers of the international community against the Muslim world and its humanitarian organizations, even though those organizations contribute greatly to saving approximately 30 million Muslim refugees. They are vicious campaigns that have escalated after September 11. Their scope has broadened to include all the nations of the world. Their allegations have been well received by some countries, given lip-service by a few others, and rejected by the rest.

These matters require further investigation. It is important that those who support, condemn, or merely incite against these organizations be well informed. This is done only thru objective analysis of the matter. This is the only real way to arrive at the truth.

Chapter II

The Campaign against Islamic Charities after 9/11

Propaganda War

The United States, according to some, is engaged in manipulating information to influence public opinion. Thom Shanker and Eric Schmitt of *New York Times* write: "[The Pentagon] missions, if approved, could take deceptive techniques endorsed for use on the battlefield to confuse adversary and adopt them for covert propaganda campaigns aimed at neutral and even allied nations[109]." It was even suggested to resurrect the Office of Strategic Influence to "provide news items, including false ones, to foreign journalists in effort to influence overseas opinion."[110]

Noam Chomsky describes democracy in the US as "a democracy of spectatorship, not one of participation". He describes the attitude of governments toward their people, saying: "There's a logic behind it. There's even a kind of compelling moral principle behind it. The compelling moral principle is that the mass of the public are just too stupid to be able to understand things. If they try to participate in managing their own affairs, they're just going to cause trouble. Therefore, it would be immoral and improper to permit them to do this. We have to tame the bewildered herd, not allow the bewildered herd to rage and trample and destroy things."[111] And since it is difficult to attain these results in a free society, controlling and changing public opinion through media propaganda is critical for these governments. "So we need something to tame the bewildered herd, and that something is this new revolution in the art of democracy: the manufacture of consent."[112]

In a nutshell he says: "Propaganda is to a democracy what the bludgeon is to a totalitarian state."[113]

America is the leader in devising public relations campaigns. Its purpose is to control public opinion, as those behind these efforts say. They learned a lot from the successes of the Creel Commission and the creation of the "Red Terror".

Chomsky speaks about how the enemy is created, even when it is an imaginary one. He writes: "Prior to about the mid-1980s, when you were asleep you would just play the record: the Russians are coming. But [George Bush] lost that one and he's got to make up new ones, just like the Reaganite public relations apparatus did in the 1980s. So it was international terrorists and narcotraffickers and crazed Arabs and Saddam Hussein, the new Hitler, [who] was going to conquer the world. They've got to keep coming up one after another. You frighten the population, terrorize them, intimidate them so that they're too afraid to travel and cower in fear. Then you have a magnificent victory over Grenada, Panama, or some other defenseless third-world army that you can pulverize before you ever bother to look at them - which is just what happened. That gives relief. We were saved at the last minute. That's one of the ways in which you can keep the bewildered herd from paying attention to what's really going on around them, keep them diverted and controlled."[114]

Speaking at the London Conference on Partnership for Peace and Development in Palestine, Dr. Wendell Belew characterizes the instruments of terror-labeling used by the American administration that relies on the media, saying that: "For an account of how OFAC determines how to go about designating an entity as a terrorist, I recommend an article by award-winning journalist David Ottaway published on the front page of the November 14, 2004 edition of *The Washington Post*. As Ottaway attests, the Process relies heavily on newspaper accounts, secret evidence and accusations by foreign governments. In one instance, OFAC relied on an article published by USA Today that the author and the newspaper had admitted to be fabricated and withdrawn from the archives."[115]

David Ottaway writes in *The Washington Post*: "The classified evidence remains out of reach and much of the unclassified evidence turned out to be allegations in newspaper clippings."[116] Concerning materials inculpating Global Relief Foundation he writes: "A Post reporter who reviewed the materials found that they included 61 newspaper articles dating back to 1999. 'We found ourselves trying to rebut newspaper reports around the world,' [Attorney] Simmons said."[117]

The impact of the media campaign against humanitarian organizations and their donors from among Muslim businessmen was apparent when the authors of the book *Bin Laden: The Forbidden Truth*, Jean-Charles Brisard and Guillaume Dasquie, relying heavily on newspapers and other print publications that appeared after September 11, 2001, brought allegations against two Saudi businessmen, Khalid Bin Mahfouz and his son Abdel-Rahman of financing terrorism. Brisard has even presented a report to the United Nations in 2002 concerning this affair. However, following legal suits in the United Kingdom and Switzerland, the two authors presented their apologies to the two businessmen in different newspapers around the world, admitting that their allegations were void of any truth. The authors also agreed to arrange for the withdrawal of the book from the market, along with clearly admitting that the allegations against the men and their families were all fabricated. In addition, the authors paid £60,000 as compensation to the businessmen, who in turn donated the sum to UNICEF. This is yet another indication of the extent of the misinformation and media war, which has targeted Islamic humanitarian organizations and their donors.

That is how public consent is manufactured and public opinion is engineered. Indeed, this is the way wars are declared. All of this comes by way of an unprecedented propaganda war waged through the media.

Campaign against Islamic Organizations Taking Root before 9/11

America's initiatives concerning Islamic organizations it believed to be connected to terrorists began well before September 11. An American magazine mentions that aggressive and vengeful conduct against Arab and Islamic organizations and their workers was spurred on by pressure from powerful Zionist lobbies in the American administration. The cases relating to the investigations and arrests of roughly thirty Muslim activists from the time of the Clinton administration are still open. During the Clinton administration the American judicial system was disrupted with the rationale of "politics before the law", whereby the law was interpreted according to the interests of pro-Israel policy organizations.

For the first time in its political history the United States witnessed, during the Clinton administration, a focused constriction of the activities of Islamic organizations accused of having terrorist affiliations, a constriction which is linked by some to the growth in influence of Zionist organizations.

Israel has found in the Islamic movement, its statements opposing Zionist oppression, a winning card to propagate the idea of terrorism threat as a substitute to the communism threat, and has been given a great opportunity to shape the future of the region, and to have great political influence.

Islamic organizations in general insisted on keeping a peaceful co-existence and dialogue within their communities in the US, shunning extremism and violence. But the propaganda machine painted all Islamic organizations and activities in the US as violent implying that the phenomenon of Islam is a danger to the US and to its interests abroad. This propaganda is fueled by persons who are known to be linked to Israel, people such as Daniel Pipes, Judith Miller, and Steven Emerson. The latter poses as an 'expert' in investigating Islamic organizations, and his inflammatory statements have incited the government to go on a witch hunt after Muslim activists.

There are many reasons behind this Zionist campaign: First the pro-Israel circles were disturbed by the access of Muslims to the intellectual, academic, and political arena, and their participation in the civilizational dialogue and political issues concerning the Muslim world and its relation with the West, and the appearance of Muslim scholars capable of defending the Palestinian issue. This is seen as a danger to the Israeli occupation policy. Second, after the fall of the Soviet Union, Israel saw its role as a strategic ally of the US in the Middle East disappear. Israel was looking for a new role. This was handed to it on the occasion of the first bombing of the twin towers in 1987. Pro-Israel groups were successful in equating the terrorist bombing in New York to the legitimate Palestinian struggle against Israeli occupation, painting with one stroke all Islamic activities as extremist, or terrorist.

In this environment of Islamophobia, during the Clinton administration, the US Congress passed laws that gave the FBI broad authority to watch and prosecute Islamic organizations, Muslim communities and their active members. One billion dollars was reserved to gather information, among other things. This formidable judicial and financial power was crowned by the issuance of the Secret Evidence Act, which allows the detention of any person suspected by the security agencies, without informing anyone of his relatives, and without prosecuting him.

These drastic laws have cast fear and unease in the Muslim communities in the US. This fear has led Muslims to distance themselves from any Islamic organization that is under watch, before even being accused of anything. Some Islamic organizations have been completely devastated by simple allegations. This has led to a drying of the financial and human sources of many Islamic organizations.

In 2000, Judith Miller wrote an article in *New York Times* warning against Islamic charities. She is the author of *Allah has Ninety-Nine Names*, about which Edward Saïd commented at the time of its publication, saying: "She trades in 'the Islamic threat' - her particular mission has been to advance the millennial thesis that militant Islam is a danger to the West."[118]

The purpose behind writing the article is to convince the reader that Islamic charities are nothing more than front organizations for terrorism and terror financing. She tries to instill fear and doubt in the hearts of Muslims so they will refrain from giving any donations to those charities. In the middle of the article, she mentions that from 6000 Islamic Organizations worldwide, Washington is investigating the operations of 30. Considering the lack of knowledge of the average American reader about Islam, the number 6000 is enough to inspire fears and doubts, but in fact it is a drop in the bucket when you consider that U.S. has about 2 million NGOs[119]. Muslims from about 2% of the US population, while Islamic NGOs form only 0.3% of US NGOs. She alleged that US officials, investigating a decade of international terrorist attacks have found a common thread with Islamic charities and relief organizations that they suspect were being used to move men, money and weapons across borders, that Osama Bin Laden relied on at least nine groups of them in his recent (before 2000) operations.

Miller tried in her article to convince the reader to believe that all Islamic charities are connected to terrorism[120]. She says that other charities "have been linked to a recent plot to bomb historic and tourist sites in Jordan, the 1993 bombing of the World Trade Center and terrorist attacks in Egypt against tourists and government officials."[121]

Another example of the early campaign against Islamic charities is what happened with the Islamic African Relief Agency in 1999. The USAID, a government organization, cut off the grants to this organization under pressure from Richard Clark who was in charge of combating terrorism during the Clinton era. Clark informed *Newsweek* that he feared that a number of American Islamic charities had possible terrorist ties and urged the State Department to break off relations with those charities. A memo from the USAID dated December 29, 1999 says that contracts with the Islamic relief agency should have been evaluated according to the national interests of the United States.[122]

In February 15, 2000, *Quds Press* mentioned that Michael Sheehan of the State Department hinted that there is a link between terrorism and charity work, especially in the Muslim world. [123]

These early campaigns spread suspicions about Islamic charities inside the US and abroad. They laid the ground to an open full blown campaign after September 11. They instilled fear of Islamic organizations, and a general Islamophobia that greatly facilitated this campaign. What's more dangerous is the sweeping allegations reaching most Islamic charities if not all, making no distinction between them, and without specifying the degree or the type of their mistakes. This has put all Islamic organizations in the dock, going beyond the US borders to the very soul of Muslim countries.

Examples of the Campaign

Anyone who considers the extent, and sheer number of America's propaganda campaigns against Islamic charities will come to realize how comprehensive these campaigns are against all sorts of Islamic organizations worldwide. The effects of these allegations and the yielding to American pressure have gone so far as to put down any collective effort to criticize or refute the terror allegations against Islamic charities. This is what happened at the international convention in Paris on January 2003, where many Islamic charities and organizations were accused of terrorism without any evidence whatsoever. Some were shut down while others had their accounts frozen without any judicial procedure or legal justice being brought to bear. This is what happened with al- Haramain Foundation, Qatar Charities, and others. Islamic charities in the US and Europe, especially those helping Palestinians have received the same treatment, which scared away donors and volunteers for fear of being labeled as a supporter of terrorism or punished.

The examples cited below represent only five percent of the cases that I have investigated. The American and international campaign is extensive and powerful and very difficult to assess and fully account for, but perhaps the following selected examples will help in understanding their true nature and purpose.

Afghanistan and Pakistan: Since the late 90s, the American Government can be said to have put pressure on Pakistan in the days of Nawaz Sharif to reduce the level of Islamic charitable activity in his country. Sharif yielded to the US pressure. In the early 1990s, there were over five hundred Arabs working for the Islamic Relief agency. By 1999, there were only two.[124]

The Committee to Support the Afghans has been shut both in Pakistan and Afghanistan, its accounts frozen. The accusation was that its money goes to al-Qaeda instead of going to the needy. The offices of Islamic Heritage Revival Association in Pakistan and Afghanistan have been raided under the accusation of terror financing, alleging that they were providing names of orphans that do not exist. The association headquarters are in Kuwait.[125]

Pakistani newspapers published a report al-Ihsan Pakistani Center, a non-profit independent organization, which the government asked to prepare advices and recommendations to regulate Islamic charities, NGOs and other citizens groups.[126]

Washington allocated 100 million dollars for Pakistan to review its Islamic school books, and get a firm control on religious (Islamic) schools, and decrease the number of religious education hours.[127]

Pakistan Central Bank froze the assets of Harakat al-Mujahedin, which was fighting Indian occupation of Kashmir, and the assets of al-Rashid Organization.[128]

Saudi Arabia: In March 21, 2002, the Saudi Government passed legislation requiring charitable organizations to present to the Ministry of Foreign Affairs details of projects they plan to finance abroad.[129] In the July 21, 2003 Congress meeting, members' questions concentrated on the World Assembly of Muslim Youth, and the Muslim World League and its alleged support of Hamas, and al-Qaeda.[130] In February 29, 2004, The Saudi Government announced the formation of the Saudi Commission for Relief and Charity Work Abroad as an exclusive - but not a supervising - organization (to deal with financing work abroad).[131]

Kuwait: Immediately after September 11, Kuwait took a series of drastic measures to organize donation collections by charities, prohibiting all cash collections and all donations to mosques even during the month of Ramadan. This is similar to forbidding Christians to donate cash to their churches during Christmas or preventing the Salvation Army to collect at entrances of shops. Charities who want to transfer money outside Kuwait need the approval of the Central Bank of Kuwait.

American ambassador to Kuwait, Richard LeBaron asked the Kuwaiti Government to further tighten the control over the charities' money collection and transfer, claiming that these actions will dry up the source of terror financing.

During February and March 2005 the Kuwaiti Government started to remove the collection boxes and booths belonging to Islamic charities. Ahmad as-Sayegh said to AFP: "We removed 25 boxes during the last three days, and this operation will continue for the next two weeks to remove more than 80 boxes." These boxes and booths belonged to five registered charities that have 123 branches around Kuwait[132].

Somalia: American delegations investigated the curricula of Islamic education in the University of Mogadishu. Al-Haramain Foundation offices in Somalia were closed down[133].

Egypt: Egyptian newspapers published a report presented by the government to Parliament to extend government control of humanitarian NGOs[134].

The Gulf Center for Strategic Studies organized a symposium, "The Future of the humanitarian Gulf organizations in the light of the US allegations of Terror Financing", where they emphasized that the US was waging hostile campaigns against Islamic humanitarian organizations since September 11, to suppress their role and reduce their activities, and give the green light to the missionary Christian organizations to take their place[135].

Qatar: Qatar Charitable Association has supported 25,000 orphans in many countries including Afghanistan, Pakistan, Bosnia, and Somalia. This support has been stopped under the allegation that the funds were used to finance terrorism[136].

The United Arab Emirates: Some economic experts declared to *Islam Online* that Western banks have reservations in dealing with 176 Islamic banks since September 11, and allege that they have links to terrorists[137].

Lebanon: The US President asked to freeze all the assets of Sanabil for Relief and Development, headquartered in South Lebanon accusing it to transfer donations collected in Europe and the Middle East to Hamas[138].

Switzerland: Al-Barakah on which funds a great portion of the Somali people depends, had its assets frozen. At Taqwah, owned by Yusuf Nada and Ali Himmat, two businessmen, had its assets frozen. No accusation of the two men's link to al-Qaeda or any other organization has been proven[139].

The US President asked to freeze the assets of Palestinian Relief Association, headquartered in Switzerland, under the allegation that they support Hamas[140].

Holland: Holland's investigation services accused Islamic Relief Fund of links to al-Qaeda and of terror financing. A report was sent to the Ministry of Finance, and the government decided to immediately freeze the Fund's assets, and officially designated the charity as a supporter of terrorism, as alleged by the United Nations[141].

Al-Aqsa Charitable Foundation assets in Holland have been frozen under the allegation that it financed terrorist activities in the Middle East. Officials of the foundation in Holland denied the allegations and insisted they collect money to support orphans and widows, and for educational projects[142].

Denmark: Rashid Eissa, the President of al-Aqsa Charitable Foundation in Denmark denied the accusations of his and his organization's support of terrorism, saying that investigations of organizations dealing with al-Aqsa, were going on for more than a month and a half and that their computers were seized.[143] He said that 2 million Danish Crones have been frozen.

France: The US President asked to freeze the assets of Benevolence and Relief headquartered in France, under the accusation that it provides financial support to Hamas[144].

Germany: The Defense of the Constitution Administration accused al-Aqsa Foundation of using the collected donations to finance Hamas activities inside Israel[145].The German Foreign Minister ordered the raid of al-Aqsa headquarters in Aachen, to raid the house of its employees and the confiscation of 300,000 Euros. He alleged that the organization promoted Jihad, and is part of Hamas, and that it transferred money to suicide bombers' families[146]. (This event is a stark example of the strong link between the American media campaign and the Israeli-Palestinian issue).

Italy: Italian security services were given the power to take action against Islamic centers, charities, and associations, especially those in Rome, and also in other European capitals[147].

Austria: The US President asked to freeze the assets of the Palestinian Association headquartered in Austria. The US treasury alleged that an official from Hamas managed the organization and used its funds to support Hamas[148].

Sweden: The US administration asked the Swedish Foreign Ministry to suspend al-Aqsa Charity Foundation, headquartered in Malmö in southern Sweden and to freeze its assets because it supports needy families in occupied Palestine[149].

Australia: Australian authorities froze the assets of al-Aqsa Charity and added it to the list of organizations with link to terrorism. The government forbade financial dealings with the organization[150].

Yemen: Under pressure from the US, the Yemeni Government closed the religious universities, and decided to establish new ones following the Al Azhar model in Egypt with "moderate" scholars. It expressed its fears of the activities of al Iman University, prohibiting from collecting donations without permission[151].

Malawi: The Malawi police in Blantyre raided the homes of five foreigners at dawn: two Turkish (the executive director of Badr International School, and the owner of a restaurant chain), one Saudi (the executive director of Saudi Trust), one Sudanese (the executive director of Zakat al Fitr Trust), and one Kenyan (a teacher at Badr International School), and detained them. Badr International School is the most prestigious university in Malawi[152].

Mauritania: The Mauritanian authorities closed definitely the Saudi Center for Religious Guidance in the capital Nouakchott and the branch of Muslim World League in Mauritania according to an official source. He said that the Mauritanian Foreign Ministry has informed the Saudi *chargé d'affaires* about the decision and banned all activities of the two Saudi organizations which have been working in religious guidance and orphans and poor support for more than 20 years[153].

The Mauritanian authority closed the Institute of Arabic and Islamic Studies affiliated with Imam Muhammad Ibn Saud Islamic University in a campaign against charitable Islamic education institutions that coincided with a wave of detentions of Islamic activists[154].

The Mauritanian police detained the manager of the charity and four employees before seizing its belongings and closing the locale[155].

On May 27, 2003, at least ten teachers at Saudi-funded Arab and Saudi Islamic Institute in the capital, Nouakchott, were arrested[156].

Jordan: Bankers in Amman reported that Amman received the demands of George Bush to freeze the assets of three Islamic financial organizations: Aqsa Bank, Holy Land Foundation, and the Palestinian Beit al-Mal Holdings Company. This freezing concerns the fourth largest financial bank in Jordan, al-Bank al-Islami because it processes 50% of al-Aqsa Bank capital[157].

Morocco: The Charitable Social Association in Rabat has been prevented from continuing its program of Ramadan meals distribution to the poor in the old city, leaving 600 needy people without meals[158].

Uzbekistan: The Uzbek Government banned all religious Islamic teaching outside government schools. A decree has been issued that bans Imams from giving private religious lessons, or teaching memorization of the Qur'an. Penalties are as high as 100 euros and 15 days of prison (the average monthly income of the

Uzbeks is 20 euros). There are ten authorized religious schools in all Uzbekistan, eight for boys and two for girls. The remaining 230 schools do not have permission to teach religious subjects and as a consequence it is expected that they will be closed.

Kenya: Mercy International Relief Organization offices have been closed. The Kenyan government banned International Islamic Relief Organization after the bombing of the American embassy in Kenya[159].

Cambodia: On May 28 Cambodia charged 3 men - 2 Thais and an Egyptian - with being members of the Jamaah Islamiyah and having links to al-Qaeda, and prepared to deport another 50 Arab and African Islamists. Twenty-eight of the suspects were Islamic teachers associated with a Saudi-funded school. Prime Minister Hu Sen presiding at a press conference announced that his government's "investigation proves this group has received financial support from international terrorist groups. The funding mainly came out of Saudi Arabia."[160]

The United Nations: The United Nations announced that it fears the work of international relief organizations in Pakistan will be halted because of the various attacks and allegations against them, especially the 51 Arab relief organizations working in the refugee camps in Peshawar and the surrounding vicinity because of the raids and harassment campaigns which started by the Kuwaiti Heritage association in Peshawar by American intelligence and the Pakistani forces[161].

News and analyses singled out Great Britain, Bosnia, Palestine, Afghanistan, and Iraq as case studies that reveal further the truth of this campaign and the causes behind it.

Conclusions:

The examples mentioned above are but the tip of the iceberg. There are countless other examples. What draws our attention and gives cause for alarm is the comprehensive geographical scope of this campaign. These resolutions, procedures, and demands have a dangerous significance and forebode even more dangerous consequences to rights and freedoms. Indeed, they forebode a conflict between civilizations and faiths.

One who considers these brief examples can see how sweeping this international campaign has been, covering basically every country on every continent. He can see how this campaign has concerned itself with every type of Islamic organization including charities, relief organizations, educational organizations, social organizations and religious organizations. This has been part of America's strategic plan from early on, well before September 11, so as not to be a reaction to September 11. Analysts have viewed this strategy as being the creation of an imaginary enemy.

After evaluating the above examples one notices the following:

1. This extensive campaign has targeted only Islamic organizations. It has not targeted any Christian or Jewish charities.

2. It does not seek to correct particular mistakes as much as it seeks to uncover mistakes or bring about a cessation of those organizations' activities, freeze their accounts, or cut off their sources of revenue.

3. It comprehends most countries of the world, both rich and poor. And it targeted the most successful organizations in education and religious guidance, the most prominent for their activities, and the ones that have many branches around the world.

4. Political pressure and pressure campaigns represent the greater part of these events. Judicial and legal proceedings have not reigned supreme in these matters.

5. Some European countries that closed certain Islamic charities and froze their assets reversed their decision after their own investigation revealed that the American allegations were baseless.

6. Organizations concerned with the Palestine issue were the primary targets all over the world. America put pressure on every country in the world that harbored relief organizations for the Palestinian people, including Europe, Australia, and the Arab world. In some countries, funding for such organizations were cut or otherwise curtailed.

7. Most countries around the world have passed new legislation that restricts the activities of Islamic charities without distinguishing those that are concerned with domestic matters from those with an international scope.

Observers are asking if all of these sweeping American measures are really a response to September 11. Are they perhaps a new strategy to take advantage of the opportunity to declare a new war, the War on Terror? Under the banner of this war, they can carry out many of their strategic goals, even though most of their initiatives do nothing to lessen the alleged threat of terror. If anything, those initiatives increase that threat.

America's Sweeping Demands

The United States did not content itself with imposing restrictions upon Islamic organizations and putting an end to their activities. They went further and started to interfere with textbooks and school syllabi in many counties, particularly in countries of the Muslim world. Qatar's a*l-Watan* newspaper mentions that the United States has demanded the Arab world abolish religious studies in its schools, and that this demand is being taken into consideration in most Arab countries. The newspaper unveiled a lengthy American study it said has reached some European Union states and was prepared by research centers subsidiary to the American State Department. Eight senior researchers specialized in the Middle East affairs, about Islamic organizations participated in the research. The newspaper mentioned sources in Britain saying the principal recommendation that came out of this study was the necessity of abolishing religious teaching in the entire Arab region because it is the vessel from which terrorists graduate, as the study claims.

Senator Joseph Biden, chairman of the Foreign Affairs Committee said that it is necessary to encourage Saudi Arabia to stop financing religious schools; otherwise there will be grave consequences for it and other countries. Prince Nayef criticized Senator Biden's position in a Saudi newspaper[162].

The American Ambassador in Egypt has asked Dr. Muhammad Tantawi, the Shaikh of al-Azhar (the most important mosque and Islamic university in Egypt) to close 25 religious organizations, under the allegation that they support terror. These organizations have been active in promoting the boycott of American products. The ambassador has also asked to put pressure on some al-Azhar faculty members who asked the Egyptian Government to take a stronger position towards the US.[163]

Diplomats from the American Embassy in Sana'a, Yemen, intensified their visits to the religious universities and education centers whose curricula concentrate on teaching religion. They collected samples of these curricula, and demanded to erase or change some quotations written on the walls of the universities![164]

The far reaching American demands, have gone beyond the activities of the organizations to reach the activities of some leading personalities in the field of Islamic charity work. One of these personalities is Sheik Mohammed Ali Hassan Al-Moayad, a 59 year old Yemeni citizen distinguished by his charitable activities who served as under-secretary and adviser at the Ministry of Endowments in Yemen. He founded al-Ihsan al-Khayri Center in Sana'a, Yemen, a charitable organization as well as a philanthropic bakery, several health clinics, and a computer learning center. He was a supporter of the Palestinian people. According to the Arab Commission for Human Rights, and the Global Justice Organization, Mr. al-Moayad was arrested on January 10, 2003 in Germany where he was traveling for medical reasons. He was then delivered to the US authorities to be tried in a Federal Court in Brooklyn, New York. In July 28, 2005, he was sentenced to 75 years in prison and fined $1.25 million for alleged support to the Palestinian Hamas.[165] The whole prosecutors' case reposed on a sole source, an FBI informant from Yemen with a checkered past[166], who later set himself on fire[167] outside the White House trying to kill himself because he believed the FBI had lied to him.[168]

Dr. Riad AbdelKerim, co-founder of Kids in Need of Development, Education and Relief (KINDER USA), a Muslim American relief organization, said certain aspects of the guidelines are beyond the scope of what many charities are able to do and called them "ridiculous and burdensome". "The Red Cross does not keep a list of everyone they give a band aid to after a tornado," he said.[169] "During times of humanitarian crisis, conducting background checks of every individual who could possibly be involved with foreign relief organizations is irrational," said Attorney L. George.[170]

The Text of America's Demands (Kuwait as an Example)

The text of America's requests for strengthened surveillance of the charities in Kuwait reveals, some say, a lot about the real purpose behind America's campaign. America was fishing for proofs during its inquiries in this matter. Its principle was "condemn first then look for evidence". In its efforts to "dry up the sources of terror funding" America issued an official request by way of the Kuwaiti Foreign Ministry, that a number of charities and commercial establishments in Kuwait provide financial documents and declarations as well as account information due to the suspicion that some of their money was channeled into financing terrorist organizations. This documentation was to be delivered to a special American delegation that went to Kuwait with the express purpose of investigating those documents. These demands provoked the reticence of Islamic organizations, which regarded themselves as being answerable only to the Kuwaiti Government.

What follows is the text of those demands, which represents merely one of many that were made upon the countries throughout the Muslim world and upon Islamic charities throughout the world:

Document Request for Charities and Business Entities

In order to assist the team of experts to better understand the operations of charitable organizations and business entities in Kuwait, we would appreciate if as many of the below specified types of documents for each organization could be made available for the team to review upon their arrival. The records request should cover the last three years.

Corporations/Businesses and Charitable Organizations.

1. All organization bookkeeping records and other financial records including, but not limited to: general ledgers, general journals, gross receipts and income records, cash receipts and cash disbursement records, sales and purchase records and journals, accounts receivable and payment ledgers, bad debt records, cost of goods sold records, loans receivable and payment ledgers, income statements, balance sheets and all expense invoices including all invoices documenting expenses paid by cash. These records should include financial and budget documents that identify the organization's sources of income, assets, and disbursements. Supporting documents on disbursements involving the use of intermediaries is also requested, and would be of particular interest.

2. Mission statement, statement of program services accomplishments, by-laws and an organization chart. The chart should depicting (sic) structure and staffing, to include domestic and foreign/overseas branch offices, if any, including addresses, telephone numbers, and a list of employees, their positions, and any identifying information.

3. All financial statements, bookkeeper's and/or accountant's work papers used in the preparation of organizational records or tax returns. Retained copies of all foreign and U.S. tax returns, including all information and payroll tax returns.

4. Full identities, associated identifiers, applications, records of payment and all other documents regarding recipients of grants, allocations, disbursements, scholarships, stipends, and other payments. These records should include files on all assistance provided to individuals or organizations in Kuwait, as well as in all foreign countries, such as Afghanistan, Chechnya, Somalia, the Philippines, and Pakistan.

5. Full identities, associated identifiers, records of compensation and all other documents regarding all officers, directors, trustees, employees, consultants and others performing services for the organization.

6. Full identities, associated identifiers and all other documents regarding individuals and entities making gifts, contributions, bequests and any other payments to the organization. These records should also contain information on any fundraising activities sponsored by the organization.

7. Documents concerning account relationships with financial institutions including banks, brokerages and money exchanges. These documents should include: bank statements, deposit slips, check registers, canceled checks, debit and credit memos, records reflecting dates and amounts of deposits, deposit slips, records reflecting the identity of checks deposited, withdrawal slips, debit and credit memos, certificates of deposit, money market certificates, purchase of cashier's checks, wire transfers, remittance orders, and applications for wire transfers, etc.

Meeting with Individuals

In addition to reviewing the above types of records, the team would appreciate the opportunity to meet with individuals who could provide information on the following:

1. The organizations' procedures for approving projects/individuals to become recipients of charitable donations, as well as procedures for disbursement of funds to recipients.

2. The sources and types of donations the organizations have received during the past three years.

3. The recipients the organization have funded for the past three years.

4. Appropriate government officials responsible for the oversight or monitoring of the organizations and their activities.

Records to be requested from Financial Institutions

If documents need to be obtained from Kuwait banks and/or other financial institutions regarding an individual or entity, the following is a list of documents to be furnished:

1. <u>Savings Account Records:</u> including signature cards, ledger cards or records reflecting dates and amounts of deposits, withdrawals, interest, debit and credit memos, deposit slips, checks deposited, withdrawal slips, and checks issued for withdrawals.

2. <u>Checking Account Records:</u> including signature cards, bank statements, deposit slips, checks deposited, checks drawn on the account, records pertaining to all debit and credit memos.

3. <u>Loan Records:</u> including applications, financial statements, loan collateral, credit and background investigations, loan agreements, notes of mortgages, settlement sheets, contracts, checks issued for loans, repayment records, including records revealing the date, amount and method of repayment (cash or check), checks used to repay loans and a record disclosing the total amount of discount or interest paid annually, records of any liens, loan correspondence files, and internal bank memoranda.

4. <u>Safe Deposit Box Records:</u> including contracts, access records, and records of rental fees paid disclosing the date, amount, and method of payment (cash or check).

5. <u>Certificates of Deposit and Money Market Certificates:</u> including applications, actual instrument(s), records of purchases and redemptions, checks issued on redemption, checks used to purchase certificate, any correspondence and any Forms 1099 issued, records revealing the annual interest paid or accumulated, the dates of payment or date interest is earned, checks issued for interest payments.

6. <u>Credit Card Records:</u> including customer's application, signature card, credit or background investigations conducted, correspondence, monthly billing statements, individual charge invoices, repayment records disclosing the dates, amounts and method (cash or check) of repayment, checks used to make repayments (front and back).

7. <u>Purchases of Bank Checks:</u> purchases of bank checks, cashier, teller, travelers' check records, or money order records including the check register, file copies of the checks or money orders, records revealing the date or source of payment for said checks or money orders.

8. <u>Other Records:</u> records of certified checks, wire transfers, or collections, letters of credit, bonds and securities purchased through your bank, savings bond transactions and investment accounts. Such records that disclose the date and amount of the transaction, method (cash or check) and source of payment, instruments, and statements of transactions.[171]

Al-Hayat newspaper reports that the Kuwaiti charities convened a conference on January 12, 2002 to deliberate on America's requests. An announcement from these organizations said: "Is it not more logical for the Americans to present specific accusations and particular organizations and then allow those concerned parties to respond?" The announcement also commended the Kuwaiti Government which demanded from the US evidence and proof of the accusations, and did not hastened to close the organizations as did some other governments.[172]

Members of Islamic charities are surprised at the extent to which America went in those demands. It is a shame for any country that claims to champion democracy and freedom to make such demands.

Surveillance of Islamic Charities

Other information gleaned from a number of articles, personal interviews, and official documents can be summarized in the following points:

- These efforts of the United States are not restricted to Islamic organizations activities outside of the Muslim and Arab world, but also within the Muslim land. More importantly, the United States arranged with other countries throughout the world to strengthen and make more stringent their internal regulations of charities. Indeed, a high commission was formed to oversee such matters led by US Secretary of the Treasury Paul O'Neill and former deputy secretary of the Treasury, Kenneth W. Dam. Likewise, Former General Counsel to Department of Treasury, David Aufhauser leads a committee to coordinate policies among various agencies of the National Security Council with respect to terror financing, with the help of Treasury Undersecretary for Enforcement Jimmy Gurule.

The purpose of this committee is to determine the identities of terrorist groups and freeze their sources of financing within the United States and to work with America's allies to broaden the scope of these efforts to freeze their accounts worldwide. This resulted in freezing more than $112 million around the world in the first stage, through the help of many countries. The committee took the following measures against Islamic charities:

a- Stopping the flow of money to the organizations and freeze their assets under the allegation that they support terrorist groups.

b- Investigating the misuse of charities' works.

c- Coordinating with countries worldwide to raise the standards of monitoring the charities' accounts.

- Likewise, a task force was formed from a number of agencies under the name "Green Quest Operation" sponsored by the Treasury Department to combat financing terrorists and disrupt their financial network. This team has arrested 38 individuals, charged 26 others, and seized around $6.8 million inside the US and more than $16 million on their way out.

Mosques and Islamic centers were not spared from being monitored and investigated. A high source from the US Justice Department said to *The Washington Post* (May 29, 2002) that the Department will allow the FBI to open a window on the activities of extremists in mosques.

A number of Islamic centers have been raided in Virginia where there is a high concentration of Muslims, and documents and computers were seized. CAIR's President Nihad Awadh said that the areas around the centers were surrounded and the neighboring houses raided without any notification or charge. Likewise, the houses of many Islamic leaders were raided and their offices searched under the threat of arms, except that none of them has been arrested.[173]

American Measures that Penalize Everyone

In the context of this all-out war being waged by America against terrorism on numerous fronts both within and outside of its borders, former Secretary of Justice John Ashcroft declared the classification of forty-six organizations on the Terrorist Blacklist whose members are prohibited from entering the United States.

Ashcroft declared the formation of a Foreign Terrorist Tracking Task Force headed by FBI chief Steven C. McGraw and said that the Task Force "will pursue both these goals - barring terrorists from entering the United States, and tracking down and deporting those who do enter the United States - to the maximum extent permitted by law."[174]

The following are a few other examples of American measures that reveal the extent to which they instill fear of Islam and of Islamic organizations:

On October 18, 2002, *The Washington Post* mentioned that: "U.S. intelligence has identified about a dozen of al-Qaeda's principal financial backers, most of them wealthy Saudis, and a top financial investigator is headed to Europe seeking a unified front to freeze their assets, senior administration officials said. Another senior official said the list targets people who have given tens of millions of dollars to Osama Bin Laden's terrorist organization through the years by routing the money through charities and legitimate businesses around the world. Jimmy Gurule, the Treasury Department's undersecretary for enforcement said that he will begin a six day visit to Europe for this purpose. " [175]

A high-level American delegation conducted talks in Riyadh that addressed the implementation of means to oversee charities. The Saudi a*l-Watan* newspaper quoting from the Emirate's *al-Bayan* newspaper reports that the American delegation which included ten officials from the Treasury Department, the Department of State, and the National Security Agency were hoping to coordinate with Saudi Arabia the implementation of such oversight procedures against those charities which American leaders suspect are financing terrorist organizations.[176]

The *Washington Institute for Near East Policy* reports in an article entitled 'Charitable and Humanitarian Organizations in the Network of International Terrorist Financing': "The Treasury Department froze the assets of 62 organizations and individuals associated with the al-Barakat and al-Taqwa financial networks in November 2001. Federal agents raided these groups' offices across the United States and subsequently in Europe and the Bahamas as well. In his remarks at the time, President Bush stated that the two institutions provided fundraising, financial, communications, weapons-procurement, and shipping services for al-Qaeda. A few months later, Deputy Assistant Secretary of the Treasury Department Juan C. Zarate testified before Congress that 'in 1997, it was reported that the $60 million collected annually for Hamas was moved to accounts with Bank al-Taqwa'. "[177]

The institute also mentions the raids performed by the US authorities on the Saudi organizations saying: "The U.S. offices of a number of Saudi organizations were raided in Northern Virginia in March 2002. Among others, the offices of the SAAR Foundation, the Safa Trust, and the International Institute for Islamic Thought (IIIT) were raided."[178] Safa Trust has been closed, and on December 2002 the American authorities raided the offices of al-Baraka, another organization in Chicago.

Some Islamic charities in America have suffered from accusations and have had their sources frozen and their employees interrogated. These include the Global Relief Foundation, the Holy Land Foundation, and the Benevolence International Foundation. The three American Islamic charities had their assets seized by the government amid accusations of financial ties to "terrorist groups" and without any judicial proceedings.[179]

However, while the three groups were effectively shut down under Executive Order 13224, which gives U.S. authorities the power to seize assets of organizations with suspected links to terrorism, Attorney Ladale George, a Chicago-based attorney who advises more than 30 American Muslim charities said "There has never been a 'judicial finding of fact'."[180]

The assets of BIF have been frozen under the USA PATRIOT Act, to help current investigations of its alleged link to terrorism.[181]

American recommendations have been sent to Arab countries to lower the number of hours allocated to religious studies from 20 hours to only 3, and to limit the teachings to worship matters, without any talk about jihad, or Jews' criticism or hate.[182]

On the morning of March 20, 2003, Federal agents raided a number of Islamic organizations in Virginia, Georgia, and Maryland, among these were the IIIT where the agents confined all its employees in the library and searched its offices under the accusation of providing funds to terrorist organizations[183], the Muslim World League in Washington D.C., the Success Foundation which is a charity foundation, as well as several Muslim owned businesses, such as MAR-JAC companies, and Sterling Management.[184]

The American Federal Authorities arrested the executive director of Benevolence International Foundation, under the accusation of using the organization's money to support terrorist activities.[185]

Heritage Education Trust and Safa Trust brought a lawsuit against CBS and the director of SEAT an American research center accusing them of lying and fabricating allegations without evidences, which damaged the organizations' reputation and threatened the privacy and safety of its employees, by accusing them of supporting terror.[186]

American Finance Secretary John Snow and Adel al Jubeir, Advisor to King Abdallah spoke in a news conference about the joint American Saudi efforts concerning the activities of al-Haramain charity and announced that so far they designated 12 charities on the terrorist list. They are: Holy Land Foundation (USA), al-Haramain (Bosnia and Somalia branches), Global Relief Foundation (USA), Mercy International (USA), al-Aqsa Foundation (Germany, Europe), Palestinian Relief Foundation (France), Interpal (Britain), Palestinian Association (Austria), Sanabil for Relief and Development (Lebanon), and al-Akhtar Fund (Pakistan).[187]

The quick move of the U.S. Government against Islamic charities after the events of September 11 and the coordinated media campaigns and sweeping allegations that immediately followed suit, the strict monitoring, harsh measures, and sweeping demands strongly point to one thing: that the declared objective of fighting terror financing is not the true motive.

Chapter III

Islamic Charities in the US Congress

Hearing Testimonies before the US Congressional Committees

The international statements and actions of America continued to rouse suspicions about Islamic charities and stir up provocations against them both inside the US and abroad. It was received with various degrees of acceptance from one country to another. The 9/11 Commission Report titled "Terrorist Financing Staff Monograph, Chapter 7 al-Haramain Case Study" revealed the magnitude of this propaganda against Islamic charities, when it says: "Much of the [U.S.] Saudi strategy dealt with terrorist financing." And among the steps included in this strategy was: "encouraging better use of the media to combat terrorist financing."[188]

The magnitude of the material and moral losses of the Islamic charities were evident on the global level. They varied from total closure to account freezing. Some were acquitted after investigations especially in Europe.

The new regulations that bind these organizations are even harsher than the sustained losses. These regulations target the strong points of the Islamic charities, namely the incoming donations processes, the spending fields, and the money transfers abroad.In addition, the seemingly unfounded accusations of terror financing have greatly undermined the charity work. Debra Morris has expressed this fact in a study presented to the International Center for Not-for-Profit Law, saying: "It is difficult to imagine an issue that could undermine public faith in charity more than the suspicion of terrorist links. Any kind of terrorist connection is obviously completely unacceptable" [189]

From a Media Campaign to Official Measures

It is important to note here that this study is not merely about the media campaigns, but about measures, decisions and tools proposed and implemented by the US administration.

As a result of this propaganda, a number of testimony hearings were presented before some congregational committees under the pretext that they were incriminating documents on the 25 and 26 of September 2003. They numbered fourteen in all. They involved Islamic charities and their alleged financing of terrorism. About 30% of the testimonies were concerning the Palestinian organization Hamas. The eighth hearing testimony was about initiatives to combat terrorism and terror financing, the Saudi charitable organizations, and the new cooperation with the Saudi Government concerning al-Haramain Foundation. The three people who participated in this hearing were David Aufhauser, Former General Counsel, Department of Treasury, Anthony Wayne, Assistant Secretary for Economic and Business Affairs, and John S. Pistole Acting FBI Director for Counterterrorism. That was the first historic official event concerning the issue of Islamic charities, organizations, and foundations. This took place after the US global media campaigns, which spread suspicions about the work and programs of these organizations without any legal or judicial document. The next event was the publishing of the 9/11 Commission Report, in which chapter seven, entitled "A

Case Study, The Haramain Charitable Foundation", presented the case study as a prominent example of terror financing. This falls into step with the U.S. administration position, which considers it a strongest condemnation of Islamic charities.

Following is a presentation of the most important aspects of these hearings and a critique of its content. The importance of this presentation lies in the fact that it contains all the allegations the US administration has against the Islamic charities. Following that is a short presentation of the Report on the Religious Freedom in the World, published simultaneously on the 10th of September 2004 by the US State Department. Because of the relation of religious freedom with the work of Islamic charities in the world, it is incumbent to present some of the report's succinct points

I-Hearing Testimonies and Accusations of Terror Financing:

In 2003, the American administration gathered a number of its leading employees and outside experts to testify before Congressional committees to convince them of the "Wahhabi" threat to the interest and security of the United States, claiming that wahhabism cultivates an environment conducive to the culture of terror. Wahhabism, they claim, differs from the other Islamic trends by its hatred of non-Muslims. Their objectives were to convince the committees of the danger of the Islamic charities in general, and the Saudi charities in particular, claiming that they spread wahhabism in the Muslim world, and finance terror.

It is relevant to notice that during a number of testimonies presented to the Committee of the Governmental Affairs on July 31 2003, and the testimonies presented to the Financial Committee on September 25 2003, great attention was given to the use of rhetorical style and emotionally charged words, rather than a rational style based on specific events, and logical proofs.

Bringing accusations accompanied with a paucity of proofs and convincing events naturally leads to this type of tactics.

An Example of Testimonies Presented before the Congress:

Any one of these testimonies reveals what can be characterized as America's unreasonable expectations and requests with respect to Islamic charities. One of these is E. Anthony Wayne's testimony before the Senate Banking Committee wherein he said: "It is important to note that many of the changes implemented by Saudi Arabia go beyond what we would have legal authority to do."[190]

Wayne also said:

"Saudi Arabia's new banking regulations place strict controls on accounts held by charities. Charities cannot deposit or withdraw cash from their bank account, nor can they make wire transfers abroad via their bank account. And Saudi Arabia has banned the collection of donations at mosques and instructed retail establishments to remove charity collection boxes from their premises, something that is undoubtedly extremely challenging for Saudi Arabia."[191]

This statement will no doubt be a source of concern for everybody concerned with freedom and human rights, since the witness would not have been so forthright with what he said had he not felt secure that the Congressional Banking Committee before whom he was testifying would accept it and would subsequently disregard its implicit contradiction with the principles of liberty and human rights.

The indication of this worrisome statement is that the American Congress considers that any act that can be perceived as violating freedom, human rights, and national sovereignty may be justified and acceptable if it is directed toward Islamic charities accused of having connections with terrorists.

None of these measures has been put into genuine practice with respect to the NGOs in the United States and Europe because they run contrary to the independence and freedom that NGOs enjoy and violate human rights and the laws of those countries. Does the expectation of the desired results mean a dissatisfaction of all those measures that contradict the principles of religious freedoms and human rights of all nations, and can not even be applied inside America itself?

Several Islamic charities' lawyers mentioned that some hate mongers among the powerful wanted to convince the public, through these successive congressional hearings about Islamic charities, that the Congress is really preoccupied with these issues, and might continue to be so through pressures and regulations.

The failure of these testimonies to present proofs, or incriminating documents, or even mention specific events indicates that not only there is no proof for these accusations, but that the accusations themselves are baseless. The witness in this case has access to any pertinent event and incriminating proof - if they exist. All the testimonies could mention were two events, which were repeatedly mentioned:

1- That the World Association of Muslim Youths (WAMY) organized a convention in Riyadh, and among those present there was one member of the Palestinian resistance.

2- Two offices of al-Haramain in Bosnia and Somalia were designated as terrorist-supporting organizations by the United Nations at the request of the US administration based on a media campaign and accusations devoid of proofs or legal verdicts.

II -A Case Study: The al-Haramain Foundation

Al-Haramain is one of the Islamic charities working in the fields of relief, funding education, supporting orphans, building mosques, shelters, and social care centers, and sponsoring imams and callers to Islam. Al-Haramain was launched from Pakistan in 1988 and established its headquarters in Riyadh in 1991. It had 45 regional offices around the world and representatives in 80 countries, which carry out executive roles especially in areas of disaster, famine, poverty, and illiteracy. It has successfully participated in crises relief in Afghanistan, Bosnia, Chechnya, Kashmir, and Kosovo. Senator Jon Kyl, Chairman of the Subcommittee on Terrorism, Technology and Homeland Security, described the organization's activities, saying: "A report on the yearly activities of the al-Haramain Foundation described as 'keen on spreading the proper Islamic culture' are listed as follows: 'it printed 13 million (Islamic) books, launched six internet sites, employed more than 3000 callers [to Islam], founded 1100 mosques, schools and cultural Islamic centers and posted more than 350,000 letters of call (invitation to convert to Islam)'."[192] In reality, these numbers are dwarfed by the huge numbers of Bibles and pamphlets distributed to non-Christians for the purpose of proselytization; 8000 Arabic Bibles have been distributed in Iraq alone by Southern Baptist missionaries who entered Iraq at the heel of the US army.[193] Tens of thousands of churches have been erected by missionaries, 300 in Cambodia alone[194], not mentioning Evangelist TV stations that broadcast around the world. Moreover, the need of Muslims in poor countries who cannot afford Qur'an copies, and do not have the means to build mosques far exceeds what is provided to them by the charities.

Describing al-Haramain International Foundation (HIF) as "one of the most important and prominent Saudi charities," the 9/11 Commission Report also remarks that "[it] has been on the radar screen of the U.S. Government as a potential terrorist-financing problem since the mid-to late 1990s, when the U.S. Government started to develop evidence that certain employees and branch offices might be supporting al-Qaeda and related terrorist groups."[195]

The report further says: "Al-Haramain, a Saudi Arabia–based nonprofit organization established in the early 1990s, has been described by several former U.S. Government officials as the "United Way" of Saudi Arabia. It exists to promote Wahhabi Islam by funding religious education, mosques, and humanitarian projects around the world."[196]

A number of regional offices of the foundation outside Saudi Arabia were subject to accusations of terror financing, and these offices were closed. On July 22, 2004, the headquarters of al-Haramain Foundation were closed, knowing that the closing decision was not achieved thru any judicial authorities whether in the US or abroad[197.]

Selected Excerpts from the Case Study Texts:

The seventh chapter of the US Congress report concerning financing terrorism released during the second half of 2004 was titled "Case study: Al-Haramain Charitable Foundation". It contained the proceeds of hearing testimonies presented to different congressional committees; the most prominent of which was the Governmental Affairs Committee hearing that took place on September 25, 2003. Here are six excerpts:

Excerpt 1: "The Saudis responded to the increase in U.S. pressure, exemplified by the delivery of the al-Haramain nonpaper in early 2003, by articulating additional counterterrorism policies. The measures were to include Islamic Affairs Ministry pre-clearance of transfers of charitable funds overseas, host government approval of all incoming charitable funds from Saudi Arabia, and monitoring of charities' bank accounts through audits, expenditure reports, and site visits. Also in the spring of 2003, the Saudi Arabia Monetary Authority (SAMA) was said to have instituted a major technical training program for judges and investigators on terrorist financing and money laundering."[198]

"The challenge was to find a way to increase oversight over charities, mosques, and religious donations without endangering the country's stability."[199]

Excerpt 2: "Turning a corner: On May 12, 2003, al-Qaeda operatives detonated three explosions in an expatriate community in Riyadh, killing Westerners and Saudi Arabians. Since then, the Saudi Government has taken a number of significant, concrete steps to stem the flow of funding from the Kingdom to terrorists. The Saudi Government, in one of its more important actions after the bombings, removed collection boxes in mosques, as well as in shopping malls, and prohibited cash contributions at mosques. This action was important because terrorist groups and their supporters have been able to siphon funds from mosque donations. Its sensitivity can not be overestimated. US Ambassador to Saudi Arabia Jordan described the removal of the collection boxes as a "cataclysmic event." It was a real action that the Saudi public has both seen and been affected by; it has forced everyone to think about terrorist financing."[200]

Excerpt 3: "On May 24, 2003, the Saudi Government followed up with comprehensive new restrictions on the financial activities of Saudi charities. These included a requirement that charitable accounts can be opened only in Saudi riyals; enhanced customer identification requirements for charitable accounts; a requirement that charities must consolidate all banking activity into one principal account, with subaccounts permitted for branches but for deposits only, with all withdrawals and transfers serviced through the main account; a prohibition on cash disbursements from charitable accounts, with payments allowed by check payable to the first beneficiary and deposited into a Saudi bank; a prohibition on the use of ATM and credit cards by charities; and a prohibition on transfers from charitable accounts outside of Saudi Arabia."[201]

"The May 12 bombings caused the Saudis to become more receptive to disrupting al-Qaeda financing than ever before; the Saudis appeared ready to take seriously the cooperative aspect of "quiet cooperation." At the same time, the U.S. Government finally developed a coherent approach to working with the Saudis on combating terrorist financing."[202]

"Similarly, FBI officials have ranked Saudi cooperation on terrorist-financing issues as "good" since the May 12 and November 8, 2003, Riyadh bombings."[203]

Excerpt 4: "Then, in January 2004 the United States and Saudi Arabia jointly designated four additional branches of al-Haramain, in Indonesia, Kenya, Tanzania, and Pakistan. The two governments held an unprecedented joint press conference in Washington to announce the designation. The names of these branches were subsequently submitted to the United Nations, which instituted an international freeze on their assets."[204]

"Continuing the pressure on al-Haramain, the U.S. and Saudi Governments jointly designated five additional branches of al-Haramain (Afghanistan, Albania, Bangladesh, Ethiopia, and the Netherlands) on June 2, 2004."[205]

Excerpt 5 : "On February 19, 2004, federal law enforcement took action against both the al-Haramain branch in Ashland, Oregon, and the imam of the HIF [a-Haramain International Foundation] mosque in Springfield, Missouri. The FBI and the IRS conducted searches of the Ashland offices of HIF as part of an investigation into alleged money laundering and income tax and currency reporting violations. Treasury took the additional step of freezing, during the pendency of an investigation, the accounts of the branch in Oregon and the mosque in Missouri."[206]

Excerpt 6 : "On February 29, 2004, the Saudi Government announced that it had approved the creation of the Saudi National Commission for Relief and Charity Work Abroad to take over all aspects of overseas aid operations and assume responsibility for the distribution of charitable donations from Saudi Arabia."[207]

"One former U.S. Government counter-terrorist-financing official said that such an entity could, in theory, replace charities such as al-Haramain by subsuming all of HIF's activities into its own."[208]

"Action against terrorist financing is only one tool in the fight against terrorism and must be integrated into counterterrorism policy and operations."[209]

Analysis of the Report:

The report "al-Haramain, A Case Study" clearly mentions that the pressures the foundation was subjected to are not a consequence of the September 11 events. It also emphasized that the case was based on suspicions (that some employees and regional offices may have helped al-Qaeda). Notice in this report the American double standard where the U.S. insists on closing al-Haramain with the harsh measures mentioned in the first and second excerpts, while they are not applied to NGOs in the US itself. Would the Salvation Army or the United Way be closed if some of their employees were inculpated in terror support or corruption? Were donation boxes removed from churches in the US for their decade-long support of the IRA terrorists? Legal scholars are asking whether it is legal to close al-Haramain offices based on the designation mentioned in excerpt 4, before doing any thorough investigation, or judicial proceeding; and whether the designation and the closing were a punishing measure. Were they a revengeful measure? Or maybe a deterrence for other Islamic charities?!

What is important here is that the 9/11 Commission Report which was issued by a commission formed by the U.S. Congress, and contained a special chapter about al-Haramain as a case study, did not mention a single specific incriminating event to support the accusations of al-Haramain financing al-Qaeda, that nebulous entity, whose features have yet to be defined.

Anyone who reads this report comes out with the strong impression that not only it did not present any evidence inculpating the aforementioned charity of supporting al-Qaeda, but such evidence exists neither in reality nor in documents, knowing that the report describes al-Haramain as a nonprofit organization which "provides meals and assistance to Muslims around the world, distributes books and pamphlets, pays for potable water projects, sets up and equips medical facilities, and operates more than 20 orphanages."[210]

Al-Haramain has been described by several former U.S. Government officials as the "United Way" of Saudi Arabia. "It exists to promote Wahhabi Islam by funding religious education, mosques, and humanitarian projects around the world," the report says.[211] Some argue that Wahhabism is a virulent form of religious extremism.[212]

In the report, al-Haramain was accused of financing al-Qaeda: "After the 9/11 attacks, a more focused U.S. Government sought to work with the Saudis to stem the flow of funds from al-Haramain to al-Qaeda and related terrorist groups. Progress was initially slow; though some U.S.-Saudi cooperation on al-Haramain occurred within the first six months after 9/11, it was not until the spring of 2003 that the U.S. Government and the

Saudi Government began to make real strides in working together to thwart al-Haramain."[213]

But how did the report arrive at this conclusion, i.e. the accusation of al-Haramain of financing terror?

Al-Qaeda is said to have its headquarters in Afghanistan, and it is known that the Afghanistan-Pakistan area was under the most strict surveillance of many countries' investigation agencies; In addition to the American agencies, there are the Israeli agencies who are described as having capabilities beyond imagination, the Russian agencies, the Indian agencies, and others, and no doubt all these agencies were cooperating in the fight against a common enemy, al-Qaeda. However the report recognizes that: "The al-Haramain Islamic Foundation (al-Haramain or HIF) is one of the most important and prominent Saudi charities,"[214] and it has been on the US radar screen as a potential terrorist-financing problem since the mid-to late 1990s, almost a decade of inspection. After the East Africa bombings in 1998, The U.S. Government began to give more attention to terrorist financing. The National Security Council (NSC) created the Counterterrorism Security Group to concentrate the administration's effort on terrorist financings, and as a result, the NSC became increasingly interested in Saudi charities and Bin Laden's use of charities to fund terrorism.[215]

In spite of this concentration on the relation of the al-Haramain with terror financing, the U.S. Government has not been able to provide the Saudis with evidence to convince them of the charity's inculpation in financing al-Qaeda. The report admits that "the U.S. Government never moved against al-Haramain or pushed the Saudi Government to do so until after 9/11." In fact the report says: "We did not provide sufficient information for the Saudis to act against charities like al-Haramain, did not push the Saudis to undertake investigations of charities like al-Haramain, and did not request real cooperation from the Saudis on intelligence or law enforcement matters relating to charities like al-Haramain."[216] Later on in the report the commission admitted that: "the intelligence was simply not strong enough against the HIF headquarters to push the Saudi Government to take aggressive action against the whole organization."[217] And it also says: "the U.S. Government had too little unilateral intelligence on HIF and on al-Qaeda's funding mechanisms generally to press the Saudis. The Principals [government most senior officials including the secretaries of key departments] did not want to confront the Saudis with suspicions; they wanted firm evidence. One NSC official Terrorist Financing Staff Monograph indicated that there was some intelligence regarding charities, but it did not rise to the level of being actionable against any specific charity. As he said, 'One individual could be dirty, but it would be difficult to justify closing down a charity on that basis'."[218]

It was admitted in the report that: "Occasionally the U.S. Government provided select pieces of information out of context," meaning they have nothing to do with al-Haramain terror financing accusations. The report adds: "as was the case before 9/11, the intelligence was simply not strong enough against the HIF headquarters to push the Saudi Government to take aggressive action against the whole organization. As an early 2002 strategy paper emphasized, the United States needed to gather more solid, credible evidence on al-Haramain, which could be released to the Saudi Government as a way to ensure continued Saudi cooperation. Although the intelligence community expressed repeated concerns that al-Haramain was deeply corrupted, others argued that there was little actionable intelligence on the charity. The intelligence presented to the policymakers was either dated, spoke to fund-raising for "extremism" or "fundamentalism" and not for terrorism, or lacked specificity."[219] The report admits that: "During 2002, the Saudis repeatedly said they would be prepared to act against al-Haramain if the U.S. Government provided them with more information, especially about specific branch offices and individuals."[220]

So why didn't the U.S. Government provide the information requested by the Saudis so that they would take the necessary measures against al-Haramain? The only explanation provided by the report was that: "Some viewed Saudi requests for information from the United States as somewhat disingenuous given Saudi Arabia's ability to gather information on HIF and its supporters."[221]

The report says that information about HIF was provided in a nonpaper at the beginning of January 2003. Its goal was to compile all government information on HIF. However, the report did not reveal the contents of the nonpaper, or the genuineness or gravity of the information in supporting the accusation of HIF link to terror financing. Nevertheless, in March 11, 2002, almost a year before the nonpaper, the United States demanded to close the Bosnia and Somalia branches of al-Haramain and to freeze their assets, and forbid dealing with them. The UN acceded the U.S. demands to designate the two branches as terror supporting groups, and subject to sanction by virtue of the UN Security Council Order no. 1267. The report states that before presenting the nonpaper in January 2003, it appeared that the U.S. Government has asked the Saudis to act on the basis of little more than U.S. suspicions or assurances that the United States had intelligence it could not release.[222] The report did not hide the fact that the U.S. Government continued to put great pressure to curtail the activities of the Saudi charities particularly those working outside Saudi Arabia, except that it admits that this pressure did not bear fruit even after the said non-paper, and that the May 12, 2003 Riyadh bombing was the decisive factor that enabled the U.S. Government to realize its goal.

Anyone who reads the above statements would have suspicion about the seriousness of the U.S. allegations and wonders whether its goal was really to stop the money flow to terrorists. This suspicion deepens when one realizes that senior administration officials testifying before the Congress have repeatedly pointed to a logical fact: That if terror financing is the life blood for the terrorist, it is also his deadly poison, his fatal weak point. Now if this is so, why wasn't it left to do its work of following the thread that leads to the truth? In other words, by following the money trail they would arrive to the terrorists and unveil their plans and then abort them. Putting a particular organization suspected of terrorism financing under surveillance is the most effective means of fighting terrorism. These charitable organizations and the financial *Hawalahs* would be the traps that catch the terrorists; therefore their remaining is crucial to the success of the war on terror.

But on the contrary, the U.S. administration is more keen on preventing Islamic charities, especially those in Saudi Arabia, from transferring money to their branches abroad, even when this was done through official banks, and even if they presented to the U.S. Government guaranties of transparency and control over the charities procedures as was done lately by the Saudi Government, which adopted new measures as mentioned in the report.[223]

All this points to one thing: If the US Government had a serious suspicion of an al-Haramain link to terror financing, it would have been natural to leave it active, and following the money trail would be the most effective means to find the terrorists and discover their plans.

Does the Case Study Offer any Clue about the Real Objective?

If stopping the money flow to terrorist is not the real objective, then what is the US Government's goal in curtailing the activities of Islamic charities, preventing thousands of orphans from support, cutting off humanitarian works for hospitals, schools, and scholarships, and stopping projects of digging wells for potable water?

Commenting on the closure of al-Haramain branches, Dr. Wendell Belew said that when charities are closed, or the financing of their activities is stopped, the first people who are hurt are those whom the charities were trying to help. Dr. Belew said that efforts should be made to remove any problems without hurting the charity recipients, or taking extreme measures against the charities such as freezing their assets, or closing their offices or branches.

Dr. Belew commented on the closure of al-Haramain Somalia branch saying that the closure of the branch in January 2004 is the best illustration of this tragedy: the forced closure of a charitable organization without a plan to continue its charitable work. On the eve of Eid al-Adha (Muslim holiday) more than 2500 orphans were driven out of the only shelter available to them, and more than 700 orphanage workers lost their jobs. This decision might engender many problems in a country torn by war and famine. These children could be recruited by armed groups. Not only that, Dr. Belew said but both the United States and Saudi Arabia will bear the responsibility of these orphans' tragedy[224], which will complicate matters. Since February 2004, there have been more than 12 news articles about the Somali orphans plight, in British, American, and Canadian newspapers.[225]

Attorneys and researchers monitoring the closure of al-Haramain see that this issue will not end, the investigations of the Saudi charities will continue. Not only that but supporters and officials in charge of these charities are targeted, and will be considered guilty of supporting terrorism since their charities have been closed, or reorganized, or merged into other organizations under a cloud of suspicions and accusations. Allegations and pressure exerted on other charities and their countries of origin will increase as long as the acceptance and yielding to these pressures are going on. A question that is repeatedly asked: What is the objective that justifies the U.S. sacrificing its reputation among people and attracting their hatred towards it because of these indiscriminate campaigns against Islamic charities?

A glimpse of the answer might be in the report itself: "others argued that there was little actionable intelligence on the charity. The intelligence presented to the policymakers was either dated, spoke to fund-raising for 'extremism' or 'fundamentalism' and not for terrorism, or lacked specificity."[226] In other words the real objective could be said to be preventing the charities from teaching Islam.

David Cole and Lynne Bernabei revealed another piece of the truth in the *Washington Times*, mentioning the following things:

"The country's [U.S.] current round of profiling has not worked to identify real terrorists, and has instead obstructed efforts to find those who truly threaten us... By drawing a wide net of suspicion over virtually every Muslim and Arab man in this country, the government wastes its resources and misdirects its attention... The entire profiling effort was a colossal failure and a drastic misallocation of much needed resources in terms of identifying and prosecuting actual terrorists."[227]

"In casting their net of suspicion broadly over tens of thousands of Arab and Muslim men, Ashcroft and the Department of Justice have done more than simply misdirect their investigative focus."[228]

"As an example, the al-Haramain Islamic Foundation, Inc. of Oregon has been unfairly accused of links to terrorists. Al-Haramain Oregon is an Islamic charity dedicated to distributing Islamic information and Qur'ans to Muslims throughout the

United States, and to educating the public at large that Islam is opposed to terrorism in all forms."[229]

"As an Islamic charity, however, al-Haramain (Oregon) has been suspected and labeled as a terrorist by many who accuse first, and find out the truth later."[230]

"This approach has penalized thousands of humanitarian donors, and many more legitimate beneficiaries of much needed humanitarian need."[231]

"When the U.S. charges major Islamic charities as terrorists, without giving them a fair hearing, the government further alienates Muslims, and provides fertile recruiting ground for al-Qaeda and other terrorist groups."[232]

Does the Religious Foundation in Saudi Arabia Offer any Clue about the Real Objective?

The Reform Movement of Muhammad Bin Abdil Wahhab:

More than two centuries ago while the United States of America was being established, most of the Arab populations' cultural and social situation was deteriorating. At that time, appeared a religious leader that led a religious and social reform. That leader was Shaikh Muhammad Bin Abdil Wahhab. He started his reform mission by building a coalition with Muhammad Bin Saud to establish the first Saudi state, and continue the reform. Muhammad Bin Abdil Wahhab's principal mission was to call to the worship of one God, and to apply the principles of Islam according to the authentic Sunnah (the sayings and acts of the Prophet Muhammad).

"Wahhabism", as some label Islam in Saudi Arabia, was never a sect, nor a school of thought within the Muslim world, but it is rather a reform and revival movement that relies on evidence from the Qur'an and the Sunnah as a fundamental pivot, and a legitimate reference. It shuns the belief in myths, and the worship of tombs and holy men. It engendered a revival in the Arabian Peninsula and in the Muslim world in general. Saudi Arabia was more obligated than the other countries in calling to Islam, since it is the birth place of Islam, and has the special privilege of the custody of the two holiest places in Islam; Makkah and Madinah. Cooperation with Muslims around the world is a religious duty, and a pressing demand from the Muslim minorities and Muslim countries in all humanitarian areas. It is no wonder that this should be the legitimate right of Saudi Arabia as it is with the Vatican, the World Churches Council, and the American religious institutions with their different denominations which carry out their work of care and call to Christianity among their followers and others around the world.

The closing of Islamic cultural offices in some Saudi embassies, and the closing or freezing of the Islamic Arabic Institutes in countries such as Mauritania under the allegation of wahhabism indicate a misunderstanding of the reality of Shaikh Abdil Wahhab's call to reform. Even projects of development in countries with Muslim minorities accomplished by Saudi charities have been considered as means to support terrorism.[233]

Some statistics from the American print media:

Senator Jon Kyl writes: "Between 1975 and 1987, the Saudis admit to having spent $48 billion or $4 billion per year on "overseas development aids," a figure which by the end of 2002 grew to over $70 billion (281 billion Saudi Riyals). These sums are reported to be Saudi state aid and almost certainly do not include private donations which are also distributed by state-controlled charities."[234]

Kyl continues: "What have the Saudis been able to buy with this unprecedented Islamic largesse? Quite a bit it would seem. For starters, the Wahhabi creed which is practiced by no more than 20 million people around the world, or less than 2% of the Muslim population, has become a dominant factor in the international Islamic establishment through an elaborate network of front organizations and charities."[235]

Matthew Levitt[236] of the *Washington Institute for Near East Policy*[237] writes about the amount of Saudi expenditure: "Experts assess there are approximately 200 private charities in the Kingdom, 'including 20 established by the Saudi intelligence to fund the Mujaheddin that send some $250 million a year to Islamic causes abroad'."[238]

Regardless of the fact that this statement lacks accuracy in determining the number of Saudi charities working abroad, the amount of expenditure is close to reality. According to statistics published in "The Charity Sector and Allegations of Terrorism" by M.A.Salloomi, the yearly expenditure of all the Gulf States' charities abroad does not exceed $550 million[239]

The alleged American objective of curtailing the Islamic charitable work is even more apparent when one notices that the American Government has continued its relentless effort in gathering witnesses before the Congressional committees (such as the testimonies before the Governmental Affairs Committee on July 31, 2003) to convince the Congress of the danger of Saudi religious activities. They alleged that Wahhabism, or Salafism, or in other words the prevalent Islamic trend of understanding Islam in Saudi Arabia, differs from the explanations in other Muslim countries regarding the relation of Muslim with non-Muslim, that it is distinguished by its hatred and enmity of non-Muslims, and thus it encourages aggression. The American administration knows more than anyone else that these allegations have no foundation, for two reasons:

First, a logical reason: the Saudi understanding of the relation of Muslim with non-Muslim does no differ from other Muslims because it is governed by Islamic laws that cannot be amended or changed. During two hundred years "Wahhabism" as some people label Islam in Saudi Arabia, has been the subject of being maligned and defamed through an accumulation of lies that have been accepted for political objectives. In the literature - Muslim and non-Muslim - that deals with the differences between "Wahhabism" and other Muslim practices in the world, it was never described as having a different understanding concerning relation with non-Muslims.

Second, a factual reason: before 9/11 and for seventy years, America, more than any other country, had a presence in Saudi Arabia represented in its companies, experts, employees, tourists, and others. In spite of that there has been not a single case where an American has been subjected to discrimination because of his religion, whether it was in applying the law, or work contracts, or even personal normal dealing.

The reform movement of Abdul Wahhab had a profound effect inside the Arabian Peninsula and abroad during two centuries, through the unique religious schools, and condensed religious curricula, which were exceptional in those times. It did not have any negative effect on people's thinking and did not bring any problem to the West in that time span, to the point that when oil was discovered six decades ago by American companies, Saudis from different classes and groups worked alongside the Americans in the oil field, in safety and security, as attested by the companies' officials themselves. There must be reasons other than "Wahhabism" that explain the new phenomenon of extremism and terrorism. Likewise, a great number of foreigners, and they number in the millions, half of them non-Muslims, are working in Saudi Arabia, and there is no known incident of discrimination between Muslim and Hindu Indian, or Muslim and Christian Filipino, or Muslim and Buddhist Thai concerning the work contracts or laws or even normal personal dealing.

The only exception is the prohibition of the non-Muslims from entering Makkah and Madinah. This prohibition is not specific to Saudi Arabia, but is the belief of all Muslims everywhere. Included in this exception is the establishment of religious places of worship for non-Muslims in the Arabian Peninsula. This also is not specific to the "Wahhabi" belief but is shared belief by all Muslims in the world, because the Prophet Muhammad said: "No two religions should meet in the Arabian Peninsula"[240] The geographic area of the Arabian Peninsula has a special religious sanctity just as the Vatican has a special religious sanctity to the Catholics. It is considered an area exclusive to Islam. If the Saudis disregarded these religious laws, one billion Muslims would refuse to do so, because this matter has been settled 14 centuries ago. The same goes for the obligation on the Muslims to defend the Arabian Peninsula, the land of the two Holy Mosques; it is the belief of Muslims worldwide. Early Muslims have been the stellar example of religious tolerance, and respect of religious freedoms. They did not forbid the existence of worship places for non-Muslims in all the lands they ruled from the Atlantic to the Pacific, except in the Arabian Peninsula, abiding by religious rules that accept no change or alteration. It is the exception that proves the rule. The tolerance of Muslims of other religions and the existence of religious places for non-Muslims during all the history of Islam is the strongest proof that the exception of the Arabian Peninsula is not a consequence of intolerance or denial of religious freedoms.

In any case, there is no Saudi or permanent resident in Saudi Arabia who is not Muslim. Moreover, the non-Muslim temporary residents, whether they are businessmen, workers, or tourists do not expect to have permanent places of worship, while they have agreed to abide by the country's rules, recognizing that temporary residents have no right to a permanent temple.

Although the Abdil Wahhab reform movement has certain flaws concerning the vision or the application, as do most movements throughout history, it rivals other global constitutions in freeing the people from subjugation and subordination. It believes in Jihad and in freedom for humankind, and it believes in tolerance, as stated in the Sharia (Islamic law) that there is no compulsion in religion and that freedom is the foundation that will ensure the understanding of the religion.

Report of the Religious Freedoms in the World:

Muslims in Saudi Arabia and elsewhere believe in what is written in the Qu'ran:

"Let there be no compulsion in religion."[241]

"Will you then compel mankind, against their will, to believe!"[242]

"You are not a tyrant over them to force them to believe."[243]

"Say 'you shall not be asked about our sins, nor shall we be asked of what you do."[244]

Now let us suppose that the Saudi charities' activities include propagating the Islamic trend prevalent in Saudi Arabia (even if this trend has been described as fundamentalist), banning this activity by applying pressure or by force, contradicts the principles stated in the US State Department report released on December 15, 2004 and titled 'International Religious Freedom Report'. The American Secretary of State announced that the release of this report is a proof of America's strong support of everyone who seeks to follow what his conscience dictates without being subject to oppression and persecution.

> *The report says: "The failure to protect freedom of religion and other fundamental human rights can undermine social order, foster extremism, and lead to instability and violence....[T]he Administration's National Security Strategy declares that the U.S. will 'take special efforts to promote freedom of religion and conscience and defend it from encroachment by repressive governments'."[245] The report blamed some countries for wronging certain religions by linking them to dangerous and deviant sects. It condemned totalitarian and dictatorial regimes for controlling religious thoughts and behavior, and for considering some religions as enemies of the state, or often times as a threat to the state's ideology.*

The report condemns also some governments for restricting the import and distribution of religious literature, and points especially at China, Turkmenistan, Bangladesh, Nigeria, Saudi Arabia, Azerbaijan, Israel, and Belgium. Although the report admits that the Nigerian Federal Government respects religious freedoms in general, it alleges that there are cases where limitations were imposed on religious activities for security and safety reasons, and that a number of northern districts in Nigeria forbid public Christianization to avoid religious violence.

Even though the report recognizes that non-Muslims in Malaysia are free to practice their religious rites, they accuse the Malaysian Government of monitoring the activities of non-Muslim minorities because it is worried that their religious doctrine might cause division among the Muslims.

It is ironic that the report also condemns Uzbekistan for restricting religious freedom because the government imprisoned hundreds of persons most of them belonging to the Hizbut-Tahrir religious group or to "Wahhabi" groups. The report criticized also

Azerbaijan for publishing articles in many newspapers attacking "Wahhabism" and Christian missions.[246]

The US State Department International Religious Freedom Report, released on November 8, 2005, claimed that in Saudi Arabia "freedom of religion does not exist"[247], failing to explain that the Saudi people and government have unanimously and freely chosen Islam as their religion and Islamic Shariah as the law of the land. Therefore government and people are both religiously and morally obligated -and committed- to defend Muslims' human rights everywhere, through political, economic, and humanitarian means. Thus in the field of humanitarian work, religious freedom is mutually practiced by both donors and recipients. It is also undisputed that democratic principles dictate the acceptance of the Saudi people's choice to abide by Islam and the Islamic Shariah. Refuting this is a violation of freedom and democracy. By selecting certain examples and presenting a biased picture, the report has lost much of its credibility. Political motives should not be part of impartial independent studies that seek the truth.

Speaking of religious freedoms, shouldn't the US Congress, a representative body of the US people, study the effects of the PATRIOT Act, Secret Evidence, and anti-terrorism laws – and the Administration's use of these tools - on the civil liberties of its own people and on the American Islamic organizations, especially since, according to OMB Watch, there was no incriminating evidence against these organizations, their employees, or their boards of directors?[248]

It is ironic that the US State Department report alleges that there are violations of religious freedoms inside Saudi Arabia, while at the same time the US administration has been said to have exerted great political pressures that resulted in the curtailing of the freedoms of religious organizations inside and outside Saudi Arabia. The pressure is even greater on those organizations that have affinity with democratic practices, and religious freedoms. The discriminatory treatment of the Islamic organizations and other Islamic entities inside and outside the US is due to their religious affiliation. In other words, their religious freedoms have been curtailed.

Nevertheless, no matter how "Wahhabism" is described as extremist, or as being a danger to global Islam, this description can not reach the level of extremism of the religious fanatical trend that excludes others from their own religion, and devotes all kinds of enmity and hatred towards Muslims. This fanatical doctrine whose followers believe that their salvation will happen at the Second Coming of Jesus, that this coming is conditioned by the establishment of Israel and the building of the Temple for the third time - for this they're plotting for the destruction of the al-Aqsa Mosque, which they claim sits on the site -, and by the advent of Armageddon where 200million among the enemies of the Christ will be killed. These enemies are the infidels, they say, and they believe that they have to help hasten the Second Coming of the Christ "By praying for their Rapture and the End of Time, might they force the Hand of God - to bring it about?" asks Grace Halsell.[249]

"A 1996 Survey of Religion and Politics conducted by the University of Akron revealed that 31% of the adult Christian population agree or strongly agree with the belief that the world will end with a battle at Armageddon. This means 62 million Americans accept this belief system," says University of Akron Professor John Green[250]. Another survey performed by the Institute of the First Amendment Studies, in Akron, Ohio in 1997 found that 60% of the U.S. Christians believe the world will end in Armageddon[251].

The United Nations; both Victim and Culprit:

The UN procedure concerning al-Haramain designation as terror supporter constitutes a dangerous precedent in the history of international law for the following reasons:

a- The United Nations is assuming the role of arbitrating in disputes between states and private institutions, whereas it is supposed to only arbitrate between member nations.

b- The UN punitive decision toward al-Haramain was not based on a court order, arrived at by legal procedures. It has been issued without hearing the defense, or allowing the accused to defend itself.

c- The two offices were not physical persons and have no criminal responsibility and therefore cannot be charged with criminal intent, an accusation addressed only to physical persons. If one of their employees has committed a crime - and up to now no one has been proven guilty of any - then the legal procedure would be to hold him responsible, bring him to justice, and if proven guilty then he alone is subject to punishment, not the organization he worked for. This was the way the U.S. dealt with United Way of America in 2002, a well known organization that collected huge donations and where misuses and financial mistakes had happened. No freezing of assets or closure was ordered. In France, the Cancer Fighting League, one of the strongest organizations in the 1990s, has been subject to mismanagement and illegal budget use. There was a trial, and a new management was formed. Again neither assets freezing nor closure was ordered.

In addition to raising legal concerns, the procedure taken by the United Nations raises humanitarian, and human rights concerns.

Finally, the testimonies relied on rhetorical style, and concentrated on negative emotional charges addressed to the audience and not on presentation of specific inculpating events.

Breaching the International Humanitarian Law:

There are official agreements of support and protection among nations concerning the humanitarian aspect in particular, but the UN and other international organizations are helpless vis-à-vis the breaching of international laws where - willingly or unwillingly - the means and mechanisms of the UN have been weakened, and its limited freedom curtailed.

Examples of the legal articles that particularly concern the humanitarian NGOs and their workers:

No general penalty, pecuniary or otherwise, shall be inflicted upon the population on account of the acts of individuals for which they cannot be regarded as jointly and severally responsible. (See Article 50 of the 4th Convention respecting the Laws and Customs of War on Land and its annex, The Hague, October 18, 1907).

"The acts are and shall remain prohibited at any time and in any place whatsoever, whether committed by civilian or by military agents...d) collective punishments." (Article 75.2 of the Geneva Protocol I, relating to the Protection of Victims of International Armed Conflicts).[252]

"Medical and religious personnel shall be respected and protected and shall be granted all available help for the performance of their duties. They shall not be compelled to carry out tasks which are not compatible with their humanitarian mission." (Article 9 of Protocol II, Protection of medical and religious personnel) [253]

Flawed OFAC (Designation Criteria of the American Justice)

It is noticed that the allegations against Islamic charities, countries, and financial institutions are usually brought by greedy American law firms who roam the countries fishing for news they can use for their financial compensation suits for the 9/11 damages, taking advantage of the new political development in America. One of the most prominent attorneys in pleading the case of Lockerby is among the first people who made trips around the world buying news about Islamic charities to use as allegations for the compensations to the families of the 9/11 victims.

Moreover, these allegations relied mostly on what the media has published. Were these allegations to be brought before justice, they would not stand. David Ottaway mentions in *The Washington Post* that the Office of Foreign Assets Control (OFAC) relied in its designations of terrorist organizations on what was published in the newspapers. He wrote: "Charity officials have also not had a chance to confront all of the government's evidence linking the group to terrorism. The classified evidence remains out of reach and much of the unclassified evidence turned out to be allegations in newspaper clippings."[254] Ottaway reiterated the complaints of the charities' attorneys that there was no legal definition of "specially designated global terrorist". He reported that Professor David Cole, of Georgetown Law Center, asked: "If the category has no definition, then how would a group who challenges the designation know what it is? It is whatever the government says it is."[255]

Ottaway asserts that the sources of allegations and designations are the media campaign propagandas, saying: "Post reporter who reviewed the materials found that they included 61 newspaper articles dating back to 1999. 'We found ourselves trying to rebut newspaper reports around the world,' [Attorney Roger C.] Simmons said."[256]

Concerning this state of things Dr. Wendell Belew said at the Conference on Partnership for Peace and Development in Palestine held in London on December 16, 2004: "Just as charities must operate with transparency, however, so must governments. Our efforts to improve and modernize the standards and practices of charities will be undermined if the same governments that call for transparency and democratic procedures fail to meet those standards themselves. Unfortunately, the policies and practices of the United States Government, for example, fall far short of the mark in many respects. The Office of Foreign Assets Control (OFAC), in particular, would have a tough time meeting the standards set by the [British] Charity Commission"[257] Dr. Belew commended the 9/11 commission in revealing part of the truth saying: "The commission's report and supplementary staff report have done an excellent job of bringing to light the flaws in the current OFAC designation process." He added: " I believe that in too many cases the actions of OFAC diminish rather than enhance national security by targeting innocent organizations and individuals....the act of designating an individual or an organization is deemed to be an action that does not afford the protection due to a defendant in a criminal proceeding...On the other hand, any American who provides goods or services to the designated entity without a license (which are handed out by OFAC) is potentially a felon, subject to severe penalties."[258]

And describing the negative effects of these procedures he said: "Once designated, an individual or organization has little recourse. There is no system of fact-finding or appeal. The sole judge of lifting the designation is the agency that made the designation in the first place, OFAC. Once designated, the entity must wait a year to petition OFAC to change its mind."[259]

"The likelihood of OFAC changing its position on a designation is severely undermined by political considerations. Senior officials of the US Government, from the President on down, have taken to issuing statements describing the designated entity in the most lurid terms and dismissing any doubts as to the guilt of the designated party. Government leaders claim credit for victory in the War on Terrorism by pointing to the designations."[260] Dr. Belew proposed a complete haul of the designation procedure; "Justice demands due process in the designation of a terrorist. The flaws in the OFAC designation process stem from structural deficiencies. As was the case with the Abu Ghraib prison scandal,

- Too few resources are allocated to deal with a challenging problem;
- Lack of transparency results in lack of accountability; and
- Unclear lines of authority contribute to confusion on goals and objectives."[261]

Absence of Facts in the US Courts

Dr. Belew insisted in the London convention that having confidence in the facts is the correct way to arrive at the truth: "Nothing good can come from policies that are developed under false perceptions of reality", he said, "As recent events have shown, even intelligence agencies can sometimes get it wrong. Western traditions of justice have a proven track record of getting to the truth by exposing allegations to rigorous examination by opposing parties. We must trust in that tradition to get at the facts about terrorism." He emphasized the importance of respecting the law, and justice to get out of the crisis: "The Rule of Law is an important gift from this great nation - and others - to the world. If we abandon this rule in the face of adversity, we will weaken our position, not strengthen it. If we abandon the rule of law in order to protect government's position on a given matter, we will diminish ourselves in the eyes of the world." Insisting on the importance of justice, he says: "The current policies of OFAC contain little justice, no mercy, and scant humility. While the flaws are a result of a bad system rather than evil individuals, these matters must be addressed speedily and effectively if we are to prevail in the struggle against terror and injustice."[262]

In this context David Ottaway writes: "US authorities face enormous obstacles in gathering evidence usable in court...The Treasury designations were being based on more nebulous 'links' to terrorists rather than hard proof of 'finding'...experienced lawyers steeped in the federal courts rules of evidence and due process found the designations 'manifestly unfair', citing the use of classified evidence and material that would normally be considered hearsay."[263] He also said: "So far, Treasury has not succeeded in obtaining a terrorist conviction against any of the three charities whose assets were frozen pending investigation - Global Relief, Benevolence International Foundation, and al-Haramain Islamic Foundation."[264] Ottaway reiterated what the 9/11 report said: "In conclusion the report asked whether the destruction of Global Relief and Benevolence had been worth the price, 'Did it enhance the security of the United States or was it a feckless act that violated civil rights with no real gain in security?" Ottaway pointed out to the lack of evidence saying: "Al-Haramain's Washington lawyer, Lynne Bernabei, asked Treasury for the evidence against her client. She said she received mainly articles from newspapers and policy journals."[265]

US-based Muslim charities have been prosecuted and effectively shut down after onlt being accused of terrorism, but not charged. This was the case of Help the Needy charity. Responding to the humanitarian catastrophe created by the Gulf War and the US sanctions against Iraq, Dr. Rafil Dhafir, an oncologist in upstate New York, founded the charity Help the Needy (HTN) which got food and medicines to thousands of starving Iraqis for 13 years.[266] Upon arresting Dhafir, Ashcroft announced that "supporters of terrorism had been apprehended."[267] Both Attorney General Ashcroft and Governor Pataki publicly referred to Dhafir as a terrorist[268], and continuously alleged that HTN was a terror-financing organization. Yet no terrorism charges were ever brought against them. Prosecutors hinted at national security reasons for holding Dhafir without bail, but no evidence was offered to support the allegations[269]. Paradoxically, the prosecutors successfully lobbied Judge Norman Mordue to prevent the charge of terrorism from being part of the trial. Why? Because the DOJ cannot win a terrorism case, simply because there was not a shred of evidence of terror link. And so in a travesty of a court, Dhafir was tried on the charges of breaking the US sanctions against Iraq, and of money fraud. Help the Needy was selectively targeted. Dhafir is no guiltier of breaking the law than is former President Carter. After Hamas victory in the Palestinian elections, President Carter "urged the international community to directly or indirectly fund the new Palestinian Government even though it will be led by an internationally-declared foreign terror organization." He added that they should "bypass the Palestinian Authority and provide the 'much-needed' money to the Palestinians via non-governmental channels."[270] This is what HTN and its founder were convicted for! "[Dr. Dhafir] is thought to be the only U.S. citizen convicted of breaking the Iraq sanctions, though groups such as Voices in the Wilderness, Veterans for Peace, Pax Christi USA, the American Friends Service Committee, the Order of St Dominic, Conscience International, Global Exchange, and the International Action Center have admitted breaking the sanctions with Iraq since before the US invasion."[271] The only non-Muslim organization that has been punished —to the best of this author's knowledge- is Voices in the Wilderness, which was "fined but never prosecuted for violating the Sanctions"[272]. Yet "Judge Norman Mordue prohibited Dhafir's attorneys from raising the question of selective prosecution because he is a Muslim."[273]

As for the money fraud claim, a court watcher, Madis Senner, a CPA and former Wall Street businessman, declares: "The fraud claim is bogus." Senner elaborates: "If [the government] wanted to question the donors about fraud, then why did they ask questions about the mosque, religious practices, family in the middle east, etc... Because they were shaking the tree in search of information."[274] The biggest crime of HTN's founder was that he was "sloppy with records"[275] Now although Dhafir was tried only for ordinary white collar crimes, the prosecution has asked that his sentence be based on post-trial judicial recognition that he is a national security threat. In other words, he was punished for a crime for which he was not tried and against which he did not have an opportunity to defend himself. This violates the Sixth Amendment.

Adding salt to injury, the US Government has squandered HTN's funds by giving it to a "Jerry Lewis-like organization where most of the donations are eaten up by salaries and trips for the workers" despite the fact that Mr. Scott Porter, HTN's attorney, has asked that the money be sent to Iraq in the form of wheel chairs badly needed by the war victims[276].

The lessons learned from this case are:

a-An Islamic charity can be brought down as a result f the allegations made by the US government, even if it is ultimately found to have nothing to do with terrorism. No Islamic charity in the US, no matter how careful, or how diligently it follows the rules, is safe from being shut down by the US Government. Help the Needy clearly illustrates this point.

b-Money seized by the government will be given to sources other than intended by the donors, thus violating the First Amendment-protected religious freedom of the American Muslims to perform Zakat as their religious duty.

c-The prosecution has used tactics in this indictment that should raise concerns among all NGOs. "[These] trial strategies [are] increasingly being used by the DOJ to take people off the streets who are not criminals. These tactics have been used against Greenpeace ...animal rights activist, and several groups of anti-war protestors," writes Jennifer Van Bergen[277].

d-A clear message is being sent that humanitarian acts like the one performed by HTN will be punished. Today, a Muslim organization is targeted, but in the future other non-Muslim NGOs might be the targets.

e-A double standard is used when dealing with Islamic organizations as opposed to others. This has been illustrated both in the case of breaking the Iraq sanctions, and the tactics used for sentencing Dr. Dhafir.

Islamic charities came to the conclusion that in reality the campaign against them is no more than a clearly fabricated case and that all that was presented to the U.S. Congress, and what came out of it, was no more than a paper war following a propaganda war.

Al-Haramain's case is like the other similar cases, it has been designated without legal procedure, away from the rule of law. Moreover, the US and other countries' administrations have treated al-Haramain branches as guilty without presenting their cases to courts so that justice could be carried out. Thus al-Haramain, its employees,[278] and the people benefiting from it have become victims of the faulty criteria and flawed systems. It has been treated at all steps of the issue with unjust measures and decisions based on political considerations rather than legal justice.[279]

In other cases the American Judicial system has proven its fairness and even-handedness. The most prominent of these cases is the collective lawsuit against the Saudi Government and a number of Saudi princes and businessmen and some Saudi banks for compensation to the 9/11 victims' families.After looking at the allegations and demands of the 9/11 victims' families, Judge Richard Conway Casey of New York dismissed the allegations against a number of defendants[280]on January 18, 2005. This confirms that many of the allegations and designations would not stand before the just law.[281]

What makes the American allegations against Islamic Charities in general, and al-Haramain in particular, even more suspicious was that on August 4, 2005, the federal attorneys filed a motion to dismiss charges against al-Haramain foundation, reserving the right to file charges in the future.[282] However, the al-Haramain attorney, Mark Blackman asked US Magistrate Thomas Coffin to deny the government's motion to dismiss. Blackman argued that the case should either proceed to trial with the current indictment or that the case be dismissed with prejudice. [283]

On August 9 2005, the Federal Court dismissed all charges against al-Haramain.[284] Thus the American investigations have failed to prove the veracity of the allegations against Islamic charities, and the dossier has been closed in favor of the charities. The US Government has chosen al-Haramain as a showcase example of Islamic charities accused of terror financing and yet it has utterly failed in indicting the charity, and the charges did not stand before the law.

Officials at al-Haramain believe that the American Government recurred to this move because no evidence was presented to the court. The proved innocence of the charity after due process of law would be even harder on the prosecutors than dismissing the charges. They obviously did not fail to notice that the Dutch courts have thrown out all allegations against al-Haramain, clearing it of all charges. Dr Wendell Belew, Jr. spokesman of FOCA announced that the Dutch Government has un-froze the assets of al-Haramain Foundation, "since it has not discovered any material evidence that would justify continued freeze on its assets."[285]

The latest news concerning the veracity of the allegations against al-Haramain were published on July 7, 2006 in the *New York Times*, relating the horrendous ordeal of the Algerian Laid Saidi who run the branch of al-Haramain in Tanzania, a tale which carries a new set of allegations against the American secret detention program. In May 2003 Mr. Saidi was expelled from Tanzania. According to the *New York Times*, "Mr. Saidi, 43, said that after he was expelled he was handed over to American agents and flown to Afghanistan, where he was held for 16 months before being delivered to Algeria and freed without ever being charged or told why he had been imprisoned."[286] Under the subtitle of *A Dire Misunderstanding*, the article continues: "In prison, Mr. Saidi said, he was interrogated daily, sometimes twice a day, for weeks. Eventually, he said, his interrogators produced an audiotape of the conversation in which he had allegedly talked about planes. But Mr. Saidi said he was talking about tires, not planes, that his brother-in-law planned to sell from Kenya to Tanzania. He said he was mixing English and Arabic and used the word "tirat," making "tire" plural by adding an Arabic "at" sound. Whoever was monitoring the conversation apparently understood the word as "tayarat," Arabic for planes, Mr. Saidi said."[287]

Mr. Saidi said the interrogators accused him of funneling money to al-Qaeda, allegations he strongly denies, and for which evidence was never produced. While he was in prison, however, the United States Treasury Department asked the United Nations to add Al Haramain's Tanzanian branch to the list of charities alleged to have financed terrorist organizations.[288]

In summary, while the US administration has taken al-Haramain as a case study and an example of terror supporting organizations, that represents the situation of Islamic charities worldwide, we have used this same example and it proved the contrary, because not only the 9/11 report on al-Haramain case study does not prove that the accusations are wrong, but that there is no evidence at all for the accusations, and indeed all charges have been dismissed.

Moreover, the Senate Finance Committee has cleared US Muslim organizations of terror financing. *The Washington Post* reported: "The Senate Finance Committee has wrapped up a high-profile investigation into U.S. Muslim organizations and terrorism financing, saying it discovered nothing alarming enough to warrant new laws or other measures, officials said. The inquiry, which took two years, was highly unusual in that the committee pored through private financial information held by the government."[289]

One would think that after the Senate Finance Committee findings, Islamic organizations would be safe from being targeted as terror supporters, but the US Government is at it again. On February 19, 2006, the Treasury Department locked the offices of KindHearts and froze its assets, effectively shutting the charity while it is under investigation. A lengthy probe would be disastrous for the charity, said Dr. Hatem Elhady, chairman of the board of KindHearts, but a Treasury Department spokesman said there is no timetable for the investigation. "That's exactly their goal. They will take too long and nothing will come out of it, but by the time they decide something, everyone will forget about KindHearts," Dr. Elhady said.[290]

In addition to the above, the fact that the names of all Saudis accused in post-September 11th charities judicial cases were acquitted further reveals the absence of evidence to condemn Islamic charities in general and Saudi charities in particular. Furthermore, the acquittal of the donors and volunteers makes the government liable to pay them both moral and financial damages, after all the lawsuits against them were proved unfounded and were dropped. For instance, the**** court issued a list of the acquitted persons and institutions. The list includes*** (Review appendix No.3 for the list).

The U.S. federal court definitively closed the files of all Saudis accused in the post September 11 charities cases, dismissed the cases on the grounds of lack of evidence, and the lack of a legal suit against the defendants. Foremost among them are: Sheikh Aqeel Al-Aqeel former president of Al-Haramain Charity, Engineer Suliman al-Buthe former general manager of Al-Haramain Charity in America, Yassin Al-Quadi, Adnan Basha, and Jamal Khalifa (deceased).

In June 2009, a great number of these names was cleared, among them are Talal Badcook, Shaheer Batterjee, Abdullah bin Laden, Bakr bin Laden, Omar bin Laden, Tarek bin Laden, Islam bin Laden, Dallah United Arab Group, Dubai Foundation for Administrative Services, Sheikh Saleh Alhussayen,Abdul Aziz bin Ibrahim Al-Ibrahim, Ibrahim bin Abdul Aziz Al-Ibrahim Foundation, Yousef Jameel, Abdul Rahman bin Mahfouz, Khalid bin Mahfouz, the National Commercial Bank, Abdullah bin Saleh Al-Obaid, Abdullah Al-Rajhi, Saleh Al Rajhi, Sulaiman Al Rajhi, Abdul Rahman Al-Suwailem, Abdullah bin Abdul Mohsen At-Turki.

Moreover, Chapters IV and V are chock- full of additional proofs that reveal the truth behind this campaign against the Islamic charities.

Chapter IV

The Declared Objectives of the Campaign: Analysis

The New Financial Procedures and the Declared Objectives.

The campaign against the Islamic charities had a declared objective of fighting terror financing, which allegedly the charities are providing. But it has become clear through the examination of the case study of al-Haramain in Chapter 3 that there is no proof to support the American allegations. Other issues and case studies examined in the following chapters further reveal the truth about the US objectives.

In spite of the many difficulties in following the money trail, there is an insistence in continuing the financial war, but this pursuit rather reveals that tracking the Islamic charities' financial transactions does not realize the declared objective, because terrorism does not need much money, and the movement of small quantities of money are not subject to control, as Jennifer Barrett says in *Newsweek*: "The current legislation is not adequate. There is no system to check the banks' deposits in cash below $10,000.

The legislation says that if a deposit is below $10,000 in cash, the bank can accept it without informing the Treasury."[291]

In spite of the obvious failure in tracking financial transactions, a great amount of money that is beyond imagination has been spent to follow this objective. Some of these obstacles have been mentioned by Matthew Levitt of the *Washington Institute for Near East Policy*. He says: "Though the PATRIOT Act provided US authorities with long overdue tools and powers critical to countering this kind of threat, plenty of domestic problems persist and hamper our ability to address this threat to national security. Law enforcement and intelligence organizations, for example, remain short on experienced analysts (especially those with critical language skills such as Arabic, Farsi, Pashtu and more), lack technologically advanced database and other computer tools frequently available on the open market, are still trying to establish smooth and seamless means of interagency communication that overcome the barriers of institutional culture, and often labor under management that is risk averse and often disinterested in strategic analysis."[292] He adds: "America also suffers from a distinct lack of foreign cooperation from critical countries that are nominal allies, most critically the Gulf States, including not only Saudi Arabia but also Qatar, Kuwait, and the United Arab Emirates."

Administrative Difficulties:

Matthew Levitt described these administrative difficulties as strategic gaps, saying: "Even within the US intelligence and law enforcement community, the financial war on terrorism has been hamstrung by bitter turf wars between the Departments of Treasury and Justice. The Departments have reportedly launched parallel task forces that do not communicate or share information. While disconcerting, operational inefficiency and territorialism between agencies pales in comparison to the more strategic gap in policymaking circles. Cracking down on terrorist financing, especially in the case of charitable and humanitarian organizations that camouflage their funding of terrorism by funding legitimate groups and causes as well, requires a political will that was markedly absent until September 11."[293] He also said: "The Financial Action Task Force on Money Laundering (FATF)…issued a list of eight "special recommendations" on curbing terrorist financing as a starting point for governments," the most relevant one concerning charities was the eighth: "Reviewing the adequacy of laws regulating non-profit organizations."[294] "In fact," Levitt says, "this is just a subset of the larger challenge of international cooperation. While the need for international cooperation cannot be overstated, there is no one central organization dedicated to combating terrorist financing."[295]

International Obstacles:

Jeremy Scott of the *BBC News Online* says: "Three independent experts contacted by *BBC News Online* agreed that even taking into account the huge difficulties faced by law enforcement and regulators in tracking money launderers, many governments have proved half-hearted a best when stumping up the necessary funding. British policemen, both serving and ex-officers working in financial intelligence, have complained to *BBC News Online* that interdiction of money laundering has been about style rather than substance. And despite having by far the biggest and most effective operation in the world, even the US has often found itself facing a huge and unmanageable mound of suspicious transaction reports."[296]

Levitt has also mentioned the difficulties in cooperating with the European States, saying: "US officials complain that European allies have contributed few names to the list of alleged terrorist financiers subject to financial blocking orders, that they have yet to act on all the names already on the list, and that those names European allies have added to the list are primarily domestic groups such as Basque and Irish groups. Europeans in return, have repeatedly expressed their frustration with US requests to add people or groups to terrorist lists while supplying insufficient evidence, if any."[297] He then stressed: "It is critical, therefore, as recommended in a recent report commissioned by the Council on Foreign Relations, that the international community establish a specialized international organization whose sole purpose would be to combat terrorist financing."[298]

In fact Levitt has warned against the gaps and exposing the tremendous difficulties in tracking financial transactions, saying: "In the United States, for example, while it is illegal to provide material support to a designated terrorist organization, it is not illegal to be a member of such an organization. Terrorists are aware of the shortcomings and limitations of our domestic legal systems and proactively exploit these gaps to their advantage. They raise tremendous amounts of money in the United States and Western Europe, abuse broad freedom of speech laws in Britain, exploit privacy laws in Germany, and manipulate banking laws in countries that allow offshore accounts." [299]

However, preventing charities from raising money, restricting freedom of speech, and changing privacy laws are not the solution. On the contrary, they go against the principles of freedom and democracy which the US claims it wants to spread in the Middle East. This does indeed send the wrong message to the people of the Middle East and the Muslim World in general, and throws strong doubts about the stated objectives of the campaign.

International Law and the Challenges it presents:

The US decisions relating to tracking financial transactions, and freezing or seizing assets are limited to banks inside the United States, whether they are American Banks or branches of foreign banks. These decisions do not apply to banks located outside the US even if they are branches of American banks except in countries that have bilateral agreements with the US. Therefore Banks outside the US are not legally bound by the US decision, because there is no international agreement to this effect.

Consequently, the US pressure on other countries to force their banks to freeze assets of suspicious supporters of terrorism is not based on legal authority, or on certainty that the assets belong to terrorist groups, but is rather based on mere suspicions.

Countries around the world are faced with a dilemma: either they respect their own internal laws and judicial systems and refuse to freeze the assets except by following the rules in place with respect to the privacy of the customers' accounts, or hasten to please the United States and put their judicial systems, internal laws, and the privacy of their accounts at the disposal of America.

It is clear that countries which chose the second venue are among the majority. Most countries hastened to review the list of persons and organizations designated by the US, and froze their assets without taking the pain to verify the credibility of the allegations that the organizations or persons are terrorist supporters, and without assessing the danger of following this path on the investors' confidence in the country, and the relationship of the banks with their customers after breaching the financial rules and traditions regarding their privacies.

The Ineffective Path:

In general, tracking financial transactions in order to stop the money flow to terrorists has been ineffective. "You can't trace a cent to any terrorist," says Attorney Nancy Luque[300]

Christopher Schmitt and Joshua Kurlantzick of *US News & World Report* emphasized the difficulty of tracking money, saying:

"If knowing where charity money goes can be tricky, tracking the origins of such money can be even more difficult."[301]

And the French reporter Ibrahim Warde of *Le Monde Diplomatique* says: "The terrorist strikes cost a fraction of the price of a single payload of a single B52 bomber. And they were funded through the simplest of money transfers. How effective is financial regulation?"[302]

Illustrating the impotence of the US administration in tracking the money, he reported the former US Secretary of Finance Paul O'Neil, who served in the beginning of the Bush administration, saying: "For the last 15, maybe even 25 years, this nation has had a program aimed at so-called money laundering, which is trying to get at evildoers who are moving cash around the world economy. And there has been an enormous amount of activity upward of $700m a year spent on this subject. And when I began asking the question of what have we gotten for the money we spent, I must say I was very disappointed that over this period of time, there's one famous case that produced a significant amount of money that was caught. We should insist that we get value for money spent."[303]

Dan Mitchell, the McKenna Senior Fellow in Political Economy at the Heritage Foundation, "pointed out that the anti-terrorist financing campaign has cost the private sector billions of dollars and has entailed a sweeping invasion of privacy, yet there is 'nothing much to show for it'. The government approach defies common sense and has turned the traditional approach of law enforcement upside down." "Thus, short of reading people's mind," he said, "there is no way to systematically track down terrorists or terrorist financing sources this way, and pursuing such a strategy is a waste of valuable resources."[304] Moreover, if, as the Government Accountability Office (GAO), an arm of the US Congress, has said, terrorist funding comes mainly from criminal activity,[305] then why is the Bush administration adamant on continuing on this path? A glimpse of the answer is in the report of OMB Watch: "[T]hese regulations …force charities to incur organizational and social costs far beyond the administrative burdens of compliance." The report summary states that "there are serious defects in the government's approach that render elements of the financial war on terror ineffective and pose significant threats to the work of non-profit organizations throughout the world. This is a terrifying consequential outcome."[306]

People associated with humanitarian organizations in the world and bank directors warned that the financial decisions and measures can not fulfill the declared objective (to staunch the finance of terrorism). However, they fulfill the bankruptcy of Islamic charities, which often have to abandon humanitarian work to defend themselves. Since the goal of stemming the flow of money cannot be attained through these measures, this again throws doubts concerning the declared US objective.

The Difficulties of Tracing Small-Scale Transactions:

The September 11 attacks have changed the focus of the US and world from pursuing the money laundering activities to tracing the financial transactions of groups opposed to the United States of America. President Bush has considered this step as "The Financial War Front".

The financial focus may be misplaced, noted Warde, because it is based on the assumption that most organized crime is motivated by financial gain. "Yet the real logic of terrorism is different," he says, "According to The FBI estimates, the September 11 operations cost less than $200,000. Most terrorists led modest lives, survived from low paid jobs, or received money from their families. The one item that may have required outside support was the cost of flying lessons"[307]

Terrorist operations do not necessitate considerable financing, as numerous specialists pointed out. "The first attack against the World Trade Center in 1993 which resulted in six dead and 1,000 wounded, cost somewhere between $10,000 and $20,000." Warde said. "It is doubtful that drying up money sources would seriously deter further terrorist acts," he concluded. Stressing the tremendous difficulties, Warde said: "Now [financial institutions] are asked to investigate and police, or get punished. Large institutions may be able to slip through the net, but smaller establishments, especially those connected to the Islamic world, have an almost impossible task proving that they are not facilitating terrorism."[308]

In reality, most who are hostile to Islam repeatedly accused Islamic charities of supporting terrorism. Warde writes: "Almost every Islamic charity is now under surveillance. Some anti-Islamic commentators have long argued that the raison d'être of many philanthropic organizations was to finance terrorism or provide a front for it. But the size and ubiquity of the charitable sector have a simpler explanation: almsgiving or Zakat is one of the five pillars of Islam."[309]

In the wake of the Islamophobia, the tendency to equate Islam with terrorism has also reached the financial sector. "Any financial flow associated with the Islamic world is presumed guilty until proven innocent."[310]

Warde concludes his article by saying: "The logic of collective punishment will result in substantial collateral damage."[311] And among the collateral damage are the Islamic charities and the needy Muslims they serve. Mr. Qumaysi, an official at the Somali orphanage, said: "It is strange that the US says the Muslim aid agencies are terrorists, but they don't bring their own agencies to replace them. Isn't this just another way of killing the orphans whose parents have died during civil strife in Somalia?"[312]

Sarah Toyne and Jeremy Scott-Joynt of *BBC News Online* said: "No one is under any illusion that the task will be an easy one. Tracing the flow of illicit money is a complicated, time-consuming business, and the cards are stacked against investigators... Experts believe the task is going to be an extremely difficult one."[313] Doubting that the reason behind the campaign against Islamic charities was the war on terror financing, Toyne and Scott said: "However, terrorism experts say that an operation such as the attacks on the US would not necessarily have been all that expensive. 'It would not be that expensive...'said Paul Rogers, professor of peace studies at Bradford University."[314]

"How do authorities trace the money in the first place?" Toyne and Scott ask. "Suspicious transaction reports (STRs) are hardly reliable, many experts fear. Some banks are less than diligent about filing them, and not only the 'correspondent banks' which sometimes consist of little more than a brass plate on a door and a nominated director in a house down the road. Even if the reports are filed, usually a required practice for any sum over about £10,000, the regulators may be too snowed under to pay attention."[315]

In fact, the US administration should realize now that tracking terrorist finances has not, and will not, bring results or be an obstacle to terrorist operations. The real objective of this campaign against Islamic charities is not declared. Toyne and Scott pointed to the lack of seriousness of the American institutions in combating financial crimes, "The US Financial Crimes Enforcement Network (FCEN), which oversees anti-money laundering efforts at the moment, is notorious in US banking circles for having a huge backlog of STRs. And banks complain of being forced to be policemen."

A senior UK banking executive said: "Banks don't have the people or those with enough experience to play Sherlock Holmes.

The processes are very skilled - they are run through 'legitimate' companies. How can you possibly detect all of them?" He added: "If we were to implement all the regulations, bankers would be doing nothing else."[316]

Undoubtedly, not all the banks apply all these rules. "It might be easier to withdraw money from a retail bank in New York or London, rather than Jersey," said Toyne.[317] This has been proven in money laundering cases. For example, when officials investigated funds stolen by the former Nigerian dictator Sani Abacha, they found that most of them went through financial institutions in London.

Compounded Difficulties in the Third World:

The difficulties in tracing money are compounded to the point that it is impossible to pursue it especially at the end stage of the financial transactions. Funds are usually transferred through accounts in free zones banks, or using unofficial means, or directly transferred without the use of banks. Toyne and Scott pointed to this fact saying: "The secret lies in an alternative banking system hundreds of years old, known in India as *hawala* and in Pakistan - and Afghanistan and the Middle East - as *hundi*. According to Professor Barry Rider, director of the Institute of Advanced Legal Studies in London and an expert on financial crime, the trust-based *Hundi* system is entirely normal and prevalent wherever there is a South Asian or Middle Eastern Diaspora. 'Say I am working in the UK and want to send money back to a village in Pakistan,' he said. "I could get a bank transfer, but that's going to be at the official exchange rate. And what good will it do my family in a village with no bank?' Instead, he says, you find the *hundi* broker - often a local businessman - give him the money, and after a short time his contacts back home will deliver the money, at the black market rate, in local currency and minus a handling fee, to your relatives. No paper trail, no fuss. And no money ever crosses the border."

Professor Rider adds: "No intelligence organization - except the Directorate of Revenue Intelligence in India, perhaps - has ever effectively cracked the system. You could count the number of successful penetrations on the fingers of one hand."[318] Therefore, the US administration might know that they are failing in their declared objective, but through this siege, they might have been successful in their undeclared one.

If the declared objective is not achievable, what could the true objective be?

In spite of the sweeping powers that President Bush has granted the US Treasury Department to conduct in-depth investigations into individuals and institutional bank accounts and the deposits and transfers conducted through them and to freeze those accounts on the basis of the least inkling of doubt, there are numerous challenges that get in the way of conducting these measures fully or with the precision required for them to realize their presumed objective of cutting off financing to terrorist organizations. There are a number of reasons for this:

- The huge number of banks that are subject to the Treasury inquiries: More than 5000 banks in America received instructions from the US Treasury, not to mention the hundreds of thousand banks and branches around the world, with millions of accounts.
- This resolution conflicts with a number of customs and legal and banking procedures both inside the United States and abroad. The powers granted the US Department of the Treasury conflict with the United States Constitution and with the constitutions of many other countries since they allow for the incrimination

of bank accounts and individuals on the basis of mere suspicion without a judicial ruling.

- There are alternative ways to transfer and move funds. Money can be transferred directly without passing through the banking system.

- This resolution poses a threat to the relationship between banks and their customers and the mutual confidence of both parties. This will affect the banking activity worldwide, and will hamper the work of the humanitarian organizations especially the Islamic charities, and this cannot continue even for a short period. Banks cannot play the role of policeman.

- There is a danger that some international corporations can use this resolution as a means to impede other corporations that either compete with them directly or that deal with their competitors by having those corporations placed on the black list without any real evidence and consequently having the accounts of those companies closed or their competitiveness eliminated. The same can be applied to countries and individuals as well. This presents a threat on the international trade environment. It is possible to overcome the difficulties presented by the American decisions, but only for a limited time, and all the same, the threat will have short term and long term effects.

Islamic charities' money transactions have been scrutinized and treated more harshly than any other transactions even more than money transactions related to organized crimes, arms and drug trafficking, and Mafia organizations. This shows an uneven treatment and reveals the injustice in this war, which does not help attain the objective of combating terror financing. The method of dealing exposes further the real objective, for even if one organization or a branch of an organization or even a person has committed a mistake, all are under accusation and all incur penalties as well.

Anyone well acquainted with these measures, difficulties, and challenges, realizes that the war on terror financing that targeted Islamic charities is not the goal, because this goal cannot be attained practically. But it has greatly succeeded in spreading doubts about the organizations and weakening their financial role, and in destroying the mutual trust they had with their communities and governments.

Finally, has the financial war that targeted Islamic charities worldwide fulfilled the declared goal, a goal that is almost impossible to fulfill according to a number of specialists in this field? Or was it a war that used these means to fulfill undeclared objectives? And what are these objectives? One has only to look at the negative effects on the Islamic charities. Charities officials in the US, Europe, and the Muslim world are wondering: "Could it be that these arbitrary financial and administrative inquiries of Islamic charities aim at weakening their financial and human resources? Is their goal to diminish, if not eliminate, the charities' role and programs in the global arena?" Some others observed: "The American administration has now complete control on financial transactions and has breached the privacy of many countries, organizations, and people under the pretext of "the war on terror financing."

Discussing the disproportionate effects of the anti-terrorism financing policies on Islamic organizations, Laila al-Marayati, Chairperson of the Islamic charity KinderUSA, argued that the US Government uses anti-terrorist financing programs as a political tool to profile and discriminate against Islamic charities. "To date, the only domestic groups targeted and shut down have been Muslim... The results of this campaign against Muslim charities were clearly illustrated in the Tsunami relief effort: not one Muslim charity appeared on the US Government's list of approved organizations to deliver relief."[319] Theresa Odendahl of Georgetown Public Policy Institute's Center for Public and Non-Profit Leadership argued that "by enforcing elaborate, draconian rules, Washington is doing mightily what it claims to be against: harming charities and the people they serve while doing little to stem terrorism."[320]

The British Investigations of Islamic Charities

Countries that respect their judicial system performed strong investigations to arrive at the truth behind the allegations against Islamic charities. Among them is the United Kingdom. According to Debra Morris, not all allegations stand in front of the truth. She said: "On March 13, 2002, the Charity Commission published its policy on charities and their alleged links to terrorism. It was announced that on September 11, 2002, the Charity commission already had inquiries open into the activities of five charities and their potential links to terrorism, and were evaluating concerns into two others. Since then, it has evaluated concerns about a further ten charities, and opened formal inquiries into five of them. Two of those charities have been closed down and another one has had its assets frozen."[321]

On August 21, 2003, the US Government designated the Palestinians Relief and Development Fund (Interpal), which has its headquarters in Britain, as a "Specially Designated Global Terrorist" organization for allegedly supporting Hamas, alleging it was "the fund-raising co-coordinator of Hamas" and "a principal charity utilized to hide the flow of funds to Hamas"[322] On August 27, President Bush announced that the US would block Interpal's bank account, and urged Britain to take action against the charity. British Muslims reacted angrily. Ibrahim Hewitt, the chairman of trustees of Interpal, said: "This is happening because America says so, because Israel says so." The Muslim Council of Britain has sent a letter of protest to the foreign secretary, Jack Straw.[323]

Interpal was launched from London in 1994. Issam Yusuf, Interpal's director has informed me that the organization was subject to investigations in 1996 under the pressure of Zionists. The investigation resulted in the praise of the organization as an example of disciplined British humanitarian organization. Its gross income of £5 million, ($9 million), 80% of it raised in the UK, reflects the popular and government's trust in it.

In spite of the fact that the media has accused humanitarian organizations in Britain and Wales of having links with terrorist groups, the investigations undertaken by the British Charity Commission concluded that "connections between registered charities in England and Wales and terrorist organizations are rare."[324]

On January 9, 2002, the US department of Finance has designated the Kuwaiti Islamic Heritage Revival based in Britain as a terrorist organization, and as a precautionary measure the British Charity Commission has temporarily frozen the assets of a charitable organization registered in Britain under a similar name, while it investigated the nature of its relations - if any - with other organizations. However after the investigation the Commission has been convinced that the organization had had no activities linked to terrorism.

The Charity Commission's director of operations, Simon Gillespie said: "We have no evidence that Islamic charities are especially vulnerable to abuse in regards to terrorism or any other wrongdoing and we fully support the work of all bona fide religious charities. We expect all charities to properly account for their activities."[325] In her article "Charities and Terrorism", Morris writes: "The good news is that, in both absolute and relative terms, the numbers of charities potentially involved with terrorist activity are small. Neither the Charity Commission, nor other regulatory and enforcement organizations have evidence to suggest that the 185,000 registered charities in England and Wales are widely subject to terrorist infiltration."[326]

The U.K. has a strong history in lawmaking and establishing regulations, and deals with issues on the principle of trust and respect of the law and the right to sovereignty. It has become quite different from the US in its dealing with this issue. It does not treat the charitable organizations as a security threat, and the British media was not a source from which the British security apparatus built their cases. The Charity Commission has been a good example of independence in dealing with the American allegations of terrorism such as the ones against Interpal, and in accepting the effective role of the British Overseas NGOs for Development (BOND), which solicited the British Foreign Minister Jack Straw to remove Interpal from the list of terror supporting organizations in countries such as the US, Canada, and Australia[327]. The Commission is distinguished in its dealing with persons rather than organizations, and clearly does not politicize humanitarian work.

The Procedures Reveal Some of the Truth:

In her article titled "Charities and Terrorism", Debra Morris says: "It is difficult to imagine an issue that could undermine public faith in charity more than the suspicion of terrorist links. Any kind of terrorist connection is obviously completely unacceptable."[328] Was the choice of these allegations of terrorist links intentional?

Concerning the same issue, the International Center for Not-for-Profit Law said: "On 10 December 2001, the Charity Commission completed its formal inquiry into the International Islamic Relief Organization, formally a registered charity. The inquiry which was opened in September 2001, followed media reports that the charity may be linked to terrorist groups... A full inquiry was conducted and the Commission made use of its investigatory powers to obtain copies of all financial records and documentation. The Commission staff established that...the charity had no income or expenditure other than accountant's fees since 1997, and had not carried out any activity since this time."[329] American allegations against the charity were not substantiated in the Commission Report.

Islamic Relief, set up in 1984, is the UK's largest Islamic charity, with a worldwide gross income of around £15 million-£5 million of which raised in the UK. The charity also receives funds from the Department for International Development. At the moment the main focus of the charity's appeals is relief efforts in Afghanistan, Palestine and Chechnya.[330] Dr. Hani al-Banna, President of the organization headquarters in Birmingham, UK, said the organization's gross income reached £26 million in 2003, its expenditure reached £31 million, and in 2004 it was £30 million. 80% of the donations come from individuals, and 20% from non-governmental foundations abroad. The British Government also provides financial support to some of its projects through the Department for International Development, and it is expected that its gross income for 2005 will be around £40 million, which reflects the extent of the UK Government confidence in it and the people's confidence in the Islamic charities in Britain. It should be noticed that this organization has 27 branches and offices worldwide, including one in Los Angeles, California.[331]

Muslim Aid, the second largest charity in the UK headquartered in London, was founded in 1985. Its income is around £ 5 million. It supports relief and development projects in Somalia, Sudan, and Bangladesh, and sends relief supplies to disaster areas as well as helping with longer term projects, as has declared its London director in February 2005. Jamie Wilson of the *Guardian* says:

"Since September 11 attention has focused on Islamic charities as conduits for terrorist funding. The Charity Commission has opened 14 investigations into Islamic charities since the terrorist attacks. No direct links with terrorist groups have been found."[332]

Europe Differentiates between Organizations:

The European Union has uncovered some of the truth through its stand concerning this issue. Levitt says: "On May 3, 2002, the European Union (EU) added eleven organizations and seven individuals to its financial-blocking list of 'persons, groups, and entities involved in terrorist acts.' Unfortunately, while the list marks the first time the EU has frozen the assets of non-European terrorist groups, it adopts the fallacy of drawing a distinction between the nonviolent activities of terrorist groups and the terror attacks that they carry out." While Mr. Levitt considers this distinction as negative, the EU considered it a right decision. Levitt continues: "By distinguishing between the terrorist and welfare 'wings' of Hamas, for example, the EU lent legitimacy to the activities of charitable organizations that fund and facilitate terrorist groups' activities and operations."[333]

"The result of all this investigation is that not one community group has been closed down and no one arrest made following the [police investigators'] visits. The Home Secretary, David Blunkett, even apologized for overzealous investigations," says Gideon Burrows of *The Guardian*. "The people who have been contacting us have been finding it very difficult to cope," said Massoud Sharajah, director of the Islamic Human Rights Commission, to the *Guardian*. "We had to produce 300,000 leaflets to distribute to Muslim people to tell them their rights when special branch or MI5 came to call."[334]

Regarding the unfair distinction between Islamic and other organizations, The *Guardian* says: "There is bitterness among some Islamic charities about the way they have been treated. Christian and secular charities are praised for sending money to Afghanistan, but Islamic groups doing the same are suspected of funding terrorism. Many are concerned there is a concerted attack on the Islamic charity and community sector in the UK. Some see it as a part of the UK Government wanting to please the United States, others believe there is a conspiracy to weaken Muslim civil society by whipping up suspicion against Islamic Charities."[335] It says: "What is clear is that negative effects on the Islamic community and voluntary sector - whether intentional or not - could be regarded as another attack on the faith and practice of the UK's three million Muslims." Fadi Itani, director of north London's Muslim Welfare House, asks: "How can they tell us not to give support for orphans or widows? Charitable giving is a pillar of Muslim beliefs, when someone attacks it; it is like attacking those beliefs."[336]

A US Treasury official said: "We know not only that money from Interpal has ended up funding violence, but that Interpal has itself been responsible for channeling money to fund terror."[337] But these accusations proved false. On September 24, 2003, only five weeks later, the Commission gave Interpal a clean bill of health. "We have moved swiftly to reach a conclusion on this case because of the possible adverse impact of our actions on the charity's beneficiaries," said Simon Gillespie the Charity Commission's director of operations." The Charity pointed out in its report that: "despite being asked, the US has failed to provide any evidence to back up its accusations." "And one occasion where money from a banned charity, the al-Aqsa Foundation, had found its way to Interpal has proved to be an entirely bona fide payment for humanitarian efforts," the report explained. Mr. Hewitt, Interpal director, said: "The Charity Commission demonstrated a degree of independence which these days, is refreshing." The news prompted David Aufhauser, the US Treasury's General Counsel, to tell a

Senate Finance Committee hearing on terrorist finance that the administration was 'disappointed' at the decision.[338]

The UK investigation outcomes and the UK officials' comments exposed the nature of the American campaign and its hidden objective. They point out that the campaign clearly targeted the Islamic charities in Europe that are concerned with the Palestinian issue in particular. This partly explains the negative turn Europe has taken in its policy toward the Palestinian issue, due to the US pressure. This again proves that there are other undeclared objectives behind this campaign.

The Islamic Charities in Bosnia

Islamic charities in Bosnia have been especially targeted after September 11. Andrew Purvis wrote an investigative report in *Time* Magazine about the American allegations against Bosnian charities titled "Money Trouble", where he said: "Benevolence [International Foundation] is the first charity to be criminally linked to international terror…Back in Bosnia, where humanitarian aid is still a major pillar of the postwar economy, US and local investigators are examining the finances of no fewer than eight Islamic charities they believe may be linked to terrorism." [339]

Humanitarian NGOs play a crucial role in Bosnia which is still suffering from the effects of a long and destructive war. Despite the intense humanitarian aid presented by these organizations to the Bosnian people, the Bosnian Government took a hostile position toward them with regard to the allegations. Many Islamic charities were subject to investigations and house searches. From being an observer, the government became a participant with foreign institutions in repetitive searches and investigations without any conclusive proof or reliable information. For example, the Bosnian police stormed the campus of The Parents' Home School for Orphans, a school managed by al-Haramain and al-Aqsa and where 300 orphans receive education, health care, lodging, transportation, food, and clothing, all for free. This storming coincided with a statement by the Bosnian Intelligence Minister, Baritcha Chulac saying that the US has asked the Bosnian Government to prohibit the Islamic relief organizations from working on its soil.[340]

The relief work in Bosnia has been interpreted as a dangerous extremist activity, and the relief aid has been looked at as support to terrorism. David Kaplan of *US News & World Report* says: "It was Bosnia, though, that finally caught the sustained attention of the CIA. In the early '90s, the ethnic-cleansing policies of the Serbs drew hundreds of foreign jihadists to the region to help defend Bosnian Muslims. Saudi money poured in, too. Saudi donors sent $150 million through Islamic aid organizations to Bosnia in 1994 alone."[341]

A US court has sentenced Enaam Arnaout, director of Benevolence International Foundation (BIF), to 10 years in prison, accusing him of financing Bosnian fighters (buying shoes for them) during the Serbo-Croat ethnic campaigns against the Bosnians.

The US Treasury has frozen the assets of both Benevolence International Foundation (BIF) and the Bosnian branch of al-Haramain. The Bosnian Interior Ministry announced that the Bosnian federal police has searched for the second time the headquarters of BIF and al-Haramain in Travnic. The Bosnian Interior Minister, Ramo Masleša, a Bosnian Croat, has described the operation as part of the Bosnian efforts to combat terrorism and dry up the sources of its financing. He pointed out that the search order was issued by the federal high court.[342]

According to Purvis, the main source of worry concerning the Islamic charities in Bosnia was that tens of persons suspected of terrorist activities (i.e. they participated in the fight with the

Bosnians against the Serbs during the ethnic cleansing war) have left Bosnia and the Balkan states during the months following the 9/11 attack; most of those were working with Islamic charitable organizations. Purvis says: "The irony is that Islamic charities have also done a great deal of good, funneling hundreds of millions of dollars in aid into the Bosnian economy since 1991, supporting everything from mosques to war orphan's education." While accusing them of "plotting evil", Lieutenant General John Sylvester admitted: "They were preaching good, and even sometimes doing good."

"Already the probe has triggered angry rebuttals from Muslim ambassadors and aid groups who say investigators are casting too wide a net," noted Purvis. "Just last week the deputy director of Bosnia's antiterrorism commission quit because he said his government was focusing too much on Muslims and not enough on known war criminals like Bosnian Serb leader Radovan Karadzic."[343]

In fact, offices of most Islamic relief organizations have been raided. The searches have brought no evidence of terror support.

Alen Cosic, the head of the local BIF Bosnian branch, denied his former boss Enaam Arnaout was a terrorist, and said that the FBI has fabricated evidence against him because it was "jealous of his success"[344]. He said large cash withdrawals without bookkeeping were normal in the aid business. "I can't say Enaam didn't see Bin Laden," Cosic said, "but he is a serious guy who dedicated his life to helping people."[345] The head of the Islamic Community in Bosnia, Mustapha Ceric, distributed at a press conference "a list of dozens of agencies in the country with a note by each one that had been investigated. All were Islamic. Targeting organizations 'on the basis of what they could do and not what they have done might cost Bosnia a lot,' he said."[346] Purvis called it "Preemptive justice"! He wrote: "Ibrahim Satti, the local director of al-Haramain & al-Masjid al-Aqsa said his agency's accounts were frozen for no apparent reason, interrupting a project to build schools and dormitories for 300 orphans mainly from the Srebenica massacre. 'If we take care of your children,' he asked, 'is that terrorism?' "[347]

"This is not a war on terror," said Anela Kobilica, a Bosnian Muslim woman from Zenica. Holding up her veil for emphasis, she said: "This is a war on Islam." Purvis commented: "In the current atmosphere, it's an easy claim to make."[348]

Jonathan Benthall and Jérôme Bellion Jourdan have tackled the issue of the role of Islamic organizations and Muslim fighters during the Balkan wars, and what happened to the mujahedin after September 11. They Say: "In the aftermath of 11 September 2001, the control of Islamist militants has intensified. Several individuals have been arrested, and some of them extradited to their countries of origin or to Guantanamo Bay to be detained by the US authorities on suspected links with 'terrorist' activities. The activities of some NGOs… have been further investigated… after a request by the USA indicating suspicion that Islamic charities were channeling funds for 'terrorism'."[349] Six employees of Islamic relief organizations have been detained in Guantanamo Bay. Among those are two employees of the United Arab Emirates' Red Crescent, both married and each father to two children, one employee of Taiba Charitable Organization, also married and father to two children, and an employee of the Charity Work Organization, married and father to five children. One of the detainees' children was afflicted with a heart condition after witnessing the police storm into their house and take her father away. One of the detainees became partially paralyzed after being shackled until his arrival to Guantanamo. Even though the Bosnian Federal Court has released a verdict number KI-115/01, dated January 17, 2002, ruling that they are innocent, for lack of incriminating evidence, and ordering that they be immediately released, the then

Socialist Bosnian Party's Government sought to extradite them to Guantanamo in the middle of strong demonstrations in Sarajevo against the unwarranted extradition. This has contributed to the defeat of the Socialist Party's Government in the elections. People close to the detainees expressed doubt as to the veracity of the accusations saying that they are pure fabrications exploited by the Socialist Party for political interests, which soon brought about their loss. Sabiha Welitsch, a detainee's wife said: "I never doubted that my husband was a victim of unfair political tendencies. I never thought that personal political interests would be reason enough to strip a person from his human rights and deprive families that have nothing to do with political conflicts from their breadwinners. We have no other resort but to ask God to vindicate them." The concerned US parties, however, would not embarrass the pro-American Socialist Party by releasing the detainees.[350]

In a desire to get to the truth of the matter concerning these allegations, I saw it necessary to ask the Mufti of Bosnia and head of its Muslim scholars, whom I met at the Kuwait convention in 2004 about the American campaign and allegations against Islamic charities in Bosnia. The following is the text of our interview:

Question 1: Why did Bosnia welcome the relief work of Islamic charities more than the others?

Mufti: We welcomed all relief organizations because we were greatly suffering from the ethnic war, a war of extinction which has religious motive. No doubt those who suffered most were the Bosnian Muslims, and that their brothers among the Arabs and Muslims are more entitled than others to help, but rather it was an obligation on them, because Bosnian Muslims do not want the help of non-Islamic charities that might want to change their religion, or take their children outside Bosnia to Christianize them. And no one can rebuild the mosques that have been destroyed by the Serbs except the Islamic organizations.

Question 2: Do you feel that Islamic charities and their employees have been targeted? And what are the motives behind that?

Mufti: The reality confirms that, and the measures taken against the charities are not secret. The declared allegations are exposed by the results, which have been the weakening or absence of these organizations, and the halt of their money transactions, the arrest or expulsion of some of the employees, all this in a country that is most in need of the work and projects of these organizations.

Question 3: Has it been proved that Islamic charities have supported terrorism in Bosnia?

Mufti: My dear brother, has terrorism been defined? Is it a label, a term defined by its results, or a relative term? If we suppose that it exists in Bosnia according to the American interpretation, then the jihad of the Muslims to defend the Bosnians against the Serbs who were ethnically cleansing them, has been over since the early 90's. The Muslims still have to regain their properties, their culture, their orphaned children; they still have to rebuild their mosques that have been destroyed by the Serbs. Can you call these development projects and relief work terrorism or supporting terrorism?! Can't you see the results on the field? The facts and statistics recorded by impartial Europeans and Americans strongly point to the real objective of the global American campaign against the Islamic charity sector.

Chapter V

Case Studies
Islamic Charities under
American Hegemony

Introduction to the Case Studies

Since the advent of September 11, the US attacks and military presence have concentrated on countries such as Afghanistan and Iraq, and some countries bordering the Caspian Sea. The vision of the United States' international sphere of influence after the fall of the Soviet Union necessitates the need for the US to secure its geo-strategic interests especially in the Eurasian Continent. America's geo-political strategy is to gain preeminence over the world's oil reserves, most of which are in that area.[351]

It is not a coincidence that most, if not all of these countries are Muslim countries. In spite of claiming the opposite, the US Government's actions and policies project a view of Islam as an opponent, and that a clash of civilizations (more precisely of religions, i.e. a new crusade) is imminent. This view has been clearly stated by Samuel Huntington in his book "The Clash of Civilizations"[352]. Is the aim of the US to subjugate the Muslim World, by striking at Iraq? The alleged US aggressions against

Muslim countries fall in step with this view. The breaking down of Islamic charities also falls in step with this view. The US position towards the Palestinian issue again agrees with this view, a blatant Israeli transgression against the (mostly Muslim) Palestinian people, and the consistent US defeat of all UN resolutions against Israel.

The following case studies in Palestine, Afghanistan, and Iraq, all of which have become victims of the so-called war on terror, reveal to a great extent the true aims and purposes of the campaign against Islamic organizations and charities. Moreover, they reveal a new negative relationship with most non-governmental organizations that are opposed to America's war in Iraq. These organizations - through their programs, activities, or positions - are seen as "competitors" to American influence.

Case Study 1: Palestine

The Palestinian issue is a global issue where different interests and principles intersect and some others clash. It is not just a Middle Eastern or even an Arab issue. Not only is it the issue of more than a billion Muslims, but of some of the Christians and the Jews as well.[353] Global forces such as the US, EU, and others compete for a resolution of the problem that may or may not be just.[354]

The American actions concerning Islamic charities had a catastrophic effect on the Palestinian people. The Palestinians are victims of the war on terror. They have been subject to hunger and terror, and have been under siege, forbidden from receiving relief and medical aid. This campaign has encompassed most relief organizations inside Palestine and the supporting organizations outside Palestine whether they are in America, Europe, or the Arab world. These organized campaigns give the impression that they are part of the policy of preemptive war, or the preparation for a future war.

The course of elimination that started by blocking the Palestinian Islamic organizations, starving the people benefiting from them, leaves no doubt as to the goal of the American terror allegations against Islamic charities. For example the US decided to freeze the assets of many financial organizations which deal with some global charities such as al-Aqsa International Bank and Beit al-Mal Holdings Company under the allegation that they were supporting Hamas.[355] The decision was preceded by a meeting of Israeli Shin Bet security police with US Treasury officials to inform them that the two organizations helped transfer money to Hamas.[356]

The Palestinian Authority decided to freeze the financial assets of most Islamic charities. About 90% of Palestinian Islamic charities had their assets frozen inside Palestine. Among these are the Islamic Assembly, the Islamic Association, and the Muslim Young Women Association, the Friends of the Palestinian Student Association, the al-Aqsa charity, an-Nour Charity Association, and the Committee of Social Care. The Palestinian Attorney General asked the banks to allow no withdrawal from the accounts of the organizations without his permission.[357]

Delinda C. Hanley of the *Washington Report on Middle East Affairs* commented on these decisions, saying: "As the al-Aqsa intifada entered its second winter, Israel's American supporters launched a particularly cruel weapon against the Palestinian people. While Israel's Prime Minister Ariel Sharon sent helicopter gun-ships, bulldozers and heavy weaponry to attack and reoccupy Palestinian territory in the West Bank and Gaza Strip, his lobbyists in the United States used political pressure and smear campaigns to block humanitarian aid from reaching the Palestinian people in time for the holidays."[358]

She adds: "As the holy month of Ramadan neared an end - a time when Muslim Americans are most generous in opening up their pocketbooks to help those in need - President George W. Bush announced on December 4 [2001] that he was ordering the closure of the Texas-based Holy Land Foundation for Relief and Development (HLF). On December 14 he took the same action against the Illinois-based Global Relief Foundation and the Benevolence International Foundation, also in Illinois."[359] The three charities are active in supporting the Palestinian people in the occupied territories.

"Accusing the Islamic charities of funding Hamas extremists," Hanley says, "the Treasury Department froze their funds, raided their offices and seized their records. Almost immediately the Canadian Government took the same actions against the three charities."

Describing the reaction of the charities, she says: "The non-profit humanitarian organizations and their supporters strongly deny any links to terrorism. Global Relief, founded in 1992, says it 'is in the business of helping innocent civilians and takes every precaution to ensure our aid does not go to support or subsidize any nefarious activity.' The Holy Land Foundation, founded in 1987... raises funds for relief efforts for Palestinians in Israel, Lebanon and the occupied territories. In recent years, the HLF expanded its mission to help Muslims face disaster in Chechnya, Kosovo, and Turkey."

"Donations to both groups," she adds, "helped feed the hungry, bring injured youths to the United States for medical treatment, and provide medical and educational support. Like many Christian charities, contributors could also sponsor a Palestinian orphan for a set monthly amount and then regularly receive letters and photographs."

"The HLF raised more than $13 million in 2000. In 2001, in the wake of the deadly tornado, it gave the city of Fort Worth $ 10,000. In December the Treasury Department froze $5 million in donation to the Holy Land, nearly half the amount it had raised during the year."

Hanley says: "In closing down the Holy Land Foundation, President Bush said that the organization builds schools to 'indoctrinate children to grow into suicide bombers' and supports the bombers' families after deadly suicide missions. The Holy Land denied connection to Hamas and providing assistance specifically to the families of suicide bombers, although they may be among the many recipients of HLF relief aid. The organization's friends note that no relief organization in the world is asked to question hungry children about their parents' religious or political beliefs or legal status."

Hanley comments: "By closing the Islamic charities, the Bush administration has demonstrated that it succumbed to Israeli pressure to link the US war on global terrorism with Israel's war against the Palestinians." She adds: "The Israeli Government, along with its public relations machines and its lobbyists in the United States, methodically set out to reverse the administration position [of making distinction between its war against al-Qaeda and Israel's war on Palestinians]. According to the November 8 *Washington Jewish Week*, leaders of the Conference of Presidents of Major American Jewish Organizations met with administration officials in the beginning of November to ask for anti-Israel groups to be added to the list of terrorist organizations. Similarly, the November 9 *Forward* reported that a concerted effort was launched to add Hamas, the Islamic Jihad, and the Lebanese Hezbollah to the list of terrorist organizations subject to new financial sanctions. 'The lobbying effort for the inclusion of the Palestinian organizations was wider than typical campaigns mounted by pro-Israel advocates in Washington,' *Forward* noted. 'The pressure on the administration has become unbearable.' American Jewish organizations were delighted with the success of their efforts."[360]

Freezing of Accounts:

Islamic charities close to Hamas have asked the Palestinian Authority to cancel the freezing of their assets, warning of a popular explosion in Gaza where unrest has reached its peak after the assassination of Shaikh Ahmad Yassine, Hamas spiritual leader.

On March 21, 2004, the Palestinian High Court ordered the release of the assets of six of the organizations which were frozen under pressure from Washington on August 2003.

Abu Heen, a leader at the Islamic Assembly said: "By the end of January 2004 we will have not a cent, and there will be thousands of people we will not be able to give aid to," he added that in spite of the official freezing of the organization's assets for seven months, they were able to reach an agreement with the Authority to allow them to spend from the assets if they provided them with the names of each recipient (persons, and associations). The agreement was broken by the Israeli raid of Ramallah's banks on February 25, 2004, and the seizing of millions of dollars under the allegation that they were being used to support terrorism. Abu Heen said: "We receive money from well known organizations most of them in Europe and the United States. These organizations are helping the poor, and not the terrorists." He expressed doubt that the Palestinian Authority would respect the High Court decision, saying: "Why don't they respect the law?" then he added: "But what law? There is no law in Gaza." He explained that the budget of the association he manages is $50 million dollars, that it provides aid to 20 thousand orphans, 50 thousand families, and pays ten thousand student tuitions. It provides education to 20 thousand students through a network of kindergartens, and elementary schools. He concluded: "We offer aid to anyone who needs it without political discrimination."

Islamic Reform Association, one of the organizations who had its assets frozen, manages twelve kindergartens, two elementary schools, in addition to four dispensaries. Jaber Alewa, an official of the association said: "We provide religious schooling and we help the poor." He added: "People have confidence in us because we spend what we receive on the needy, unlike others" hinting at the Authority's institutions which are facing accusations of corruption.[361]

The Palestinian Authority Yields to Pressure:

On August 24, 2003, the Palestinian Authority issued a decision ordering all banks to freeze the assets of 12 Islamic charities and private organizations, due to pressure from the US and Israel. As an illustration let us listen to the comments of the general manager of the Islamic Association about the hardship caused by the freezing of his organization's assets: "This year, (2004) we did not offer any aid and we won't be able to because our assets are frozen. We do not have a cent." He added: "When we wanted to come to the aid of our own families in Rafah, we had to go to the streets to collect money from the passersby. This year has been the worst for the Palestinian people. Islamic organizations used to support 15 thousand orphans. Who will support them now? Nobody will!" He added that the charity also used to support five thousand needy families, and provide tuition for 10 thousand university students.[362]

Dr. Haytham Manna', President of the International Bureau of Humanitarian NGOs, commented on the possibility of applying these standards, saying:

"What is the definition of suspect operations? Can the Ford Company or the J. Carter Company follow the movements of each organism operating in the southern countries? Is it possible to deprive a European charitable institution of taking care of the wounded, or to ask them to fill set forms in private hospitals that they finance? How to make the distinction between the various victims: between a man with beard, a woman with scarf, an orphan who lost his father in a suicidal operation, without falling in the misdemeanor of racism or selectivity? Is it the duty of the non-governmental organizations to shift into right political organizations, which adopt the strategies of the American administration's action in order to avoid becoming suspect?"[363]

Startling Statistics from Palestine:

Here are some statistics concerning the prisoners, the sick, handicapped, and children who increasingly are in need of food and medication, at a time when charities' assets were being frozen inside Palestine and abroad:

Statistics released by the Palestinian Prisoner's Club show that in 2004 there have been extreme cases of sickness among the prisoners that needed special medical care. There were 800 cases that needed urgent surgical operations. *Al-Jazeera* news channel received information from the Prisoner's Club that said the medical situation of the Palestinian prisoners has been deteriorating rapidly during the last three years, and that the prisons' administration has adopted a policy of neglect and denial toward these medical cases.

The Prisoner's Club in a statement to a*l-Jazeera* said: "The proportion of the handicapped among the prisoners has reached 10% all of them wounded by bullets and bombs. A number of them had their limbs amputated, and others are hemiplegics… The human situation is dismal. The harsh treatment, malnutrition, widespread parasites, lack of cleaning products, subduing the prisoners with gas, all have contributed to the deterioration of the prisoners' health situation. Heart, joints, teeth and kidney diseases are widespread, as well as seizures and some cancer cases." Eissa Qaraqe' President of the Palestinian Prisoner's Club said: "90% of the prisoners have been subject to harsh and ferocious beating during their arrest, which has engendered serious diseases. The policy of medical neglect is intended to slowly kill the prisoners. Most surely those who are released from the interrogation rooms carry physical and psychological diseases." He said in another report to a*l-Jazeera*: "Poisonous gases used by the Jewish prison guards to subdue the prisoners have left them with serious diseases. Disorienting noise instruments installed in the prison cells have also caused diseases. Utter neglect of the lives, health and future of thousands of prisoners. Prison camps such as the Negev, Hawara, Qadumim, Benyamin and others are unsuitable for human life." The Palestinian Minister of prisoners affairs, Hisham Abder-Razzaq said to a*l-Jazeera*: "More than 900 prisoners inside the Israeli prisons are suffering from different illnesses." Horrific statistics have reached a*l-Jazeera* about unprecedented violations the Palestinian prisoners are subject to. According to statistics issued by the Ministry of Prisoners Affairs, there were about 7400 prisoners up to July 2004. A report from the Ministry says: "More than 2000 children have been arrested since the beginning of the Intifadha, 470 of them are still in the Israeli prisons."[364]

The Outrageous Conditions of the US Aid Agencies:

Palestinian NGOs have faced unprecedented demands to accept conditions imposed by the US aid agencies. *Al-Hayat* newspaper has published some of them: "The Palestinian NGO network has warned against an American-Israeli plan to strike at and subdue the Palestinian civil society by putting political conditions on the humanitarian aid and financial help the NGOs receive from the US aid agencies, such as the USAID which demanded lately from the citizens groups to sign a document of "terrorism testimony" as a prerequisite condition for financial help from the agency." The newspaper adds: "This step is in the context of the policy of oppression and harassment practiced by Israeli and foreign entities to dry up the sources of human and financial support to the Palestinian people, and which resulted lately in the Palestinian Authority's decision to close charities linked to the social branch of Hamas in Gaza."

The document states that an organization receiving US aid should: "Give no financial or material support to any individual or organization known or could be known to call for, plan, support, or participate, or has participated in a 'terrorist activity' …that it should stop such support to any organization described as such immediately after signing the agreement." While in Gaza thousands of families have lost their only source of income provided by the charities, the same fate threatens thousands more in the West Bank. [365]

Difficulties Faced by UNRWA:

Peter Hansen, former Commissioner-General of the United Nations Relief Work Agency for Palestinian Refugees in the Near East (UNRWA) has presented to the UN a report where he discussed the difficulties UNRWA faces in the occupied Palestinian territories. He pointed out that the Israeli authorities have arrested 25 of the agency's employees between June 2003 and July 2004. The report maintained that the Israeli authorities offered no information concerning the reasons of the arrests, and did not allow the agency to contact the detained employees, or know where they were detained. The report explained that the Israeli Authorities have put strong restrictions on UNRWA's employees' freedom of movement under the pretext of security reasons. The report pointed out that Israel continued to impose restrictions on the employees' travel and on the compounds that belong to the agency outside the check points and across the frontiers. It also pointed out that the Israeli occupation army has opened fire on schools in Gaza and the West Bank, which resulted in the death of 29 UNRWA students and injury of 147 during the period covered by the report. The number of Palestinian refugees registered with UNRWA reached 4 million 187 thousands and 711, 68% of them live outside the 59 officially recognized refugee camps. A large portion of the refugees, 42%, live in Jordan, and 22% in Gaza; the rest are distributed between the West Bank, Syria, and Lebanon.[366]

Islamic and Jewish Organizations in the Field:

Delinda Hanley of the *Washington Report on Middle East Affairs* says: "The Anti-Defamation League (ADL), which for years has sought to close the Holy Land Foundation, posted a rambling five-page document on its web site enumerating its accusations… While his American supporters worked over US policymakers, Israel Prime Minister Sharon and his government began to use the word 'terrorist' to describe not only all Palestinian militants, but Palestinians of every stripe, and even President Yasser Arafat. America's mainstream media quickly followed suit."[367] Hanley exposes Israel's means of ensuring increased American support, saying: "Israel used the calculated assassination of Hamas leaders to provoke predictable retaliation in the form of 'terrorist attacks' and 'suicide bombings' and gain unquestioning American support for Israel's own heavy-handed 'response' to terrorism." As consequences of Israel's anti-Palestinian campaign, President Bush "closed down the charities without waiting for a complete investigation or a court ruling. Deprived of income of charitable assistance this winter, Palestinians face only hunger and cold, as well as continuing Israeli raids, destruction and closures."[368] Moreover, the Justice department allowed Israeli-American victims of "terrorist" attacks to sue Islamic charities who contributed to the organizations who attacked them. David Boim, an American killed in the West Bank can sue the Holy Land Foundation for damages because it allegedly contributed to Hamas.

By contrast, American-based Jewish organizations are increasing their support for Israel, not only for humanitarian and social services, but also for military purposes and to support illegal settlers. The Israel Now, a tax-deductible "charity" was launched by the United Jewish Communities to fund the purchase of armored vehicles, bulletproof glass for houses in illegal Jewish settlements, and support services for Israel Defense Force soldiers. The Libi Fund, another US tax deductible "charity" raises funds for Israeli soldiers who guard settlers in the Upper Galilee and the Lebanese border. The One Israel Fund purchases bulletproof vehicles for Jewish settlements. Private Jewish foundations which distribute more than $1 billion annually have surpassed the Jewish Federation donations.[369]

If charities that contribute to foreign terrorist organizations can be sued by victims of attacks carried out by those organizations, why can't the families of Palestinian Americans killed by Israeli soldiers or settlers sue the Jewish American "charities' that support these settlers? Why aren't the soldiers and settlers who kill stone-throwing children - and even children fleeing the field or at check points - not called terrorists?

The amount of the US financial support to Israel is staggering: In the aftermath of the 1991 Gulf war, the US granted Israel an additional $2 billion annually in the form of federal grants and securities. The total US grants to Israel has reached $5 billion a year, or $13.7 million daily. There are other financial aids received by Israel from Jewish charities in the US and private donations, totaling $1.5 billion.[370]

The double dealing and contrasting differences in treating the Islamic charities and the Palestinians on one side and Israel and the Jewish organizations on the other, expose the truth about the incentive behind the war on the Islamic charities concerned with the Palestinian issue. Additionally, in the aftermath of the free democratic elections, in which Hamas came out victorious, the U.S. and European governments cut financial and humanitarian aid to the Palestinian people and tied any further aid with political concessions. Thus they revealed to the whole world the strings attached to this aid, and by the end of 2005 and during the year 2006, even Arab and Islamic aid to the Palestinian people have stopped for different reasons. This case study and the above facts further expose the objectives of the American campaign against the Islamic charities: suppressing the Islamic charitable organizations as a way to incur spiritual and material defeat and thus arrive at the elimination of the Palestinian and other issues, an unprecedented way to settle political problems. The means and the goals both are united in the elimination of the Palestinian issue.

Case Study 2: Afghanistan; the First Victim

Christopher Schmitt and Joshua Kurlantzick of *US News & World Report* have illustrated the extent of the catastrophe in Afghanistan, when they wrote: "To date, the US Treasury Department has frozen the assets of 66 people and organizations believed to be linked to al-Qaeda -and the list is expected to grow. A number of them such as the foreign charities Wafa Humanitarian Organization and the Al Rashid Trust, actually do relief work, but are also suspected here and abroad of funneling money to al-Qaeda or other terrorist organizations."[371] Is mere suspicion sufficient to close down charities, depriving Afghan refugees from the help the aid they desperately need?

Yielding to pressure, Pakistan has taken drastic measures against Islamic charities. Schmitt says: "Pakistan has deported 89 staffers of Islamic charities suspected of links to terrorism and ordered closed some 76 non-governmental organizations it said were involved in undesirable activities."[372]

Should the Afghan refugee population at the Pakistani frontier be left to die because of the measures taken against the Islamic charities and their employees even inside Pakistan?

The Consequences of Eliminating Islamic Charitable Work:

Afghanistan's need for charity and its choice of Islamic organizations accepts no substitute and the open media campaign before, during, and after the war supports the opinion that these charities are themselves targeted. The consequences of this campaign are evident:

1. Islamic charities, their members, and their employees have been harassed and they have become unable to approach Afghanistan or the neighboring countries. This fulfills the goal of taking away the Islamic charities from the people who feel closest to them regarding their religion, not to mention the Afghans' human rights and the right to life. A void has been created by banishing these charities. A stark example is the war on WAFA Foundation, a small organization interested in solving drought problems, by drilling wells, presenting some medical instruments to the children's hospital in Kabul, and directing some successful relief programs. Another example is the Rashid Trust. The whole world has witnessed the war and came with the impression that it was a revengeful war against the Afghan people, completely destroying its infrastructure. *Al-Hayat* newspaper in London said: "In a letter addressed by UN Secretary General Kofi Annan to the Organization of Islamic Convention, he promised to form a Committee for Afghan Human Rights. He explained in the letter that the proposed committee will not be able to effectively investigate the Ganji Fort event before some time. Will it be after the Northern alliance receives the ransom of the captives in its prisons, or after Guantanamo is filled beyond its capacity? There are now 2000 prisoners in an area of 117 square kilometer."[373]

2. The media and field campaign against Islamic charities have created a void in the charity field. Non-Islamic organizations, some of which dedicated to Christian missionary work especially the Christianization of Muslim orphan children, moved in swiftly to fill the void, and to change the religious map of Afghanistan. An educated Afghan told a*sh-Sharq al-Awsat* Arabic newspaper that the matter has gone beyond the spread of slavery and bondage. Christian missionary organizations take Muslim children whose parents have been killed in the war and put them for adoption in Christian families to change their religion. This happens in complete secrecy, the lady said.[374]

New education curricula which are devoid of any Islamic identity have been issued. Co-education has been encouraged, a practice alien to the Afghan people. Media that is offensive to their tradition and belief have been promoted and encouraged.

Here are some facts concerning the Christianization effort in Afghanistan: The situation in Afghanistan has created a fertile ground for the Christian missions. The International Mission Board (IMB) was very active in the area, and during the attacks on Afghanistan which occurred after the 9/11 events, many relief initiatives were announced that were clearly linked to missionary operations. The president of IMB said in a letter addressed to the missions: "As bleak as physical conditions seem, the spiritual situation of the Afghan people is even worse. While the United Nations rushes to distribute tons of food and warm clothing to Afghanistan's destitute, the country is closed to missions' agencies that could fill the spiritual void in people's hearts." [375]

Franklin Graham's Samaritan Purse has planned to build a hospital in Afghanistan as a means to strengthen its mission. On

Christmas Eve of 2001, it sent Christmas gifts to one million Afghan children, and more than 100 thousand notebooks.[376] Aid should "share the love of Christ" said the Rev. Franklin Graham. "The love of Christ" is shared in the form of adoptions of orphaned children, and religious pamphlets tucked into relief kits. Commented Janice D'Arcy in her article entitled "Some Organizations Mix Missionary Work with Aid."[377]

3. The ferocious war that has taken place in Afghanistan, and its consequences, is in fact a war against the aims and means of the world's charitable organizations, Islamic and otherwise. All charities of the world working for decades might not be able to remedy the damages brought by the weapons of mass destruction, and the effects of starvation and disease brought by this war. It might take much longer for Afghanistan to heal its wounds.

This destruction is considered a depletion of the humanitarian organizations' capabilities if not their total elimination, as expressed by Ramsey Clark, former US Secretary of Justice who described the bombings as war crimes and crimes against humanity according to the second article of the Charter of the United Nations, and crimes against Islam. [378]

4. The war in Afghanistan has revealed the true nature of the New World order, and of the so-called international law and human rights, as well as that of international organizations. The nations of the world were unable to make a strong stand in front of the injustice incurred to the Islamic relief organizations, even though their stand would be in accordance with the international laws. Pierre Hazan of the French newspaper *Libération* said: "America treats the International Justice like a supermarket; it uses it when it serves its interests. It never happened that the US was defeated in its democratic values its justice and equality principles like it was after September 11."[379]

The question that needs to be asked is: what punishment will America face for its mistaken air strikes against mosques, hospitals, weddings, and receptions which have resulted in the deaths of 400 Afghan civilians?[380]

More important: what is America's objective behind this behavior and actions toward the international laws?

5. The war in Afghanistan and the War on Terror whose scope has been broadened and globalized have shown themselves to be fueling, instigating, and nurturing the seeds of terrorism. The general and sweeping campaigns provide a fertile ground for it. Is this really what is needed at the new historic era?

The war on Afghanistan, accompanied by the harmful campaign against Islamic charities, and the marginalization and demeaning of the international independent institutions, derailing their goals, all this confirms that a new era has come; the era of American hegemony, the domination of one power, America, with the elimination or marginalization of all perceived new competitors, and among them Islam and its institutions, but also any international organization that hinders the fulfillment of the goals of what has been called the American Empire.

Finally, when we contemplate the so-called war on terror in Afghanistan, we notice that peace has been excluded from the area where the participating nations and the NATO have brought chaos and war –not peace-. The afghan resistance and the Taliban and the so called al-Qaeda have since mid-2005 and during all 2006 engaged in fierce battles, which according to media and political reports are turning to their benefits, thus defeating all the objectives of the war. This reminds us the late President Richard Nixon who said that the decisive factor in victory is the strength of the great ideas, because ideas cannot be defeated by armies. Unfortunately, it is the victims of this kind of war who pay the stiff price, where whole populations including children, women, and whole communities are destroyed, or totally deprived of their human rights.

Case Study 3: Iraq; Motives and Objectives

Iraq is a good example of what appears to some to be the elimination of any new competitor to American influence. Most NGOs including Islamic charities and human rights organizations have been marginalized. The Iraq war itself from the causes of the war to its results exposes the truth behind the "war on terror".

The UN Commission Report confirming that no Weapons of Mass Destruction (WMD) existed in Iraq was not an obstacle to the American raid on it, neither was the fact that Iraq was a sovereign nation and a member of the UN. Human rights organizations had no role in protecting the people of Iraq, their properties, their safety and honor, or the environment. Islamic charities had no role in Iraq either despite the dire need for relief. On the other hand, organizations known for their affiliation to the extreme Christian Right have been supported and allowed to change the country's Islamic culture. Religious motives concurred with economic and political objectives.

Thomas Friedman wrote in *The International Herald Tribune* in January 2003: "Any war the United States launches in Iraq will certainly be, in part, about oil. To deny that is laughable."[381] Patrick J. Buchanan insisted that "the real reason was empire and making the Middle East safe for Israel."[382] This is in accord with the strategy for reshaping the Middle East that was spelled out in the Project for the New American Century[383]. Paul Findley has also pointed to the supposed scheme of enlarging American influence in the world, the opposition of the establishment of an international criminal court, and the withdrawal from the Anti Ballistic Missile Treaty, and explained that the war on Iraq doesn't fall out of this context, saying: "Oil and Israel are the real reasons for the war"[384] With an oil reserve of 112 billion barrels, or 11% of the world oil reserve, Studies have shown that the last drop of oil will be in Iraq.

Studies published by the US Energy Information Administration[385] estimate that the oil reserve is around 200 billion barrels, and that the average American and Canadian oil reserves do not exceed ten years whereas the Iraqi oil reserves exceed 100 years, and the Iraq oil extraction is the least expensive among the world's oil producers whose reserves do not exceed 97 years. According to the US administration's studies and the British Petroleum estimations in 2002, Iraq will be the most capable country to fulfill the needs of the international market.[386]

To control the sources of energy means to control all the competitors, such as the European Union, China, India, Japan, and the entire Muslim World, countries, oil, and all.

Former Secretary of Justice, Ramsey Clark, recorded in his book "The Fire This Time: US War Crimes in the Gulf" the explicit details of these alleged crimes and killing of around two million Iraqis due to famine and sickness after the intentional destruction of all Iraq's infrastructure and the imposed embargo on Iraq. "Both the sanctions and this war are genocide." Ramsey Clark said[387]. In a letter addressed to the United Nations, he said that an attack by the US on Iraq "will violate the Charter of the United Nations, international law and the friendship of all who seek peace and respect the dignity of humanity." "An attack by the US on Iraq," he said, "would also violate the Constitution and laws of the United States and expose President Bush to impeachment by the House of Representatives under the Constitution of the United States for the highest of crimes, those against peace and humanity, to judgment by the United States Senate and trial in federal court for crimes charged."[388]

Just before the publication of Clark's book, the 77[389] Tactical Fighter Squadron has published and distributed "a recreational song book" where it described what it will do in the Persian Gulf, and that the Iraqi people should get ready for extinction[389]. One of the less offensive verses in the song book runs as follows:

> *"Phantom flyers in the sky,*
> *Persian-pukes prepare to die,*
> *Rolling in with snake and nape,*
> *Allah creates but we cremate."*[390]

Let us describe in brief the transgressions that happened and are still going on against international political, human, and charitable organizations in Iraq, and against the human rights of the Iraqis, their honors, religion, property, and dignity.

Christian Missionary Efforts:

The German news agency mentioned that missionary expeditions led by Reverend Franklin Graham, one of the most influential religious figures in the US, were sent to Iraq. Franklin Graham stated that his organization The Samaritan Purse was in contact with the American relief and aid agencies in Amman, Jordan, to facilitate the organization's mission in Iraq. Graham has never hidden his extremist opinion of Islam, for he stated previously at the beginning of the war on Afghanistan that Islam is a "very evil and wicked religion."[391] The same Franklin Graham delivered the invocation prayer at Bush's presidential inauguration.

President Bush granted Franklin Graham, his spiritual father, the privileges of Christianization in Iraq. He prepared to extend his Christianization activities in Iraq, and reported that he sent numerous church representatives armed with bibles and food to support the Iraqis in their suffering. Other churches such as the Southern Baptist Convention, the most important protestant church in America and a staunch supporter of the war in Iraq, announced that it was quite ready for work in Iraq. Its spokesman said: "We want to help them to have freedom and true freedom in Jesus Christ."[392] He did not hide his church's long term plans, saying: "The long-term goal is to develop relationships with the people…and share the unconditional love of Christ to transform their lives spiritually."[393]

The "War for Souls" in Iraq:

Taking advantage of the disastrous condition of the Iraqis, American Christian missionaries have dropped in Iraq like vultures, declaring a "war for souls". David Rennie wrote in *The Telegraph*: "Organizing in secrecy, and emphasizing their humanitarian aid work, Christian groups are pouring into the country, which is 97% Muslim, bearing Arabic Bibles, videos and religious tracts designed to 'save' Muslims from their 'false' religion. The International Mission Board, the missionary arm of the Southern Baptists, is one of those leading the charge."[394]

"John Brady, the IMB's head for the Middle East and North Africa, this month appealed to the 16 million members of his church, the largest Protestant domination in America," wrote Rennie. "Southern Baptists have prayed for years that Iraq would somehow be opened to the Gospel," the appeal began. "That 'open door' for Christians may soon close." "Southern Baptists must understand that there is a war for souls under way in Iraq," the bulletin added, citing Islamic leaders as his chief rivals.[395]

Likewise, John Hanna, an evangelical who before going to Iraq has attended a seminar for missionaries to the Arab world, said: "last time we only took 8,000 Arabic bibles to Iraq. In future missions the goal is one million." Mr. Hanna described Islam as 'false' and said: "the Muslim religion is an antichrist religion." Jerry Vines, a former head of the Southern Baptist Convention has described Prophet Muhammad as a "demon-obsessed pedophile."[396]

After the fall of communism, the neoconservatives look at Islam as the only remaining foe, a stubborn opponent, and therefore there are serious efforts to infiltrate its societies especially in the Middle East where the stakes are higher because of the compounded belief in "Armageddon" which the Christians say will take place in Palestine between the forces of good (read the US and Israel) and the forces of evil (read the Muslims and other non-protestant Christians), and which will end, by the victory of good over evil, and will be crowned by the second coming of the Messiah who will rule the earth for 1000 years.

Fahmi Huwaydi of a*l-Majallah* magazine commented on this war over the souls, saying: "It appears to me that their fanaticism and hatred of the Muslims have made them eager to make the Muslims abandon their religion more than they are to convert them to Christianity. In other words they want to declare Islam's defeat more than they want Christianity's victory."[397]

The Council on American Islamic Relations (CAIR) has described the Christian missionary expeditions accompanying the American forces as keen on linking up the reconstruction of Iraq with the Christianization of its Muslim people.[398]

The missionary efforts to Christianize Muslims under the guise of humanitarian aid have been greatly helped by the forced absence of Islamic charities. In one of the IMB bulletins, it was reported that aid workers handed out copies of the New Testament. Another bulletin said Iraqis understood "Who was bringing the food…it was the Christians from America."[399] Franklin Graham was blunt about his group's role and the role of Christian missionaries in general. "If we are going to depend on Muslims to go in and help Muslims, well, they aren't coming," he said.[400] And no wonder, most of their charities have been either closed down, or had their assets frozen, or have been greatly hindered by the new regulations.

Bush's Religious Leanings with Respect to Iraq:

New York Times raised the problem of President Bush's religious motives towards Iraq, saying, "Pres Bush's conviction that he is doing God's will, has surfaced more openly since September 11." The paper says that Bush's providentialist outlook promotes tunnel vision, discourages debate and reduces diplomacy to arm-twisting. Worst of all it says, it sanitizes messy actualities of war and its aftermath.[401]

As for the war in Iraq, God is in world affairs, Bush says, calling for the United States to lead a liberating crusade in the Middle East, and "this call of history has come to the right country."[402]

No doubt that missionary-crusader mentality has cast a shadow over Bush's personality. Bush considers Bill Graham who is known for his hatred of Islam and his aggressive Christianization efforts, as the man who brought him to the Lord and the man who made him keen to read every day Oswald Chambers' book, a priest whom *Newsweek* said he died in 1917 while exhorting the British and Australian soldiers to march on Jerusalem and to seize it from the Muslims[403]

The number of Christian missions in Iraq is expected to reach 100 in 2003.

Fallujah: An example of US rebellion against international institutions and their goals

Newsweek published an article titled "Rules of Engagement" where it mentioned horrific statistics in the war on Fallujah:

"The Lancet recently published a study that used interviews and extrapolations to estimate the total [number of dead] at 100,000 or more, mostly from aerial bombardment," the article says. It is "a lot of innocent dead," the article adds, "far more than were killed, say, on September 11 - and many Iraqis accuse the Americans of reckless disregard for civilian lives." [404] Many other British newspapers published the same statistics, with the addition that the number of wounded is much more than the number of dead. "The American military's major detention centers in Iraq have swelled to capacity and are holding more people than ever," the New York Times said. The number of detainees has reached 8900 detainees.[405]

The Fallujah case and the Iraq war in general are a strong example of what has been called the American hegemony and perhaps a flavor of things to come: huge number of innocent civilian victims, and the forced absence of free press and international humanitarian and political organizations. These predictions made by some combined with the exclusion of the "competitors" can be said to be occurring under the banner of "the war on terror".

Naomi Klein wrote in the *Guardian* an article titled "In Iraq, the US does eliminate those who dare to count the dead" in response to the US Acting Ambassador's objections to her previous article. She wrote: "It is quite rare for US embassy officials to openly involve themselves in the free press of a foreign country." She pointed out to reports of hundreds of civilians being killed in Fallujah. "This information came from three main sources," she said, doctors, Arab TV journalists, and Clerics. She said that:

"statistics and names of the dead were gathered from four main clinics around the city and from Fallujah General Hospital. While doctors reported the numbers of dead, it was al-Jazeera and al-Arabiya that put a human face on those statistics. With unembedded camera crews in Fallujah, both networks beamed footage of mutilated women and children throughout Iraq and the Arab-speaking world. The reports of high civilian casualties coming from journalists and doctors were seized upon by prominent clerics in

Iraq. Many delivered fiery sermons condemning the attack, turning their congregants against US forces and igniting the uprising that forced US troops to withdraw. US authorities have denied that hundreds of civilians were killed during the April 2004 siege of Fallujah, and have lashed out at the sources of these reports."[406]

Then Klein wrote about the second Fallujah attack on October 2004, saying US troops once again laid siege to the city, but this time the attack was reported to have included a new tactic: the elimination of the doctors, journalists, and clerics who focused public attention on civilian casualties during the previous attack.

Eliminating Doctors:

Klein wrote about the elimination of doctors during the second siege on Fallujah:

"The first major operation by US marines and Iraqi soldiers was to storm Fallujah General Hospital, arresting doctors and placing the facility under military control. The New York Times reported that 'the hospital was selected as an early target because the American military believed that it was the source of rumors about heavy casualties' noting that 'this time around the American military intends to fight its own information war, countering or squelching what has been one of the insurgents' 'most potent weapons'.

The Los Angeles Times quoted a doctor as saying that the soldiers 'stole the mobile phones' at the hospital, preventing doctors from communicating with the outside world...Two days earlier, a crucial emergency health clinic was bombed to rubbles, as well as a medical supplies dispensary next door. Dr. Sami al-Jumaili, who was working in the clinic, says the bombs took the lives of 15 medics, 4 nurses, and 35 patients. The Los Angeles Times reported that the manager of Fallujah General Hospital 'had told a US general the location of the downtown makeshift medical center' before it was hit... When fighting moved to Mosul, a similar tactic was used: on entering the city, US and Iraqi forces immediately seized control of the al-Zahrawi hospital."[407]

Eliminating Journalists:

Naomi Klein also wrote about the elimination of journalists:

"The images from last month's siege on Fallujah came almost exclusively from reporters embedded with US troops. This is because Arab journalists who had covered April's siege from the civilian perspective had effectively been eliminated. Al-Jazeera had no cameras on the ground because it has been banned from reporting in Iraq indefinitely. Al-Arabiya did have an unembedded reporter, Abdel Kader al-Saadi, in Fallujah, but on November 11 the US forces arrested him and held him for the length of the siege. Al-Saadi's detention has been condemned by Reporters Without Borders and the International Federation of Journalists…It's not the first time journalists in Iraq have faced this kind of intimidation. When US forces invaded Baghdad in April 2003, US Central Command urged all unembedded journalists to leave the city. Some insisted on staying and at least three paid with their lives. On April 8, a US aircraft bombed al-Jazeera's Baghdad office, killing reporter Taraq Ayyoub. Al-Jazeera has documentation proving it gave the coordinates of its location to the US forces. On the same day, a US tank fired on the Palestine hotel, killing José Couso, of the Spanish network Telecinco, and Taras Protsiuk, of Reuters."[408]

The Elimination of Muslim Scholars:

Lastly, Klein wrote about the targeting of Muslim scholars, saying: "Just as doctors and journalists have been targeted, so too have many of the clerics who have spoken out forcefully against the killings in Fallujah. On November 11, Sheik Mahdi al-Sumaidaei, the head of the Supreme Association for Guidance and Daawa, was arrested according to the *Associated Press*, 'al-Sumaidaei has called on the country's Sunni minority[409] to launch a civil disobedience campaign if the Iraqi Government does not halt the attack on Fallujah'. On November 19, AP reported that US and Iraqi forces stormed a prominent Sunni mosque, the Abu Hanifa in Aadhamiya, killing three people and arresting 40, including the chief cleric - another opponent of the Fallujah siege."

Quoting General Tommy Franks who said: "We don't do body count," Klein asked: "What happens to the people who insist on counting the bodies - the doctors who must pronounce their patients dead, the journalists who document these losses, the clerics who denounce them? In Iraq, evidence is mounting that these voices are being systematically silenced through a variety of means, from mass arrests to raids on hospitals, media bans, and overt and unexplained physical attacks."

Klein concluded her letter to the US ambassador by saying: "Mr. Ambassador, I believe that your government and its Iraqi surrogates are waging two wars in Iraq. One war is against the Iraqi people, and it has claimed an estimated 100,000 lives. The other is a war on witnesses."

The Committee of Muslim Scholars in Iraq announced in the Doha, Qatar convention, on February 24-27, 2005, that up to February 2005, 20 scholars and members of the committee have been killed, among them Shaikh Harith a-Dhari, and Shaikh Muhammad Bashar Faydhi. Eighty other scholars have been detained in the American prisons in Iraq.[410]

Fallujah; a War Crime:

In an interview with *Left Hook*, Professor Naom Chomsky described the American attack on Fallujah as a major war crime. He condemned the US President saying: "The President of the United States is subject to death penalty under US law for that crime alone."[411] Contrasting the atrocities of Fallujah to the genocide of the Muslims in Srebrenica where women were trucked out of town and all men were slaughtered, he said: "With Fallujah, the US didn't truck out the women and children, it bombed them out. There was about a month of bombing, bombed out of the city, if they could get out somehow, a couple hundred thousand people fled, or somehow got out, and men were kept in and we don't know what happened after that."[412]

"The first major step in the offensive [was] the capture of the Fallujah general hospital…people lying on the ground, soldier guarding them, and then there is a story that tells that patients and doctors were taken from - patients were taken from their beds, patients and doctors were forced to lie on the floor and manacled under guard." He added: "That's a grave breach of the Geneva conventions, Geneva conventions say *explicitly* and unambiguously that hospitals must be protected, hospitals and medical staff and patients must be protected by all combatants in any conflict. You couldn't have a more grave breach of the Geneva Conventions than that." He pointed out that the Congress passed a War Crimes Act in 1996 which states that: "Grave breaches of the Geneva Convention are subject to the death penalty. And that doesn't mean the soldier that committed them, that means the commanders. They weren't thinking about the United States of course, but take it literally, that's what it means."[413]

The *New York Times* coldly explained that it was done because the US command described the Fallujah general hospital as a propaganda outlet for the guerillas because they were reporting casualties. "I don't know if the Nazis produced things like that," Chomsky remarked. Commenting on whether the casualties were inflated, he said: "Well our Dear Leader said it was inflated, so that means that since we're like North Korea, it has to be inflated. But suppose it was. I mean the idea of carrying out a major war crime, explicit, because the hospital was a propaganda weapon…, I mean you really have to work to find an analog to that." "And that's just one war crime, one part of the general atrocities," he added. He pointed out that according to the principles of the Nuremberg Tribunal, which the US initiated and carried out, it concluded that the supreme international crime is invasion, and he said: "That supreme crime includes within it all the evil that follows. So therefore the doubling of malnutrition rates, the maybe 100,000 casualties, the grave war crimes in Fallujah, they're all footnotes, they're footnotes to the supreme international crime."[414]

"The level of destruction and terror and violence carried out by the powerful states far exceeds anything that can imaginably be done by groups that are called terrorists." Asked about the claim of "civilized world" combating "barbarism" he pointed out to the atrocities committed by the US and the West and said it was "beyond barbarism." "It's absurd," he said, the worst atrocities committed since the Mongol invasions happened in Germany "the stellar example of Western civilization…the model of democracy. Yeah, it's the worst barbarism since the Mongol invasion." Then he asked: "What kinds of correlations can one make?"[415]

AP/Ipsos nine-country survey finds considerable skepticism about the eligibility of the United States to propagate freedom and democracy in the world. The majority of the countries disagree as to the eligibility of the US. France: 84% disagree, Germany: 80%, Britain: 70%, and the US itself: 53%.[416]

Furthermore, human rights and freedom of expression have become new competitors to the American hegemony in this fourth world war, "the war on terror"; and might end up being themselves victims of this war.

These atrocities have been forewarned in an open letter written by Helena Cobban, author of five books on international issues, to President Bush advising him to turn back from the war on Iraq and to use other means that have been proved successful. She wrote: "A unilateral attack on Iraq for which there is no completely evident justification and no UN mandate will be seen nearly everywhere as a policy simply of 'might makes right.' It is terrifying to think how other governments might follow that lead."[417]

The Outcry of Amnesty International:

Amnesty International published numerous reports exposing the extent of the allied American and British forces transgressions. The reports raised many points, the most prominent of which are the use of lethal weapons on civilians, torture, harassment, violence and lawlessness, and unprecedented breaches of human rights. "U.S. Central Command (CENTCOM) reported that it used 10,782 cluster munitions, which could contain at least 1.8 million submunitions. The British used an additional seventy air-launched and 2,100 ground-launched cluster munitions, containing 113,190 submunitions. Although cluster munitions strikes are particularly dangerous in populated areas, U.S. and U.K. ground forces repeatedly used these weapons in attacks on Iraqi positions in residential neighborhoods."[418]

Another report from Amnesty released on April 11, 2003, further exposes the extent of the humanitarian crisis. In the report Amnesty International "urges the US/UK forces to live up to their responsibilities under international humanitarian law as occupying powers. These include the duty to restore and maintain public order and safety (Article 43 of the Hague Regulations)." Amnesty also reminds "the occupying powers that they are obliged to ensure, if necessary, the provision of food and medical supplies to the inhabitants of the occupied territories (Article 55 of the Fourth Geneva Convention)[419] One year later, a subsequent report by Amnesty International indicates that the situation has even worsened.[420]

The consequences of driving away and marginalizing the "new competitors" are clear in the extent of malnutrition and lack of medications. Karl Vick wrote that according to surveys by the United Nations and aid agencies, "roughly 400,000 Iraqi children suffer from 'wasting', a condition characterized by chronic diarrhea and dangerous deficiencies of protein." He said that 20 months after the fall of Baghdad, "Iraq's child malnutrition rate now roughly equals that of Burundi…It is far higher than rates in Uganda and Haiti."[421]

Medact, a charitable organization of health professionals, published a report about the health situation in Iraq, titled "Enduring Effects of War; Health: Iraq 2004", describing the situation as catastrophic. Mike Rowson, director of Medact asked that immediate decisive action should be taken to put a limit to the health crisis in Iraq.[422]

After studying the three case studies, the following conclusions are evident:

1. There is a weakening of the role of the United Nations and its organizations whose decisions should have been taken, for instance, regarding the absence of weapons of mass destruction in Iraq. The alleged American use of internationally restricted weapons, particularly in Afghanistan and Iraq, thus transgressing against the rules and laws of the United Nations, further weakens the United Nations' role. These transgressions have been and still are creating a humanitarian crisis with consequences that international political and humanitarian organizations are unable to cope with.

2. Human rights organizations are being marginalized, both with respect to their ability to issue resolutions, criticisms, and condemnations, as well as in the extent of their presence in the fields where Israeli or American occupation is going on and where national resistance movements are taking place. Examples abound: the elimination of resistance movements, the siege of the

Palestinian people, Ganji fortress in Afghanistan, Iraqi prisons, of which the most infamous is Abu Ghraib, the war of extermination in Iraq and especially in Fallujah.

3. Islamic charities and relief organizations are being eliminated or marginalized while Christian organizations are given greater opportunities, in spite of their being of a different religion than the indigenous people. Some of the people working for the remaining Islamic charities have been arrested, labeled as terrorists, and even interned in Guantanamo.

In any case, the outcomes of the war in Iraq and the so-called war on terror have increased these statistics. In fact the US occupation of Iraq has engendered horrendous destruction of Iraq's infrastructure and the Iraqi people even more so than during the rule of Saddam Hussein. The numbers speak for themselves: according to a study by Bloomberg School of Public Health at Johns Hopkins University and the School of Medicine at Al Mustansiriya University in Baghdad, Iraq, in cooperation with the Center for International Studies at Massachusetts Institute of Technology, entitled *The Human Cost of the War in Iraq A Mortality Study, 2002-2006*, "approximately 600,000 people have been killed in the violence of the war that began with the U.S. invasion in March 2003."[423] Between March 2003 and July 2006, 31 percent of deaths are attributed to the coalition.[424] Professor Gilbert Burnham, lead author of the study said: "We're very confident with the results."[425]

Added to these human tragedies, the American invasion has resulted in:

- The ignition of a fierce sectarian war that could engulf not only Iraq but the whole Middle Eastern region, and which threatens to change the regional and international balance of forces.

- A failure to fulfill security and democracy in Iraq. On the contrary, the million of Iraqi refugees attest to the "democracy by the sword."
- A complete failure of the US administration in Iraq.

Iraq is truly a case study of the failure of the new American strategy at the beginning of this new century for the defeat and failure of the US administration to accomplish any of its stated objectives has exceeded by far the usual norms of defeat.

The three case studies of Palestine, Afghanistan and Iraq contribute to understand the truth behind the war on 'terror' and the real goal behind the slogan of 'freedom and democracy'. They reveal the magnitude of the violations of the international humanitarian law, the extent of these violations during the waged wars and the dire consequences on the civilians. The absence of international organizations and especially the United Nations whose laws and regulations have been flagrantly ignored in the case of Iraq are an indication of the nefarious intents of the occupier. Islamic charities have been adamantly prevented from entering Iraq thanks to anti-terrorism laws and secret evidence. Banning Islamic charities from using international transactions and *hawalas*, restricting their means of collecting donations, and using drastic measures against many Islamic charities in most countries, all this has contributed to the tragedies in Palestine, Afghanistan, and Iraq and has made their people innocent victims of the war on terror. People in these countries have been denied basic needs, food, medication, and education. Closing the doors of Islamic relief organizations has only compounded the problem and increased the number of victims. This has been accompanied by a media black-out and a cover up of the tragedy in the main media outlets.

Chapter VI

Mistakes of Islamic and non-Islamic Organizations: A Double Standard

Islamic Organizations: Mistakes, Real and Alleged

This chapter does not deal with the many successes achieved by the Islamic charities. It deals with mistakes committed by some Islamic organizations, their regional offices, their employees, or the volunteers working for them. There are also misunderstandings that need to be clarified.

Some of those who work in the Islamic charity sector point out that these mistakes are present in most other sectors and are sometimes inherent to the charitable work, and moreover they are few. As the proverb says: "He who makes no mistakes makes nothing." These mistakes are:

1. Government connection:

Non-governmental charity sector constitutes a global sector that is independent from the public government sector and from the private business sector. The success of the chary sector is the fruit of its independence. Its strength comes from its private not governmental administration. Though it is supporting the government, it is independent from it. Thus its appellations: Independent Sector in some countries, Non-Governmental Sector in others, and Non-Profit Sector in yet other countries. The United Nations labels it as the Third Sector, because it is not part of the First (governmental) Sector, or the Second (business) Sector.

Numerous reports, analyses and media campaigns negatively describe the charitable work in the Arab world in general and in the Gulf Cooperation Countries and Saudi Arabia in particular, saying it is connected to the government, is part of the government sector, works according to the government agenda, and is administered by government officials. This affiliation is considered a mistake for which both governments and charitable organizations should be equally held responsible. Before discussing this connection let us review some of the analyses concerning this issue:

Benthall and Bellion, authors of "The Charitable Crescent" wrote: "Though the large Saudi foundations describe themselves as *waqf* (endowment) in Arabic language publications, they would more recognizably be characterized as para-statals or GONGOs (Government-Organized Non-Governmental Organizations)."[426] The authors reached the conclusion that many governments use the charitable work for political goals, but that the administration of this sector by the government is not accepted. "One response has been to recognize that no charitable organization is in fact immune to political analysis, and that humanitarian and development aid in particular has an inescapable political dimension."[427] In their opinion all organizations have their own private agendas which serve the political interests of their governments. The US administration views the connection of the charity sector to government as politically problematic. The following excerpts highlight the extent of the US worries concerning this aspect. "The documents establish clearly that the Saudi money flowed from several sources, all of them closely tied (and in some cases directly controlled by) senior members of the Saudi royal family. The main source of funding was the Saudi Committee for Support of the Intifada, a governmental agency run by Interior Minister Prince Nayef bin Abdul Aziz."[428]

"In foreign policy, Nayef's support for Tawhid translates into support for jihad, and so it is he - not Abdulah - who presides over the Saudi fund for the support of the Palestinian Intifada."[429]

David Ottaway of *The Washington Post* considered this connection as negative saying that the Minister of Islamic Affairs, Saleh Al-Shaikh "is the direct supervisor of one charity supported by the Saudi Government, al-Haramain."[430] He added: "The collision of Saudi missionary work and suspicions of terrorist financing in San Diego illustrates the perils and provocations of a multibillion-dollar effort by Saudi Arabia to spread its religion around the world."[431]

"Another avenue of interest involves the global finances of the al-Haramain Islamic Foundation, a large Saudi-Government-supported charity set up to propagate Wahhabism and sometimes referred to as the 'United Way of Saudi Arabia'."[432]

In an article in the *National Review Online*, Josh Lefkowitz and Jonathan Levin described the International Islamic Relief Organization (IIRO) as "the 'humanitarian assistance' arm of the MWL [Muslim World League], a quasi-official missionary and propaganda arm of the Saudi kingdom. In March 1997, MWL Secretary General Abdullah al-Obaid thanked King Fahd for his continued support, noting that the Saudi Government had officially provided more than $1.33 billion in financial aid to MWL since 1962."[433]

John L. Esposito, a scholar at Georgetown University said the Saudi theological efforts have resulted in "the export of a very exclusive brand of Islam into the Muslim community in the

United States" that "tends to make them more isolationist in the society in which they live."[434]

"The worldwide export of Wahhabi Islam began in 1962, when Saudi Arabia's ruling Al-Saud family founded the Muslim World League in Mecca to promote 'Islamic solidarity'. The Saudis were seeking to counter the fiery pan-Arab nationalism of Egyptian leader Gamal Abdel Nasser, who was calling for the Saudi monarchy to be overthrown."[435]

The 9/11 Commission Report points out that the dangers of the charitable work in Saudi Arabia was that it was connected to the government sector. The report says: "Although both the Saudi Government and al-Haramain say that it is a private organization, al-Haramain has considerable ties to the Saudi Government. Two government ministers have supervisory roles (nominal or otherwise) over al-Haramain, and there is some evidence that low-level Saudi officials had substantial influence over various HIF offices outside of Saudi Arabia. The Saudi Government has also historically provided financial support to al-Haramain, although that may have diminished in recent years."[436] The report emphasized the negative aspect of this connection saying: "religious and civic duty and government and religious functions in Saudi Arabia are intertwined. This dynamic creates complications for the Saudi Government."[437] And about the connection of the religious charitable work and the Saudi Government, the report says: "The Saudi Government's efforts on terrorist financing were domestically unpalatable. It had been content for many years to delegate all religious activities, including those of charities, to the religious establishment and was reluctant to challenge that group…The challenge was to find a way to increase oversight over charities, mosques, and religious donations without endangering the country's stability."[438]

Testifying before the Senate Judiciary Subcommittee on Terrorism, Matthew Levitt from the *Washington Institute for Near East Policy* said: "Saudi diplomatic personnel stationed abroad play a critical role in the financing of radical Islamic organizations in the West, particularly the United States and Europe. A long list of Islamic extremists have been linked to the Saudi-funded al Nur Mosque in Berlin."

"Most of the charities that get the most money are headed by members of the royal family or members of the ruling elite."[439]

"The crucial test of Saudi efforts to curb terror financing is the willingness to hold elites accountable. Will the Saudi crack down on the terror financing conducted by prominent members of their business class, elites tied to the royal family, charities, and banks?"[440]

"As one US official told *Time* in September 2003, '…the Saudis still appear to be protecting charities associated with the royal family and its friends."[441]

National Review Online wrote: "Saleh Al-Shaikh, the same man who is chairman of al-Haramain's board of directors, is President of WAMY…Given the government's deep ties to IIRO, MWL, and WAMY, it is little surprise that the Saudi Government has taken no visible steps against these organizations."[442]

The Israeli author Dore Gold was keen on proving the Saudi Government connection to the charity work when he said: "In recent years, the connection between the Saudi Government and its Wahhabi charities was graphically laid out in court testimony given in Canada by a local representative of the Muslim World League: 'Let me tell you one thing. The Muslim World League, which is the mother of IIRO, is a fully government-funded organization. In other words, I work for the Government of Saudi

Arabia. Second, the IIRO is the relief branch of that organization, which means we are all controlled in all our activities and plans by the Government of Saudi Arabia."[443]

Senator John Kyl emphasizes this connection saying: "It needs to be emphasized here that contrary to Saudi claims that charities such as al-Haramain, the Muslim World League (MWL), the World Assembly of Muslim Youth (WAMY) and the International Islamic Relief Organization (IIRO) are independent and non-governmental, there is conclusive evidence from Saudi sources that they are tightly controlled by the government and more often than not run by government officials. It is also the case that as early as 1993, the kingdom passed a law stipulating that all donations to Muslim charities must be collected in a fund controlled by a Saudi prince."[444]

Simon Henderson who testified before the Senate Judicial Committee considered this connection as a commingling of government and private activities, saying: "Some of this money goes via official Saudi channels, some goes via what are claimed to be non-official channels, and some goes via Islamic charities linked to the Saudi Government."[445] He said: "Saudi Arabia has set up other organizations which it claims are non-official. They are a conduit for Saudi Government purposes and the Islamic charitable donations of Saudi individuals." He also mentioned that the "Saudi High Commission for Relief of Bosnia and Herzegovina, founded in 1993 by Prince Salman, the governor of Riyadh province in Saudi Arabia and a full brother of King Fahd, has reportedly spent more than $600 million on mosques, schools, cultural centers and orphanages."[446] "The Saudi Islamic Affairs Minister and WAMY President, Shaikh Saleh Al-Shaikh, is also 'superintendent of all foundation activities' for the al-Haramain Islamic Foundation." He added: "The direct involvement in charities by such senior members of the royal family as King Fahd, Prince Sultan and Prince Salman illustrate the difficulty of working out where an individual prince's government role ends and his private activities begin."[447]

In principle, there is no doubt that these charities belong to the citizens groups. They are independent from the government, but they are monitored by the government through its judicial sector. While it has a nominal supervision over the charities,(and over the years it gained more supervision power and influence) the state provides judicial reference and guaranties. The charities, as any other organization, are held accountable by the judicial branch for any mistake they commit.

Interference of the government sector into the private charity sector is a fundamental mistake because this sector is globally considered a private sector, independent from the government. It gains strength and safety when it is part of the state sectors (the non-governmental sector) but not part of the government, and when all sectors refer to a fair and independent judicial system. In this manner, the charitable sector takes the political and administrative pressures off the governments and governments' officials. For example, the US Government presented the excuse that it was not responsible for the American-based NGOs' support to the rebels of Northern Ireland when it was faced with British complaints.

In fact, this management structure (i.e. independence of the three sectors, governmental, private, and charitable) allowed the governments to benefit from the gains of the charitable organizations without assuming any responsibility for them. It is the case of the US Government which does not embrace charitable or religious work and does not consider it part of its duties or job, but it does support it in many other ways, preserving its independence from the government, so that the government is not accountable for its mistakes or transgressions. However, the actual administration, probably due to its leaning to the Christian religious right, or its own religious beliefs, could be said to have breached this administrative principle. Here are few examples:

The US Government presents financial grants to religious charitable organizations through the White House. In 2002, among the more than 500 religious charitable organizations, 21 were chosen to receive a total of $25 million; among them is Operation Blessing International headquartered in Virginia and presided by the ultra-right televangelist Pat Roberson. Pat Robertson already raises a considerable amount of money through his TV program "The 700 Club". In fall 2002 the Department of Health and Human Services awarded Robertson's Operation Blessing International a half-million-dollar faith-based grant. [448]

For the first time in the US history, the Bush administration created an office for religious affairs, The White House Office of Faith-Based and Community Initiatives (OFBCI). It appears that the religious organizations' role in providing social services has increased since the creation of this office by executive order in the beginning of 2001. John J. Dilulio was its executive director. Soon a public debate in both the social services and religious circles has started about the merits of this administration.[449] The OFBCI has introduced new rules and regulations which allow religious organizations to partner with government, thus giving them control over public funds. Among these new rules: faith-based organizations are eligible to participate in the Department of Education programs, they should be able to compete on an equal footing with other organizations for federal funding, and for USDA assistance. The rules remove the regulatory prohibition against religious organizations making employment decisions on a religious basis[450].

In its "Guidance to Faith-Based and Community Organizations on Partnering with the Federal Government" the OFBCI guides the mostly Christian organizations on how to help themselves to the Federal Government Grants available to them. The document shows them how to apply for grants, provides experts to help organizations apply for the grants, and staff to assist them to understand the regulations. Although "all faith-based groups that receive Federal funds are subject to basic audit requirements, these audits are intended only to examine the Federally-funded parts of an organization's operations", says the document. But organizations should not worry, because most of them "will not be audited by the government"[451]; the government does not even bother with those that spend less than $300,000 a year, they can perform a self-audit.

What about the Supreme Court ruling that faith-based organizations may not use direct government support to support inherently religious activities? "Don't be put off by the term 'inherently religious'," the document says, "it's simply a phrase that has been used by the courts in church-state cases"[452]!

"How do we separate our religious activities from our Federally-funded social service program?" the organizations might ask "You may conduct this program in a room in the church hall and still have a Bible study taking place…in the same hall"[453] the guide answers.

"Can people who receive Federally-funded services from us also participate in our religious activities?" The guide answers, "Yes…you may invite participants to join in your organization's religious services or events…For example, a church that receives direct government aid to provide shelter to homeless individuals… may invite them to join them."[454] And a poor homeless person might as well answer the "invitation" to ensure a roof over his head.

What about religious activities in the presence of those whom they are helping? "A faith-based group may gather volunteers and employees together to engage in religious activities…An example might be a soup kitchen where volunteers say a prayer together before the meal is served."[455]

"Can we use Federal funds to purchase religious materials?" ask the organizations. "No," says the document. But there is plenty of money freed up from the social programs and available for that.

Can Federal fund be used to pay the salary of the church's staff members that perform the Federally-funded services? Yes, the staff member may even be a rabbi, priest or any other preacher. What if the staff member works only part-time? No problem. "It is fine for a faith-based organization to employ someone on their staff to perform religious duties" while he works on a Federally-funded program.[456]

What about equal opportunity employment? "There is no general federal law that prohibits faith-based organizations that receive Federal funds from hiring on a religious basis," answers the document.[457]

Should religious symbols be taken out while providing Federally-funded services? "You don't have to remove the Star of David or the cross in your building in order to deliver a Federally-funded service there," says the document.[458]

An article in OMB Watch (Office of Management and Budget Watch) summarizes the situation: "A needy person receiving aid through a voucher program or sub-award may have to sit through religious services before they actually receive aid from their social service provider. Yet the extension of the church-state relationship did not stop there."[459]

The Bush administration has asked to earmark $3.7 billion for the support of religious associations. According to *AFP (Agence*

France Press), "US President George W Bush asked his Justice Department to take steps to release some 3.7 billion dollars in federal monies aimed at helping religious charities."[460]

Examples abound about the US Government support of humanitarian charitable organizations without bearing their responsibilities. However, through this new administrative arrangement, the US Government and the European and other Western government have achieved the goal of moral and financial support of religious charitable work, which remains part of the non-governmental sector, independent from the government, and thus forming a third sector which contributes to the country's development, and realizes some of its goals and programs, without the government assuming its mistakes and transgressions. These are referred to in the judicial system, if at all.

2. Tying in Religion with Relief Work

Numerous news articles and reports view that the major mistake of Islamic charities was the mixing of relief work with *da'wah* (equivalent to missionary work). Some call it spreading fundamentalism. *National Review Online* writes: "Nonetheless, the Saudi Government continues to use an elaborate network of mosques, schools, 'charitable' and 'humanitarian' organizations, and official diplomatic facilities to aggressively propagate Wahhabism, the extreme brand of Islam that Senator Jon Kyl said 'presents a clear and present danger to our Constitution and the principles of freedom enshrined by our Founding Fathers.'"[461] Dore Gold, an ultra conservative Israeli advisor to Israeli Prime Minister Sharon, writes in the *New York Post*: "Saudi Arabia in this period also created its large Muslim international charities, such as the Muslim World League, which exported the kingdom's Wahhabi version of Islam. These charities were not nongovernmental entities or international organizations like the International Red Cross."[462]

Described as a "hatred's scribe', Gold has opposed every major peace initiative over the past two decades in the Middle East.

In Islam, charitable work is an inseparable part of religion. Benthall and Bellion have understood the nature of this connection and have shown that it is a source of strength for Islamic charitable work. Quoting a Muslim scholar, they say: "However, as a matter of degree and emphasis it is a fair claim that 'Among sacred books, the Qur'an seems to be the only one in the world which sets out precisely [in 9:60] the basic principles of the budget and expenses of the state'. It is doubtful too whether any other religion has an equivalent to the Islamic principle that hungry people have the right to share in the meal of those who are well fed."[463] This means that the Muslim state's budget should include spending in charitable, religious, and *da'wah* fields. The authors emphasize that the institution of *waqf*, the Islamic equivalent of the charitable trust or foundation, is an integral part of the religion and history of Islam, saying: "It spread over almost the whole of the Islamic world, so that, for example, between a half and two thirds of the lands of the huge Ottoman Empire was *waqf* at the start of the nineteenth century."[464] "It has been hailed as a key institution in early Islamic history in facilitating interaction between the religious and the economic spheres."[465] They have been historically connected and are not separate. The authors emphasize that this connection between proselytizing and relief exists in Western organizations, though they are not correlated as in Islam: "Just as the international Christian relief and development agencies habitually work through local churches in Christianized communities in Africa, benefiting from the grass roots support and trust to which they have access, so there are opportunities for international Islamic agencies to work through local religion based associations in Islamic communities."[466]

Even Western secular humanitarian organizations have roots in religious principles. Jonathan Benthall writes:

"The liberal humanitarianism underpinning Western humanitarianism, even in its 'secular' form, is arguably itself underpinned by a heritage of Judeo-Christian values."[467] This problem has affected for a long time the Red Cross organization which was founded in 1863 without the recognition of the priests during the Serbian wars. Ottoman soldiers refused to recognize the emblem of the cross because it reminded them of the Serbian wars. They have adopted the Red Crescent instead. Benthall explains: "Western humanitarianism was molded by Catholic monastic orders, by the Geneva Calvinist founders of the Red Cross, by the Salvation Army, by the Leprosy Mission, and by the Oxford Quakers who helped to found Oxfam. Church organizations dominated international aid until the Nigerian civil war of the late 1960s, with the founding of the secular agency Médecins Sans Frontières (MSF). Even today strands of Christian humanitarianism are strongly represented by Caritas, World Vision, the Order of Malta, Christian Aid, and the Nordic churches."[468]

If this is the situation of Western non-Islamic relief organizations, which are from countries established on the principle of separation of church and state, Islamic charities, which are established on the belief of strong relation between charity and Islam, should not be blamed.

Benthall and Bellion have depicted the Islamic *da'wah* as a response to the Christian organizations transgressions in aggressively seeking to Christianize the Muslims. They present Sudan as an example: "The missionaries in Africa have brandished the motto that says 'give up the religion of Islam, and we will free you from hunger, poverty, fear, and sickness.' Armies of missionaries have crossed Africa with food in their left hand and crosses in their right hands. It was in these terms that the Sudanese organization Da'wa Islamiya depicted, in its 1995 report of 15 years of activities, the missionary danger, in order to justify the activity of *da'wah*, the call to Islam. The play of events in Sudan has strikingly illustrated the relationship between the politics of aid and the religious question."[469]

Karin Von Hippel from King's College, University of London, wrote about the strong relation between Islamic charity work and Muslim creed, saying: "Indeed, one of the basic tenets of Islam is charity, and charity given in a way that does not humiliate the receiver."[470] This relation between relief and *da'wah*, regardless of its beneficial aspects, is not a matter of choice because it is originated from religious motives and Islamic laws which provide the base for regulations between donors, recipients, and intermediaries. These Islamic laws strengthen the charitable work and make it more effective, because they are based on the belief of: "fulfilling the trust and fearing God (since all wealth belongs to God)." This has had a beneficial aspect on the attested results of Islamic charitable work in spite of the meager means available.

It is a mistake to strip Islamic charitable work from its religious identity, and to tie it with standards and specifications set up by other religions and cultures, such as to limit its motives to humanitarian ones, and to compel its activities and relief work to be devoid from religious principles, and psychological, spiritual, and social reforms. Islamic relief work comprehends all these aspects.

In addition, Islamic charities and their employees believe that calling non-Muslims to Islam is a divine mission, and an obligation. They also believe that psychological healing from crises, famine, and wars include the belief in God and the acceptance of His decree. This belief alleviates the effects of psychological and social shocks, and helps people recover. But most importantly, they have to abide by the Qur'an's rule which says: "Let there be no compulsion in religion." And indeed there was no reported instances where coercion was used or where relief was conditioned by the embrace of Islam.

3. Support of Jihad Movements

Some individuals have presented direct financial help to factions of the Afghan mujahidin during their struggle against the Soviet Union. Some Arab governments, especially in the Gulf region, have supported the Afghans with money and American-made weapons. This was not a secret, but was indeed a source of pride for both states and organizations. The United States was at the forefront of countries that, directly or indirectly, supported the mujahidin with money, weaponry and training. The American media adopted the term *mujahidin* (then called freedom fighters) instead of rebels or Afghan fighters, when it reported Brzezinski, then US National Security Adviser, visiting Afghanistan, and meeting with the Afghan leader Yunes Khales.

There is no doubt that some of the Islamic charities supported some mujahidin factions, and this was well known to the US intelligence agencies which at that time did not object to their support.

Islamic charities have been hurt in the past and are still hurting in the present by the US Government's ambiguous and changing standards and policy concerning them and concerning Muslims and Islam in general. During the cold war, Islam was an ally to the West, as Muslim countries were fighting communism, and the Afghan Mujahidin were called freedom fighters. Robert Fisk, who was working for *The Times* in 1980, said that "the editor of *The Times* would always insist that Afghan guerillas were called 'freedom fighters' in the headline."[471] In 1982, the US Congress provided nearly $3 billion in covert aid for the mujahidin, more than all covert operations in that decade. The CIA provided the mujahidin with US-made Stinger missiles; it was the first time the CIA provided US-made weaponry[472]. The Reagan administration "arduously negotiated a six-year 3.2 billion aid package evenly divided between economic and military assistance"[473] to Pakistan in exchange for cooperation in helping the Afghan mujahidin. Commenting on the US support to the Afghans, Zbigniew Brzezinski said in 1998, that it was an excellent idea, "Indeed, for almost 10 years, Moscow had to carry on a war unsupportable by the government, a conflict that brought about the demoralization and finally the breakup of the Soviet Empire." Once the Russians have fled, however, the US abandoned its Afghan friends, and with the breakup of the Soviet Union, the US no more regards Afghanistan, and other Muslim countries as allies.

A number of American scholars and writers have criticized the ambiguous American policy and its response to the so-called "terrorism": Anthony Cordesman and Abraham Wagner have exposed in the third volume of their book "Lessons of Modern War" the extent of the US financial support of the Afghan war against the Soviet, as did Larry Goodson in his book "Afghanistan's Endless War". The causes and goal of this US about-face and ferocious campaign against Islamic charities may be to get rid of a previous ally it no longer needs, but rather is becoming a hindrance, or a danger to its objectives.

Benthall and Bellion have deftly explained the correlation between Islamic creed and aspects of relief and jihad. They quoted a Muslim intellectual who said about the Afghan jihad against the Soviets that it is

> *"fard ain [an individual obligation as opposed to a communal obligation] for military and medical experts or anyone with a special skill that the mujahidin need. They should help the mujahidin in the field of their competence and capacity. In general, it is incumbent on all Muslims to provide material and intellectual help in order to live with them in the heart even if they cannot live with them in the body."*[474]

"Thus different types of commitment were appealed for," said the authors, and among them to provide relief for the Afghans.

"This was the set of rationales that sparked off the origin and growth of the Islamic relief agencies," they concluded. "The initiative came largely from private agencies whose mobilization in the Afghan cause was tolerated, even encouraged by certain Middle Eastern states that sought to make use of the cause to further political or strategic aims."[475]

Although many attest to the efficiency of the Saudi charity relief work and its successes in the educational, medical, and relief field, some biased analysts have tried to link this work with jihad operations. Matthew Levitt writes: "A recently disclosed 1996 CIA document shows that as early as 1994 Washington was warning that in 1992 Saudi nationals gave some $150 million to Islamic charities active in Bosnia implicated in terrorism."[476] Have the charities been convicted of any wrongdoing in that time? Were the Saudi nationals doing something that was even contrary to the US policy in that time? One might ask why did the US and NATO forces intervene in the Bosnian war if not to defend the Bosnian Muslims against the Orthodox Serb's aggressions? Why are the Saudis accused of doing the same?

Hinting that not even the US is immune to such mistakes Kaplan wrote: "Saudi officials liken the situation to US funding of the Irish Republican Army. During the 1970s and '80s, IRA activists raised millions of dollars from Irish Americans, despite British pleas that the funds were backing IRA terrorism."[477]

However, if it is proven that some Islamic charities have been supporting jihad during the Bosnian war, this would be a mistake for which they would be accountable, because they would be transgressing the declared objectives of their organizations.

4. Financial Activities (Sources and Recipients of Funding)

Some accusations against Islamic charities spring from suspicions about their financial transactions (income and expenditures). This is due to the wealthy Western countries' misunderstanding about the financial dealings in many African and Asian communities. In most Arab, Muslim, African, and Asian countries, banking transactions are limited to large sums of money. Charity organizations would not present aid to the poor in the form of $20 or$50 check. Western countries where people are used to credit cards would be suspicious of this. Does this mean that widows and orphans in poor countries would have to have bank accounts or carry credit cards to receive aid?

It is customary in a capitalist system where the "culture of credit cards" prevails over the "culture of cash" to raise suspicions about these transactions. Charities most often work in poor areas afflicted by crises where it is often impossible to apply the same financial standards used in the West. The nature of crises and disasters impose the use of cash. During the recent war in Afghanistan, the United States Government dropped $70 million in cash from military airplanes to Afghan citizens[478].

Another source of misunderstanding was that employees in the US administration offices concerned with this issue, not to talk about the public at large, have little understanding of the Arab and Islamic culture. It is a duty for the Muslim to help those in need without asking who they are. Generosity is a prized characteristic among the Muslims who usually do not ask those they help for their identities.

On the other hand it might be possible that some individuals have a relation with or are employees of a charity, while keeping other personal relations with resistance movements without commingling the two activities. This of course might also be the case of government employees or private institutions' employees holding multiple relationships between government institutions and private ones. However, according to a study by Johns Hopkins University, not all NGOs are subjected to the same standards among the nations of the world, starting from their names to their programs and work traditions.

Transgressions of Some Non-Islamic Organizations

Using crises to execute hidden agendas

International organizations affiliated or cooperating with the United Nations perform commendable humanitarian relief work both inside their countries of origin, and abroad. There is no doubt that some have had great positive effects in disasters and crises areas. It is also known that each organization has its own hidden agenda. The problem for some non-Islamic charities resides in how they can execute their hidden agendas; especially that 70% of the crisis and disaster areas are in Muslim countries or Muslim minorities areas. A sizable number of the Non-Islamic organizations are forcefully working to change the indigenous people's culture and religion.

It is necessary to point out to the transgressions committed by some organizations and how these are addressed, and to compare the governments' response to these transgressions with their reaction to the mistakes allegedly committed by Islamic ones.

It is appropriate to present here examples of mistakes committed by Humanitarian organizations which are no less important than those committed by some Islamic charities and for which they have been closed. Did these Non-Islamic organizations face the same fate as their Islamic counterpart? Were they forced to close? Were their assets frozen? Were they defamed?

The shameless behavior of some international humanitarian organizations inside the United States and around the world, especially in hot spots and civil war areas belies their claims of supporting human rights and having high moral standards. Among their actions are: support of regional and international terrorism, US churches spending close to a billion dollars to cover up sexual scandals committed by their priests, using relief work for the purpose of changing people's religion and culture, distributing expired food and medication to relief recipients, sex in exchange to food, administrative corruption, and the list goes on and on.[479] We only cite in this book some of the transgressions that are more relevant to the issue.

1. Support for Regional and International Terrorism

Inside the United States there are independent militia and other organizations that can be characterized as terrorists, which enjoy, albeit, low level of social support through their members and sympathizers, and which get financial support and donations under the protection of the law. The number of military militia is estimated to be between 40 and 100 militia organizations which claim to include three million members. Independent estimations put their number closer to 25 thousands. These militias are active in more than 30 states especially in Texas. Their arsenals include hand guns, rifles, semi-automatics, explosives, and bombs. Some have warehouses stock full of armaments. These militias finance their activities in illegal ways such as tax evasion and bank robberies.[480] In its introduction to a Robert Fisk article titled "A Strange Kind of Freedom", the *Independent* wrote: "We all know about the perils of Islamic fanaticism. But, says Robert Fisk, the biggest threat to liberty in the US may come from other kinds of fundamentalism: Jewish and Christian."[481]

The Lebanese *Daily Star* newspaper described another example of terror support by Christian organizations, pointing to the role played by the World Council of Churches in supporting the rebels in Southern Sudan and the separatist movement in Biafra, Nigeria. "The support extended by the World Council of Churches to the Southern Sudanese rebels…has been ongoing since the 1950s," says Mohammed al-Roken in the *Daily Star*. "In the early 1970s Paul Steiner, a German priest, was captured in Sudan. In fact, the Southern rebels would not have been able to continue fighting had it not been for the help they received from these Western charities. In Nigeria, the World Council of Churches and other Western humanitarian organizations actively aided the secessionist movement in Biafra for more than three years. This aid was never criticized for what it was - overt support for terrorism that should have been stopped. In both these examples, Christian charities were used as conduits for Western foreign policy goals. Western countries could not extend military aid to the secessionists in Sudan and Nigeria overtly, so they used church-run charities to do the job for them."[482] By contrast organizations that sent donations to the Palestinian resistance have been targeted as terror supporters, even though the Palestinian resistance is an internationally legitimate resistance and not a separatist or rebel movement. The Gulf Center for Strategic Studies also pointed out to the scandalous double dealing, saying: "The scandalous double dealing has become clear when it has been proven that the World Council of Churches has supported and still is supporting the separatist movement in Southern Sudan through donations and grants that have reached millions of dollars."[483]

Karin Von Hippel writes: "It must be pointed out here that it is not just the extreme Islamic groups that utilize this method of influence: Christian fundamentalist organizations in the United States, for example, have been supporting certain sides in conflicts that are perceived as threatening Christianity, with the case of southern Sudan as the most obvious."[484]

2. Support for Separatist Movements

The abuse of charitable work to further political aims is a practice shared by many Western organizations. On October 1st, 2004, during a reception in Asmara, the International Rescue Committee has launched a program for the creation of an alphabet for the 4000 years old Badawit dialect. Five books were published in this language, and 19 schools have already started to teach it in Eastern Sudan to further the attempt to separate this area from the rest of the country. The armed rebels in Eastern Sudan have adopted the Badawit dialect to be taught in all areas under their control. Badawit is talked by about two million people in Sudan. This program has aroused many questions as to its goal, and suspicion that it is meant to threaten the Arabic language, the official language of the country, and thus to promote the separatist efforts in Eastern Sudan. The International Rescue Committee refused to talk about the existence of any political motive behind the program.

The program encourages more then 100 Sudanese cultural entities to revive their languages and cultures, after the treaty between the Sudanese Government and the rebels led by Garang has given all the districts the right to choose their local dialects to be taught in schools besides Arabic and English, and be the official languages used in local government institutions.[485]

Moreover, the British television channel 4 has revealed details of the British Sewa International's support of Hindu extremist groups in India. Sewa International, a project arm of the Hindu Swayasevak Sangh charity, has continuously supported Hindu terrorist groups with millions of pounds under the cover of relief work. This money has been and is still being used to terrorize both Muslims and Christians in India, killing them and burning their properties. Alleged links between the RSS charity and the Hindu Nationalist Organization Rashtiya Swayamsevak Sangh (with the same acronym RSS) and the misuse of the donation funds have been brought up to the UK Charity Commission. The Indian Government refused to grant visas to the Commission for an inspection visit."[486]

News media and human rights activists have revealed additional worrisome news at the end of November 2002, about the American India Development and Relief Fund's (IDRF) support of the Hindutva (Hindu supremacist movement) terrorist groups by sending them millions of dollars. These organizations are supposedly collecting funds to help the poor in India, but in reality the monies are sent to branches created by Rashtriya Swayamsevak Sangh (RSS) which is considered the mother organization of the Hindu organizations in India.[487] "Hindutva... uses terror to dominate," [488]writes Angana Chatterji, professor of Social and Cultural Anthropology at the California Institute of Integral Studies. The IDRF sustains the network of Hindutva organizations which promulgate terror among Indian Muslims and Christians. Their massacre of the Muslims in Gujarat is well documented.

Benthall and Bellion write: "The abuse of charitable activities to fulfill personal, political, or military aims can also be considered a practice shared by various traditions...We cannot therefore fairly characterize the raising of funds for arms rather than alms as a monopoly of Muslims. At various times, certain Christian clergy have been involved with facilitating the supply of arms in order to benefit causes they were passionately committed to. During the years before the founding of the Irish Free State in 1921, for instance, a large number of Catholic priests and monks were in trouble with the British police and military authorities. And during the Nigerian civil war of 1967-70, a number of Christian clergy became deeply committed to the cause of the Biafran enclave. Arms kept Biafra going and it was well-known that, in the early days, the Churches had condoned the dispatch of mixed cargoes [i.e. including both aid supplies and arms] to Uli airport."[489] "The major Western aid organizations have never existed in a political vacuum," the authors wrote. "The borrowing of the humanitarian fig leaf by governments either to excuse themselves for taking no action against war crimes, or to make their own wars more palatable, has become highly sophisticated."[490]

"Humanitarians seek aid without politics, a universal ideal, but for the foreseeable future the worldwide reality is the politics of aid,"[491] concluded the authors.

Indeed some American-based NGOs are playing a great role in government changes to create new pro-US Governments that fulfill the US political and economic aims in the region. It is noticeably what happened in Kyrgyzstan, Kazakhstan, Georgia, and many other countries. In Ukraine, for examples, all indications point out that US and European supported NGOs have been behind the Ukrainian street revolts that caused the collapse of the pro-Moscow Government and the establishment of a pro-Western government. According to official Ukrainian statistics, local NGOs has increased during the period between 1992 and 2005 to reach 30 thousand organizations, and that the US granted three billion dollars to the Ukrainian Government for political reforms, and $28 million to non-governmental organizations that are close to Victor Yushenko who later won the presidential elections. "This sort of change-Privatization, scarcity, increased prices-is why Yushenko's candidacy is really valued in the West, not for democracy, 'civil society', or any of the other slogans the West trumpets…Yushenko fits the New World Order bill like a glove"[492]. Here hundreds of millions of dollars granted annually to research institutes and foundations, among them the National Democratic Institute for International Affairs, headed by Madeleine Albright, former US Secretary of State, which has 160 branches in Ukraine with 18,000 Ukrainian employees.

A report published by the Ukrainian parliament in 2004 confirmed that were it not for the West financing of Ukrainian-based NGOs these would not have existed at all. This selective financing was limited to organizations that supported the opposition in order to influence the presidential elections outcome. Parliament member Pyotr Simonenko did not hesitate to say that these organizations are a cover for the intelligence agencies active in Ukraine. The same happened in Kyrgyzstan, Kazakhstan, and Georgia.[493]

Steve Gutterman of the *Associated Press* mentioned the worries of the Russian Government about foreign secret services: "Russia's security chief yesterday accused US and other foreign intelligence services of using non-governmental organizations that promote democracy to spy on Russia and bring about political upheaval in former Soviet republics." [494] Russian Federal Security Service Chief Nikolai Patrushev said: "Under cover of implementing humanitarian and educational programs in Russian regions, [the NGOs] lobby the interests of the states in question and gather classified information on a broad spectrum of issues." Russian officials have accused the United States and other Western nations of using government-funded groups to aid opposition forces that have brought down governments in former Soviet republics in the past two years. Non-governmental organizations accused of involvement in espionage include the US Peace Corps. The US Government money "funneled through NGOs that promote democracy, was a major force behind the protests that swept Western-leaning opposition leaders to power in Georgia and Ukraine, and was also a factor in Kyrgyzstan."[495]

3. Voluntary Donations to Assist Terrorism

American Jewish organizations are increasing their support for Israel, not only for humanitarian and social services, but also for military purposes and to support illegal settlers. Delinda Hanley of *Washington Report on Middle East Affairs* writes: "American Jewish money has long gone toward closing the funding gap in Israel's social services, due to the nation's heavy spending on military and defense. At Sharon's urging, the Israel Now campaign was created in the spring of 2001 with a two-year goal to raise $400 million. The tax deductible "charity" was launched by the United Jewish Communities (UJC)… to fund the purchase of armored vehicles, upgraded security systems to protect schools and community centers, counseling for Ethiopian and Russian immigrants, bulletproof glass for houses in illegal Jewish settlements, and support services for Israel Defense Force soldiers. By mid-November, according to the November 16 *Washington Jewish Week*, almost $86 million had been raised, nearly $5 million from the Washington DC area alone."[496]

Leaders of many American Jewish federations claim that collected donations are used in general for humanitarian aid, but in reality, as *The Washington Post* confirmed, the Israeli Government gets more than 80% of the donations. American Jewish groups collectively raised $2.9 billion in 2000![497]

Exposing the double standard of the US justice system, Hanley writes: "The Justice Department says that charities in the US that knowingly contribute to foreign terrorist organizations can be sued for damages by victims of attacks carried out by those organizations. On that basis, the US Government said that the family of David Boim - a 17-year-old American who was shot and killed at a bus stop in the West Bank - can sue the Holy Land Foundation…Can the families of Palestinian Americans who have been crippled, blinded, tortured or killed by Israeli soldiers or Jewish settlers sue Jewish American charities that have contributed funds for their support? Is a soldier who targets a stone-throwing or football-kicking child not a terrorist because he wears a uniform?" Hanley concludes: "The Bush administration is skating on thin ice when it stops donations given by good people in good faith from reaching sorely abused Palestinians and other Muslims suffering around the world."[498]

Biased viewpoint and double standard:

The campaigns of searches and harassment have been the exclusive lot of Islamic charities whose assets combined together do not even come close to the assets of one of the Christian charities, such as the Salvation Army which collected in 1999 alone nearly $1.5 billion, or the YMCA of the USA which ranked second after the Salvation Army, or the United Way, and many other organizations that far exceed the Islamic organizations combined in human and financial capabilities. Some of these Christian organizations are supporting separatist movements around the world.

Peter F. Drucker wrote in his book "Managing for the Future": "Few people are aware that the non-profit sector is by far America's largest employer. Every other adult - a total of 80 million-plus people - works as a volunteer, giving n average nearly five hours each week to one or several nonprofit organizations. This is equal to 10 million full-time jobs. Were volunteers paid, their average, even at minimum rate, would amount to some $150 billion, or 5 percent of GNP. And volunteer work is changing fast."[499]

Recent statistics reveal that the non-profit sector employs around 11 million people, in addition to 90 million volunteers. Donations in 2003 exceeded $240 billion, 34% of them were reserved to religious purposes. Non-profit organizations in the US includes 1.3 million charities, 13,000 are Jewish organizations, and 6,000 are Islamic organizations.[500]

Saudi public-relation agent Micheal Petruzello, said to *Insight on the News Magazine* that the Saudi Government was providing about $120 million per year to "international organizations such as the UN, the Red Cross and the Red Crescent Society for distribution to the West Bank and Gaza. The US is using the same channels. So you can't say the Saudis are giving money to suicide bombers any more than the US is doing."[501]

American charities presented humanitarian services in Southern Sudan with the help of the warring factions, including the John Garang separatist group which was fighting the Sudanese Government, even though the US might have considered the military separatist movement a terrorist movement. Humanitarian aid presented to such groups by US charities was not considered outside their role as humanitarian organizations, and thus they were not considered as transgressors, or terror supporters. Likewise, humanitarian services presented during the Russian-Afghan war by the Saudi Red Crescent, and other Islamic charities in general, should not be considered outside their role as humanitarian organizations, even though these services could not have been accomplished without the help of the Afghan fighters. Yet hearing testimonies presented to the US Senate Governmental Affairs Committee on July 31, 2003 considered similar humanitarian services presented by Saudi Islamic charities during the Afghan-Soviet, Bosnian-Serb war, Kosovo-Serb, and Chechen-Russian wars as support for terrorism!

Companies supporting the illegal Israeli occupation of the Palestinian territories.

Many Americans and multinational companies support the illegal Israeli occupation of the Palestinian territories and have not been the subject of any investigation or persecution by US government. In the report produced by the Divestment Task Force of the New England Conference of the united Methodist church twenty companies are identified as supporting in significant way the illegal Israeli occupation of the Palestinian territories. Under the title "Companies recommended for divestment: updated Nov.27.2007.

the organization website 508 lists the following companies a long with the reasons of the divestment recommendation

- **<u>Alliant Tech Systems (NYSE-ATK)</u>** is engaged with Israeli company in the rubber coated bullets. such bullets are frequently use against Palestinians, as well as Israeli and international peace activists engaged in peaceful demonstrations to protest against Israel's confiscation of Palestinian land.Rubber bullets often blind, disfigure or kill those who are hit by them. Alliant company is also engaged in other contracts that support the Israeli military which enforces the occupation. The company produces fuses for cluster bombs and guided multiple launch rocket systems.

- **<u>BLOCKBUSTER (NYSE :BBI)</u>** has Kiosks settlement in the occupied Palestinian land. These settlements violate the Fourth Geneva Convention and the Universal Declaration of Human Rights. Companies providing services to these settlements which violate the law, contribute to their growth and appeal for the Israelis. They make it harder to withdraw Israelis from the occupied territories an essential step for any lasting peace agreement with the Palestinians

- **<u>BOENING (NYSE : BA</u>** has been a major supplier of F.15 Eagle fighters and AH-64 Apache attack helicopter to Israel. These Aircrafts have been used to attack Palestinians in the Occupied Territories, resulting in many civilian causalities. Boeing makes missile systems, F-15 soft wares, apache helicopters and Joint Direct Attack Munitions (JDAM) a guided air-to- surface weapon.

- **<u>CATERPILLAR (NYSE : CAT</u>**) supplies bulldozers to Israeli Defense Forces (IDF). The IDF uses these to destroy Palestinians homes, orchards, and olive groves in the Occupied Territories. They are also used to clear

Palestinian land for illegal Israeli settlements, segregated roads and the "the Separation barrier". Despites years of corporate engagement by investors, Caterpillar is expanding it's role in the occupation recently announcing a joint venture with InRob Tech to develop unmanned remote controlled bulldozer for Israel.

- **CEMENT ROADSTONE HOLDINGS (NYSE : CRH)** is an Ireland based multinational. CRH benefits from monopoly on cement production within Israel. through it's 25% holdings in the Israeli group Mashav Initiating and Development Ltd which is the holding company for Nesher Cement. Nesher claims on it's web site to be the Israeli's sole producer of cement. Cement is being used in the construction of the separation wall inside the West Bank, which the International Court of Justice has ruled illegal. Cement is also used to build settlements in Palestinian land.

- **GENERAL DYNAMICS (NYSE: GD)** Land systems in the USA manufactures the GD 883 diesel engine for Israeli Merkava 4 battle tanks. It has supplied 1.000 M60A3 Main Battle Tanks to Israel. These tanks are frequently used against Palestinian in the Occupied Territories. It also produces equipment used in F.16 Fighting Falcon Jets sold to Israel. General Dynamics will be the general contractor for the production 3.500 MK-84 "general purpose" bombs spare & repair parts for Israel in a sale purposed by Pentagon in April 2007

- **GENERAL ELECTRIC (NYSE: GE)** supplies the propulsion system for Israel's AH 64 Apache Assault Helicopter, which is used in Israeli attacks on Palestinian towns. It also possesses contracts with Israel to sell engines for a variety of military aircrafts. In addition, GE possesses several Israeli service contracts for engineering support and testing.

- **GLOBECOMM SYSTEMS INC.(GSI) (NASDAQ :GCOM NEWYORK)** in partnership with Tadiran Spectralink of Elisra Group (Israel) has a contract to supply the IDF with equipment and facilities for communication between all branches of the IDF ground forces. The system includes mobile stations installed on HMMWV vehicles. These vehicles are used by IDF in the occupied territories.

- **ITT CORPORATION (NYSE: ITT)** provides the Israeli Defense Forces IDF with intensifier tubes for night vision goggles and has previously provided battlefield communication radios Night vision goggles are used by pilots, co-pilots and crews of fix wing and rotary wing aircraft especially helicopter crews. They enable Israel to attack refugee camps and villages in the mid night, the time when many of these raids and assaults take place. Battle field communication radios allow the military to communicate with troops over a secure channel.

- **LOCKHEED MARTIN (NYSE LMT)** is the single biggest overseas supplier for the Israeli armaments industry. It had received at least $4.4 billion since 1995 for supplying arms including missile system and fighter planes to Israel. It has many ongoing contracts, including manufacturing F-161 fighter bombers used by IDF against Palestinians. Lockheed Martin Missile and fire control in Orland, Florida produces the hellfire missile system for apache attack helicopter use by Israeli against Palestinians. According to military publication, Israeli main battle tank the Merkava MK-4 produced by Lockheed Martin Skunk Work Group.

- **MAGAL SECURITY SYSTEMS (NASDAQ: MAGS)** is an Israeli company that is providing intrusion detection fencing for separation wall. It is listed in the government of Israel web site as one of the contractors engaged in the construction of the Separation Wall

- **MOTOROLA (NYSE : MOT)** is engaged in 400 million NIS ($93 million) project to provide radar system for enhancing security at illegal West Bank Settlements deep inside Palestinian territory. Motorola has also a $90 contract to provide the Israeli Army with advanced (Mountain Rose) cell phone communication systems. It is wholly owned subsidiary in Israel has contract to develop encrypted wireless communications featuring vehicle mounted antenna that will enable military use in the occupied territories and other remote areas

- **NORTHROP GRUNMAN(NYSE:NOC)** collaborates with Lockheed Martin in producing the Israeli F-161 Sufa (Storm) aircraft by providing the AN/APG-68 (V) 9 multimode radar that provides for high resolution ground mapping. With Lockheed Northrop also produces the long Bow System which is when installed in Apache Helicopter, greatly enhances the Apache lethality. The Long Bow System includes fire control radar and Hell Fire Missile. In 2000 and 2001 the Congress was notified of more than $500 million and $509 million respectively, in pending Apache Long Bow attack helicopter sales to Israel.

- **OSHKOSH TRUCK CORPORATIN (NYSE : OSK)** through contracts worth hundreds of million dollars, supplies mobility Tactical trucks to Israeli military. These include cargo trucks with vehicles, wreckers and tractors. This type of equipments is used by Israeli military in the occupied territory. Israel also has $145 million contract with OSHKOSH Truck Corp. to build more than 900 armor kits for Israel's Medium Tactical Vehicles.

- **RAYTHOEN (NYSE : RTN)** is a major arms contractor for Israeli Military. It supplies Patriot, sparrow, Sidewinder Maverick and TOW missile. Maverick is precision air – to – ground missile that used against small mobile and hard targets. Missiles are frequently used against Palestinians in crowded residential areas such as refugees camps. They are also used in targeted assassinations of Palestinians without trail, evidence or opportunity for defense.

- **SILICON GRAPHICS (NASDAQ :SGIC**) has a contract to provide Israeli Air Force F- 15 pilots with visual system training. SGI's system will also allow training for F-16 pilots using night vision goggles and sensors. An SGI graphics system serves as image generator for Israeli Air Force UH-60/CH-53 Helicopter Aircrew Weapon Systems Trainer. These aircraft has been used in attacks on Palestinians in the occupied territory

- **TEREX (NYSE:TEX)** subsidiary American Truck Company (ATC) signed a $54 billion agreement to supply 302 medium tactical trucks and associated logistical support to Israeli army. Terex also supplied TATRA trucks used by Israeli army to mount artillery systems during the time it owned a controlling interest in that company. Terex owns Amida Industries which manufactures mobile floodlight towers used by Israeli Army in the occupied territory. It also owns Terex Demag Cranes which are leased in Israel through Riwal the major crane supplier for Israel's separation wall. Terex's ATC still has a contract with Israeli Army for training, services and spare parts.

- **UNITED TECHNOLOGIES (NYSE:UTX)** produces black hawk helicopters which are used by Israeli military to attack Palestinian cities, refugees camps and villages. Many civilians have been killed in these attacks. On Feb 1. 2001 United Technologies Sikorsky Division announced a many $211.8 million contract with Israeli

Air Forces. United Technologies Pratt and Whitely Division produces engines for Israel's F-15 and F-16 air craft which are used against Palestinians. In 2005 Israel awarded Pratt and whitely a contract worth up to $600 million for fleet management of these engines over the next 10 years.

- **VEOLIA ENVIRONMENT (NYSE;VE)** owns Connex. Connex is a central partner in a new $500 million light rail system designed to link Jerusalem to illegal settlements of the occupied west Bank. It owns 5% of the consortium building the system and secured a contract to operate the system for the next 30 years.

- **VOLVO (NASDAQ:VOLV)** bulldozers have photographed and video tapped destroying Plalestinian homes. They have also been used in Israel's construction of the Separation wall which is on Palestinian land and has been declared illegal by the international Court of Justice. Mayers Cars and Trucks in Israel is a Volvo distributer and according to Israeli sources,it is one of the main providers of construction equipment for the settlements and the Separation Wall.

- **Tobacco companies and restaurant chains supporting terrorists:**
  Hundreds of Jewish non-profit organizations have become experts in the unconditional support of Israel. Some organizations openly support the destruction of al-Aqsa Mosque. Large companies have reserved a percentage of their profit to support Israel. Philip Morris, the maker of Marlboro, Merit, and Benson cigarettes reserves 12% of its net profit to support Israel. The Arab Committee for Human Rights has released a study showing that Israel receives $9.6 million every day from this company.[502]

Another staunch supporter of Israel is McDonald Restaurant Chains that are in all parts of the world, a symbol of globalization. Mc Donald has announced many times through the media its support for Israel. During an interview with a*l-Watan* Saudi newspaper, the US consul in Saudi Arabia confirmed that McDonald Restaurants Company supports Israel with the equivalent of one day's income of the global restaurant chains, adding that everyone is free to spend his wealth the way he likes.[503]

In 2002, Jewish groups have raised in a short time, in a single emergency campaign, more than $119 million as part of aid to Israeli terrorism. These campaigns and donations have never been subject to investigations or prosecutions neither from the US Government, nor from the US Congress.[504]

4. Exploiting Relief Work as a Means for Religious Conversion and Cultural Change:

Some non-governmental organizations have adopted the policy of granting scholarships to students in poor countries for political and cultural purposes. The American billionaire philanthropist George Soros' "Open Society" is one such organization that has so forcefully applied this policy that it has encountered political and administrative problems with the former Soviet Government. "Soros is the uncrowned king of Eastern Europe," writes Neil Clark of the *New Statesman*, "His Central European University, with campuses in Budapest, Warsaw, and Prague, and exchange programs in the US, unashamedly propagates the ethos of neo-liberal capitalism and clones the next pro-American generation of political leaders in the region." Clark adds: "Armed with a few billion dollars, a handful of NGOs and a nod and a wink from the US State Department, it is perfectly possible to topple foreign governments that are bad for business."[505]

This policy of granting scholarships which is adopted by industrialized countries or some of their NGO's, targets bright minds in developing third world countries. While this has no doubt benefited the poor developing countries, it has often caused them more harm, because most often these bright people do not return to their countries preferring to stay where they enjoy greater remunerations. A brain drain thus occurs in countries that can least afford it. Those who return, become the conduit of the West's culture and ideologies in their own countries; a tremendous gain for the West.

Developed countries which offer scholarships to third world countries students are in fact preparing them to be "good ambassadors" who will be at the top social, political, and economic ladder, and through which the West can ensure its access to information about the third world countries. This in addition to the many valuable studies and researches these graduates have performed which provide an impressive data base that allow the developed countries to better ensure their interests in third world countries.

Besides the governmental aid, it is important to review the aid provided by non-governmental organizations especially that the non-governmental sector is a power that should not be made light of. Its strength lies in its efficient specialized structure. It covers all fields and interests, has high financial capabilities, and benefits from freedom of movement in the West, and has global reach with its center and pivot in the West.

Non-governmental organizations are seen on both sides of the Atlantic as being the overreaching arms of the West. Organizations concerned with family issues, women issues, human rights issues for example often promote the West's visions concerning these issues. Some have sought to found affiliated organizations in the Muslim world that espouse these visions, thus ensuring cultural and intellectual globalization, and globalization of the principles that might contradict the religions and cultures of these countries.[506]

Christianization has accompanied most relief work in the third world countries, the poor ones in particular. In his book "Lords of Poverty" Graham Hancock has written about the exploitation of relief work for religious and cultural changes. While he was reporting a famine crisis in Ethiopia, he said that he was not the only one sightseeing the area, there were many international organizations, including the FAO, UNICEF, WHO, and also the World Church Council. Graham wrote: "According to Ted Engstrom, who was President of World Vision until June 30, 1987, 'we analyze every project, every program we undertake, to make sure that within that program evangelism is a significant component. We cannot feed individuals and then let them go to hell."[507] This policy led to grave charges being leveled against the giant charity. The charges came from relief workers on the field. According to these witnesses, "World Vision employees frequently use the threat of withholding food supplies to coerce Salvadoran refugees [who are mostly Catholics] into attending Protestant worship services."[508]

"Whenever religion is mixed injudiciously with relief work there are human costs to be paid." Hancock remarked. "In Somalia," Hancock writes, "International Christian Aid, World Vision, and a number of other US charities wasted valuable donors' dollars by recruiting Christian zealots to manage their programs in the refugee camps that had been set up following fighting along the border with Ethiopia. In addition to antagonizing and outraging the Muslims amongst whom they worked, these people were generally young, untrained and inexperienced. Robert Smith, a born-again World Vision official in Somalia, caused puzzlement - and some hilarity - amongst suppliers of equipment and materials by signing all his requisition telexes with the words 'God bless Robert'."[509]

Nevertheless, we should not neglect the positive effects of these organizations in the relief field; neither should we paint all of them with the same brush. But what is noticeable is that many non-Islamic charities are ignorant of the specific cultures and customs of the countries of the "South". Their notion of compassion is paternalistic and ethnocentric. "They hail from societies which believe themselves to be more highly evolved than others (that is from developed as opposed to underdeveloped societies) and which are deeply convinced of the superiority of their own values and of the supremacy of their technical knowledge."[510] They consider the Western civilization as the ideal civilization that others should follow, and that it has reached the highest point in the long history of humanity. The goals of these organizations concur with Francis Fukuyama's "End of History" theory. That is why they have been accused of acting as custodians on others. Their long term goals are to change the religious, and social map of the world, and to play with internal conflicts to reach their goals. Most Muslim countries and Muslim minorities look with suspicion at these non-Islamic charities as the arms of the Christian Red Cross, a symbol they consider, that carries religious connotations behind relief aid façade. These organizations are sometimes suspected and feared, and some other times rejected all together.

Institutes to Christianize Muslims:

A score of universities in the US have opened centers and institutes that have among its objectives to Christianize Muslims around the world, to penetrate by any means Muslim societies and change their religion. This is often done through charitable work or by other covert ways. At Columbia International University (CIU) in South Carolina "Christian missionaries are being trained to go undercover in the Muslim world and win converts for Jesus. Their stated goal: to wipe out Islam," [511]writes Barry Yeoman in an article titled "The Stealth Crusade" in *Mother Jones Magazine.* CIU offers workshops and intensive courses to missionaries in ways to camouflage themselves as aid workers, teachers, and businessmen, to proselytize in Muslim countries. "The number of missionaries trying to convert Muslims has jumped fourfold, from several hundred in the early 1990s to more than 3,000 today," writes Yeoman. "We see Islam as the final frontier," said David Cashin, a professor of Intercultural Studies at CIU who used to don Muslim clothing to lure Bangladeshis in Kaliakoir. "Cashin regards the Islamic world as a hinterland that must be penetrated before the Messiah can return. 'History is coming to an end,' he says. 'If you believe Christ is coming back, why has he delayed 2,000 years? We haven't finished the task he set out to do.'"[512]

The missionaries growing movement to hunt Muslim souls by passing as aid workers has raised hackles, because their work disrupts the delivery of humanitarian aid and fuels resentment of Westerners. "But to those at the heart of the movement, including [CIU seminar teacher] Rick Love's students, any damage done by their work is outweighed by the importance of their mission: to wipe out Islam...'If they don't have a chance to experience Jesus, they're going to hell,' [says a CIU student]."[513]

Christian missionaries are aggressively pursuing proselytization in every area of the Muslim world they can reach. Using a practice they call "contextualization" to win converts in a foreign culture, Christian missionaries take on the behavior of the culture, even adopting the rituals of another religion (an outright dishonest practice that puts missionaries integrity into question). "The idea is to get away from the old-fashioned practice of importing American-style Christianity," writes Yeoman. "Instead, missionaries today are more likely to take on Muslim names, dress in veils and other local clothing, prostrate themselves during prayer, and even fast during Ramadan."[514]

Christian missionaries have put Christianization before relief work, endangering the lives of those they claim to rescue: Robert

Macpherson, Security Director of CARE, who served in Somalia in the early 1990s, remembers when 200 organizations were working to stave off famine in the war-battered area, recalls the dangers of the situation. "It was dangerous, dangerous, dangerous," he said. "Evangelicals have only made matters worse by showing up at food-distribution sites and handing out Christian literature, giving the impression that food aid was contingent on conversion to Christianity. 'The next thing we know, they got themselves in the middle of a riot,' Macpherson recalls. Angered by the missionaries, Somalis climbed over one another to steal food and set trucks on fire. 'They were desperate,' he says. 'They were dying. This was an emergency'."[515]

In 1997, Evangelical groups held a meeting in Basle, Switzerland for the purpose of Christianizing the World. In October 1978, the American Lausanne Committee and World Vision International held the North American Conference on Muslim Evangelization, in Colorado Springs, Colorado. Nearly 150 key evangelical leaders have attended the conference, and presented 40 papers about Islam and its relation with Christianity. Their declared goal was to evangelize the whole Muslim world. They appropriated a billion dollars for that purpose and created the Zwemer Institute of Muslim Studies, after the missionary Zwemer who was active in the Middle East in the early twentieth century from his headquarters in Bahrain, and who headed an evangelical conference in Cairo in 1906.[516] "The Lord will truly meet with his people when they concern themselves with the unfinished task of evangelizing the Muslim world" reads the introduction to the Glen Eyrie report.

Finally, this orchestrated assault on Muslims, their cultures, and their religion, by different parties, running the gamut from Hindutva's terrorist groups, to Soros' "Open Society" project which incites upheaval, to Christian charities that support separatists, to Evangelicals who are adamantly set to Christianize the Muslim world by all deceiving means, all this is going on unabashedly, without being even criticized by the Western governments, while Islamic charities are being scrutinized and harshly punished or closed for alleged mistakes that do not even come close to what other charities have committed.

Chapter VII

The Motives and Objectives[517]

Indications and Results that Point to the Real Motives

There are numerous indications that point to the motives behind the campaigns against Islamic organizations and proofs confirming that the hidden motives are different from the declared ones. Some of these are:

1- Perception of competition:

One of the causes of the campaign against Islamic charities might be the fact that they had certain effects and power among Muslim communities. Jonathan Benthall and Jerome Bellion have pointed to this fact, saying: "At the domestic level within Muslim countries and among Muslim communities in non-Muslim states, social welfare programs carried out by voluntary Islamic associations came to the West's attention over the same period when it was realized how effective they were in mobilizing political support in countries where state support cannot satisfy welfare needs and demands."[518]

The authors highlighted this aspect of competition, when they said: "The especially interesting point about Islamic institutions is that not only do they have an extensive popular outreach, but they have developed international programs sustained by an alternative form of universalism to that of Judeo-Christian West."[519]

As an illustration of this competition, they write: "During the 1980s, relations between the Arab NGOs and the Western ones were marked by defiance. The Islamic NGOs, and the Islamist parties of Afghan resistance, condemned the activities of the Western humanitarians, attributing to them activities they considered harmful to Afghan society. In a conflict characterized by an intense 'politicization of humanitarian aid', the Western NGOs were accused of supporting the most moderate political parties [in the eyes of the West]: the French NGOs, for instance, were considered to be supporters of Ahmad Shah Masood."[520]

The Role of the Cultural Heritage:

In her official biography, Queen Margarethe II of Denmark said: "We are being challenged by Islam these years, globally as well as locally. There is something impressive about people for whom religion imbues their existence, from dusk to dawn, from cradle to grave…A counterbalance has to be found, and one has to, at times, run the risk of having unflattering labels placed on you. For there are some things for which one should display no tolerance."[521] The queen is quoted as voicing disapproval of "these people for whom religion is their entire life."[522]

This hatred toward Islam expressed by a high political personality in a country that claims to be one of the most tolerant in Europe, has become apparent in the Western world. This hatred comes from the European cultural heritage as explained by Leopold Weiss in his book "The Road to Mecca". He wrote:

[The West] has only become more tolerant. Mind you, not toward Islam, only toward certain other Eastern cultures, which offer some sort of spiritual attraction to the spirit-hungry West and are, at the same time, too distant from the West world-view to constitute any real challenge to its values...when a Westerner discusses, say, Hinduism or Buddhism, he is always conscious of the fundamental differences between these ideologies and his own. He may admire this or that of their ideas, but would naturally never consider the possibility of substituting them for his own. Because he a priori admits this impossibility, he is able to contemplate such really alien cultures with equanimity and often with sympathetic appreciation. But when it comes to Islam - which is by no means as alien to Western values as Hindu or Buddhist philosophy - this Western equanimity is almost invariably disturbed by an emotional bias. Is it perhaps, I sometimes wonder, because the values of Islam are close enough to those of the West to constitute a potential challenge to many Western concepts of spiritual and social life?...to find a truly convincing explanation of this prejudice [against Islam], one has to look far backward into history and try to comprehend the psychological background of the earliest relations between the Western and the Muslim worlds. What occidentals think and feel about Islam today is rooted in impressions that were born during the Crusades. ...The damage caused by the Crusades was not restricted to a clash of weapons: it was, first and foremost, an intellectual damage - the poisoning of the Western mind against the Muslim world through a deliberate misrepresentation of the teachings and ideals of Islam. ...It was at the time of the Crusades that the ludicrous notion that Islam was a religion of crude sensualism and brutal violence, of an observance of ritual instead of a purification of the heart entered the Western mind and remained there. ...The shadow of the Crusades hovers over the West to this day; and all its reactions toward Islam and the Muslim world bear distinct traces of that die-hard ghost."[523]

The French philosopher Gustave Le Bon described this enmity toward Islam in his book "La Civilisation des Arabes":

"After such an account, the reader might be asking himself why the influence of the Arabs is so unrecognized today by scientists whose freedom of thought should place above any religious prejudice. This question I have posed to myself as well, and I think there is only one answer: That in truth, the independence of our opinions is more apparent than real, and that we actually do not possess the freedom to think on certain subjects as we wish. There are always two men within us: The modern man that resulted from our personal studies, from the moral and intellectual environment surrounding us, and the ancient man slowly molded by the influence of his ancestors, and whose unconscious soul is nothing more than the synthesis of a long past. This unconscious soul is the one, and the only one that speaks in the majority of men, and under diverse names, maintains in them the same beliefs. It dictates to them their opinions, and the opinions thus dictated seem too free in appearance not to warrant respect.

However, the disciples of Muhammad have been for centuries the most fearsome enemies Europe had known. When they did not make us tremble with their arms such as during the times of Charles Martel, during the period of the crusades, or when they were threatening Europe after the conquest of Constantinople, the Muslims humiliated us with the crashing superiority of their civilization, and it is only recently that we escaped from their influence.

The inherited prejudices we hold against Islam and its disciples have been accumulated during too many centuries not to be part of our organization. These prejudices are as natural and as inveterate as the hatred - sometimes hidden, always deep - of the Jews against the Christians.

If we add to our inherited prejudices against the Mohammedans that other equally inherited prejudice, and which increases with each generation through our detestable classic education, that the sciences and literature of the past came exclusively from the Greek and the Latin, we will easily understand why the immense influence of the Arabs on the history of the civilization of Europe is this widely unrecognized.

It will always seem humiliating to some minds that it is to infidels that Christian Europe is indebted for coming out of barbarism, and a matter this humiliating in appearance can only be reluctantly admitted."[524]

The proliferation of the southern organizations - especially those that are financially independent and do not submit to political bargain - has strengthened the idea of the "civil society" on the global level, which has engendered a need to think and act according to a global, not a Western concept. Activists of the South possess their own independent institutions and refuse any hegemonic or coercive relationship. They aspire to cooperation on a par with the rest of the world, built on mutual respect. This springs from the organizations' officials' belief that the field is open to everybody and the world's needs require more of these independent organizations, not less.

Dr. Haytham Manna, President of the International Bureau for Humanitarian NGOs, has emphasized this point in the defense of the Islamic charities, saying:

"The aggression that the Islamic or southern humanitarian organizations actually undergo imposes a re-examination and a re-evaluation of the structure, role, and action of these organizations. However, this requirement of neutrality of these organizations in their own vision of the world, cannot have any meaning since each organization in the world, has already its own program and objectives, thus their denomination —"World doctors", "Catholic rescue", "Islamic rescue" - which links the members, regroup an ensemble of shared concepts in what concerns the world's vision, the definition of non-governmental organization, and of what should be the solidarity of the international action. Then it seems impossible to interfere in their direct quarrel and in their initial destination, no

matter the country's origin and the reason behind their creation. In spite of their will, the humanitarian and charitable organizations exceeded their immediate mission that consists on helping a family, educating children, diminishing war tragedies, and thus became the protection's central guaranties of economic and socio-cultural rights in the world. In this sense, far from belonging to a partisan political program or to a government, they become the society's collective patrimony.[525]

2- The lack of incriminating evidence

The American media and field campaigns against the Islamic charities have started in all parts of the world after the events of September 11 under the banner of the "war on terror". Three years afterward, the campaigns are still going strong, openly accusing the charities of supporting terror.

The American mass media have deftly used this opportunity to spread a wide net of suspicion on every entity that falls under the title of Islamic charity organizations. The US administration has taken field, legal, and legislative measures against those charities supposedly linked to terrorism in a way that raises many questions about the campaign and the corresponding accusations, which necessitates judicious study and scrutiny of the evidences and the outcome of the campaign:

Is it really geared toward eradicating the so-called "terrorism"? Is it really a campaign to dry up its financial sources, even though, as seen in September 11, terrorists do not need much money to carry out their acts? Are these organizations implicated in supporting terrorism?

Are there other hidden objectives for this campaign, for which the "war on terror" is only a front? Does the incrimination of a delinquent organization necessitate this global mass media campaign? Wasn't it sufficient to bring the incriminating evidence to the courts and concerned governments within the US or abroad?

After thorough study and investigation, it is apparent that the stated objectives are only a front concealing other goals. These goals transpire through the evidences and results of the campaign which have been presented in this book. Analysis of the media and field campaigns, statements and writings of officials in the political, information, cultural, and humanitarian fields, and in research institutes, all point out to this conclusion.

For one thing: the media blitz against Islamic charities has raised the following question: was it a cover up or a substitute of the lack of evidence? Others wonder whether this deceptive media campaign was to form a global opinion that is hostile to the charities, or at least to cast doubt about their financial integrity. The media campaign was deceptive and misinforming because:

Reports and news did not rely on documentation. Commenting on these accusations, the British Jurists Society's Chairman said: "None of the forwarded accusations can hold out before the court."[526]

Moreover, participants in the International Conference held in Bahrain in November 27, 2002 declared: "There is no money laundering in Islamic banks." The difficulty of following money transactions in the age of electronic banking was highlighted by Rayburn Hesse, former chief of financial intelligence at the US Department of State, who said: "No one knows how much money moves outside the traditional commercial banking system... With the advent of e-mail and cell phones, it is much harder to trace their kinds of transactions."[527] Some bankers insisted that "the nature of banking system in the area, and the amount of money transferred outside the banking system make it almost impossible to trace the flow of money." An Omani banker said:

"The United States can never be certain whether the money ends up in terrorists hands or is used for humanitarian purposes."[528] In brief, the futility of this endeavor is summed up by a Swiss banker who said: "Looking for money transactions that support terrorism is like looking for a needle in a straw pile."

Did America want to make up for these insurmountable difficulties by mounting this media campaign, churning misinformation and fabricating accusations against the charities? The comprehensive campaign has included all Islamic institutions and even Islamic banks. It was characterized by distortions, cover ups, intimidations, alarmism, and misreading or misunderstanding of certain events, with the conspicuous absence of strong evidence; tactics reminiscent of the McCarthy era. The United Nation has warned that the "war on terror" has been marked by haphazardness and confusion.[529]

The United Arab Emirate Central Bank Manager has warned in October 30, 2001that: "There is an orchestrated media campaign to tarnish the image of the Islamic banking system in the Gulf." Moreover, "a commission chaired by L. Paul Bremer, a counterterrorism expert, [and later the military occupation governor of Iraq] concluded that the government is unable to trace fundraising by terrorists," announced *The Washington Post*.[530]

Lack of evidence and the difficulty of conviction have pushed the US to heavily rely on secret evidence to ensure that the defendants and their lawyers do not get access to alleged evidence. According to this new lopsided legal situation, the existence or lack of existence of evidence has become irrelevant.

A review of the 9/11 Commission Report confirms that there are no criminal charges against Islamic charities, and there is nothing in the report that indicates that any person of those responsible for the attacks belonged to any of the Islamic charities, whether in the US or abroad, or has received financial aid from them. Nowhere in the official report is there evidence or a specific event that proves Islamic charities have supported terrorism in any country of the world.

So why is the US administration barking at the wrong tree? Was this propaganda war a cover up of its failure to find and punish the culprits in the 9/11 attacks? Or to distract the American people from the clumsy way their institutions have treated the whole affair?

Open Target:

America's inclusion of the Saudi Commission for Relief and Charity Work Abroad on the list of those implicated in the September 11 attacks as being an organization that supports terror confirms the specific targeting of Muslim charities without incriminating evidence or any specific misconduct. Needless to say, the organization has stopped all activities since its designation.

The New York South District Court has added a number of Saudi organizations, and Saudi and other Arab individuals, to the list of defendants by request of the lawyers of the 9/11 victims' families. The Saudi Commission for Relief and Charity, which was created in March 2004 to exclusively be in charge of charity works outside Saudi Arabia, has been included in the list.

It is interesting to note that Attorney Martin McMahon predicted such move in a statement to the Saudi newspaper, *al-Watan*, explaining that problems facing Islamic charities will not be solved by changing their names. Changing names or changing faces will have no effect on the legal issues Saudi charities face in foreign countries especially in the United States. They will rather pay dearly because of an organization with a new identity that lacks practical experience. McMahon also said that concerning the US law, the heir (successor) organization will bear the responsibility of the defunct ones, exactly like a company which cannot avoid legal allegations by simply declaring bankruptcy or by selling out, or by merging in another one. In other words, the legal allegations will continue, and what is more, the allegations of terror support will include the new organizations as well.

McMahon's predictions were right. The commission did not even start its work that it was accused of terror support, although the accusations sprung from the fact that the commission is exclusive and is not a coordinating or supervising entity, which permits the organizations to keep their names and identities, and thus each organization is left to face the allegations independently.

Finally, the fact that it was hard to bring any tangible evidence against the charities, in spite of the tremendous efforts to scrutinize their financial transactions and their activities, and in spite of the comprehensive campaign of allegations that touched almost every Islamic organization under the sun, is a proof of their financial and administrative discipline in their country of origin, especially that they are subject to governmental supervision and financial control. Some are required to submit annual budgets sanctioned by approved accountants. In some Arab countries, the organizations' finances and administration are under direct control of the government, a situation much different from the one in the West where the charities' only official relation with the government is the tax exempt status. If this financial discipline was observed before the events of September 11, it is irrational to think that the charities would behave otherwise after the 9/11 events.

Some Islamic organizations that have been accused of supporting terrorism, had legal connections with international organizations, and were abiding by the United Nations' rules and regulations. One of the requirements of this relation is that the international organizations have the right to be informed of the charities' projects, their field works, and their annual budgets. But what might have roused the suspicion of some skeptics was that Islamic organizations, especially the ones in Arab countries, do not publish their reports in languages other than their own, because they consider charity giving an internal affair, as it is the case with organizations in other (developed) countries.

The violation of the Islamic charities' rights in America and elsewhere has transgressed all rules of law. The most fundamental legal assumption that one is innocent until proven guilty has been thrown out. Instead of demanding that the accusers prove their accusations, now the accused are required to prove their innocence.

In fact the propaganda campaign that has touched all Islamic charities without exception and most Islamic banking systems lacked objectivity. If these campaigns have targeted few Islamic charities and spared the rest, one might not be as suspicious, but to target all Islamic charities and cast a doubt on all as potential terror supporters leads one to question the motives of these campaigns.

3-Targeting all humanitarian organizations concerned with Palestine

One of the key points in American actions concerning Islamic charities is the Palestinian issue. Islamic charities in the US and elsewhere that have been specifically concerned with helping the Palestinians by building schools, hospitals, providing for orphans and widows, and helping the poor have roused the ire of Zionist Jewish organizations in the US, which started a blizzard of misinformation and warnings against Islamic charities. Islamic charities have been targeted by this media campaign even before the September 11 events. In an article in *The Jewish monthly*, Steve Emerson, *a* "ubiquitous 'terrorism expert' who eagerly presents his biases as objective analysis"[531], and whose" career suggests his priority is not so much news as it is an unrelenting attack against Arabs and Muslims"[532] ("He's poison," says investigative author Seymour Hersh)[533], smeared Muslims with a broad brush, asserting that "unfortunately, nearly all of the Islamic organizations in the United States that define themselves as religiously or culturally Muslim in character have today been totally captured or dominated by radical fundamentalist elements."[534] He warned the Senate subcommittee of the existence of "a vast interlocking network of activists and believers collaborating with one another from country to country. The nexus of Islamic fundamentalists stretches from Cairo to Brooklyn, from Khartoum to Brooklyn, and from Gaza to Washington."[535]

The September 11 events were a catalyst that launched this campaign to the forefront, where the Jewish organizations have cleverly used it to their advantage: immediately after, the Holy Land Foundation, based in Richardson, Texas and with branches in California, New Jersey, and Illinois, has been closed. *Az-Zaitouna* Arabic newspaper published in the US commented that President Bush's order on December 4, 2001 to freeze the assets of the Holy Land Foundation was a gift to the Israeli Government.[536] In the presidential executive order, the US President announced that the causes of this closure was the support of families and sons of Hamas and Islamic Jihad members. Thus the largest Islamic charity in the US which is concerned with the plight of the Palestinians has been arbitrarily closed, its assets frozen, without legal due process. The same happened to Global Relief Foundation, another Islamic charity providing aid to the Palestinians. The campaign moved afterwards to Palestine itself, where Islamic banking institutions were targeted such as al-Aqsa International Bank and Beit al-Mal Holdings Company, both based in the Palestinian occupied territories.[537] This has been followed by the closure of organizations that supported the Palestinians in Europe and other parts of the world, such as the al-Aqsa Charity Association in Aachen, Germany. More than 60% of the Palestinian population has fallen under the poverty line because of the global siege on charities providing aid to them, as stated in official reports. In his report to the UN Security Council, Teje Roed-Larsen, UN Special Coordinator for the Middle East Peace Process, warned of the Human catastrophe that faces the Palestinian population, denouncing the killing of three UN employees, and the destruction of the UN food storehouse in Gaza by the Israeli Defense Forces (IDF). "The IDF's security measures were creating a humanitarian catastrophe in the Palestinian areas," he said[538]

Just as there is a connection between the campaign against the charities and the Palestinian issue, there is also a connection between the fundamentalist religious right and Israel, which some authors call "the umbilical cord" between America and Israel which is the belief of the extreme right that God said "They that bless Israel I will bless, and they that curse Israel, I will curse."

Officials at the Islamic charities have sensed this strong connection between the American campaign against them and the Palestinian issue: It is sufficient that a charity employs or even deals with a single Palestinian who has a direct or indirect relation with Hamas or Islamic Jihad, to have its assets frozen or even the charities closed. Strong lobby forces are behind this demonization of Islamic charities, and who gains tremendously by keeping this campaign going strong. In his book "Silent No More", former Senator Paul Findley wrote: "Another factor that keeps false images of Islam alive is the aggressive lobbying that occurs in Washington on behalf of U.S. aid to Israel...In this lobbying, the specter of Muslim-sponsored terrorism is a frequent theme. It is used to rationalize the Jewish state's harsh treatment of Palestinians, most of whom are Muslims, and to justify Israel's periodic military assaults against Lebanon, where Muslims predominate. The terrorist image is the foundation of Israel's demand for regular U.S. grants of high-tech weaponry, as well as financial aid, to bolster its defenses against possible missile attacks from Syria, Iraq, and Iran, as well as other states where Islam is dominant."[539]

Fahmi Huwaydi of *al-Majalla* Magazine has pointed out to this connection saying : "The Israeli Government was successful in winning over the American leadership by convincing it that the repression of the Palestinian resistance was part of the war on terrorism. This has engendered grave results that all pour into one conduit: the attempts to completely destroy the Islamic Palestinian resistance by any means. Some of these results are:

Giving free hand to the Israeli prime minister in persecuting the Palestinian population by destroying their houses, uprooting their orchard trees, cutting their utilities, bombing the residence of the Palestinian Authority, kidnapping and killing Palestinian activists, and terrorizing the innocent Palestinian population all over the territories. This has led to the abortion of all attempts to peace during the last eight years.

- Condoning Israel's aggressions: In its official statements, the US administration has considered Israel's actions against the Palestinian a self defense, giving therefore for the first time in history the right of the occupier to defend the continuation of its occupation, a situation in complete contradiction with the international rules and agreements which have acknowledged the right of people to resist occupations by all means even armed struggles.
- Condemning Palestinian resistance movements: Washington has announced that Hamas and Islamic Jihad are terrorist organizations. As a result their assets were frozen, their members were hunted and killed by the Israeli Government, and all who helped or sheltered their members have been considered as terrorists. It is important to point out that this is the first time that a

Palestinian resistance movement has been designated as a terrorist organization which engendered measures to eliminate the Palestinian resistance.

- Pressuring the European Union countries: Washington has put pressure on the European Union countries to adopt the same position towards the Palestinian resistance. The European Union's previous position toward the Palestinian resistance was characterized by its neutrality, and cautiousness, but this has changed when the EU has asked the late Palestinian President Yasser Arafat to dismantle the infrastructure of the two organizations because their armed struggle was considered terrorism.[540]

The engine driving the US to adopt this policy against the Palestinians and the Muslim world in general is the Jewish PACs and the pro-Israel Christian Zionist lobby. Their strategy is to raise people's fear against an alleged Islamic threat and to equate the Palestinian struggle with terrorism. "Terrorism, everybody is talking terrorism now. The Israeli code of fear is now shared by the world," exclaimed Ramsey Clark. "In any American newspaper, you will find that the terrorism against the US and Israel is treated identically and must be addressed in unison. Of course this is not the case; it is their presence in Palestine."[541] Former Congressman Paul Findley argued that US Middle East policy is not designed by US officials but it is the creation of two religious communities in America, (Jewish and Christian Right) communities that have attained great political power. For over 35 years, successive US administrations have engaged by proxy in what must be described as a war of territorial conquest undertaken by the State of Israel, he said and added: "We continue this proxy war."[542] Israel's occupation of the Palestinian territories puts it in continuous confrontation with the Islamic resistance movements which it could not subdue, for this it needs a greater power. Moreover, Israel's apartheid plan, its "ethnic cleansing can only be implemented in the shadow of a major war against the Arabs, a war to Balkanize the region."[543]

But does this policy serve the interests of the United States? "Indeed, I hold that Christian Zionism threatens not just the lives of Palestinians and other Arabs," says Grace Halsell, "but the very existence of the United States. Because of the cult of Israel, we have become a nation that does not have its own Middle East policy, but the policy the Government of Israel tells us to have."[544]

Is there any doubt left that one of the prominent goals of this campaign against the charities is to impoverish the Palestinians to the brink of famine, bring them down to their knees and thus squash the Palestinian Intifadha, and to eliminate the resistance and strengthen the Israeli occupation?

4- Support for American religious fundamentalism and its ideology

Religion was never absent from the American political decision-making processes, especially those that concern the Middle East. Because of the domination of Evangelical fundamentalists, and Christian Zionists, in the political arena, notably during George W. Bush administration, whose political positions and decisions are inspired by their ideology, a global war on "terror" was unleashed, Israeli Prime Minister Sharon was given free hand to butcher the Palestinian population in Gaza and the West Bank, and a ferocious war is going on against the people of Iraq. Grace Halsell, former White House staff writer for President Lyndon Johnson, journalist and author of numerous books, among them "Prophecy and Politics" and "Forcing God's Hand" wrote: "Grounds for their [Christian Right] growth were made fertile by the presidencies of Ronald Reagan and George Bush, each of whom was indebted to the New Christian Right for his election."[545] Frank Kermode, author of "The End of the World," said about former President

Reagan: "America had for eight years a president who believed that he was living in the end time and rather hoped it might arrive during his administration."[546] It should be noted that in 2004, the staff of the Church Report Magazine was "pleased to name President George W. Bush as this year's most influential Christian. Whether battling terrorism, securing funds for the Faith-Based Initiative Program or comforting injured soldiers at Walter Reed Hospital, President Bush exemplifies the qualities of being a Christian and a leader. Even when faced with difficult decisions that may not always be the most popular ones at the time, the President stands firm in his faith and strong in his convictions."[547]

The Islamic charitable work was capable during the last decades to reach the areas that used to be the exclusive monopoly of the churches, places in remote areas of Africa, and Asia, and to contain the spread of Christianization Al-Roken noted in *the daily star:* "During the 1980s and 1990s, Islamic charities were thorns in the side of Western, mainly Church-run, charities that had hitherto monopolized aid to Asia and Africa"[548]. The real aim of the campaigns targeting Islamic charities is to restore the monopoly of Western organizations and "to weaken the bonds that have been built between the Gulf States and recipient nations, and to distort the image of wealthy Arabs and Muslims." The article concludes: "What is important is for the Gulf states to wake up to the plots targeting the humanitarian efforts they spent the last twenty years building."[549]

Christian Zionists' Influence on the American Administration

A direct relation exists between politics and the religious belief in certain prophecies. Some Churches teach their followers that it is their obligation to fulfill the will of God - as described by the church - and that God has chosen some people to help in this task.

Christian Zionist movements have a prominent role in the formulation of the US politics today, and are a strong force behind the current US President George W. Bush. The political implication of their beliefs is apparent in the following aspects:

* The belief that the Jews are God's "chosen people". Therefore the support of Israel is not only a political decision but a religious obligation. "What is the message of the Christian Zionists?" asks Grace Halsell, "Simply stated it is this: Every act taken by Israel is orchestrated by God, and should be condoned, supported, and even praised by the rest of us. 'Never mind what Israel does,' say the Christian Zionists, 'God wants this to happen.'"[550].

* The belief that God has promised the land of Palestine to the Jews. This means not only the support of the creation of Israel as a nation exclusively for the Jews, but also the support of settlements and the Judeaization of the West Bank.

* The belief that Jerusalem is part of the "Promised Land" to the Jews and this means the support of Israel in gaining international recognition on annexing and Judeaizing Jerusalem and taking it as the eternal capital for the Jews. Christian Zionists believe that "Christ cannot return to earth until certain events occur: The Jews must return to Palestine, gain control of Jerusalem and rebuild a temple, and then we all must engage in the final, great battle called Armageddon."[551]

* The belief that one of the conditions of Christ's Second Coming is the rebuilding of the temple. Many Jews believe that the site on which the temple should be built is the Haram al-Sharif which encompasses the al-Aqsa Mosque, Muslims' third holiest mosque. The mosque is an obstacle, they claim and it should be demolished. "Militant Jews …want a Jerusalem that is pure Jewish - without evidence of inhabitants of the other monotheistic faiths and their shrines. Surprisingly, millions of US evangelical Christians endorse

and financially support this Jewish plan… Christian Zionists give generous donations of money as well as their gold wedding rings and gold earrings to finance the mosque's destruction. They know its destruction might well trigger wars culminating in Armageddon, but they welcome this."[552] To add insult to injury, Franklin Graham who said in his last book that Christianity and Islam are "as different as lightness and darkness," was the honored speaker at the Pentagon's Good Friday service on April 18, 2003. Inviting Graham to the service means that the Pentagon endorses his attacks on Islam, complained many Muslim groups.[553]

This fanatical thinking is the cause behind targeting Islamic charitable organizations on the global level no matter what their activities are, whether helping in education or orphanage projects, giving aid to the poor and the refugees. Banks and other Islamic organizations were not spared. The campaign has even reached the religious curricula in Muslim countries. This confirms the belief that this campaign was really not a reaction to what happened on September 11, but has taken advantage of this event to dry up the sources of the Islamic religion in the Muslim world, to please the fundamentalist Christian right, to fulfill the Jewish Zionists dream to keep away the Islamic - but not Jewish - religion from the Palestinian issue, and to yield to the pressure of the Jewish lobby such as B'nai B'rith and to the pro-Israel fundamentalist right.

5-False Stereotyping of Islam and Muslims:

This campaign was launched by organizations, groups and individuals in the political, military, and information fields who are masquerading as specialists on Islam, but in fact their aim is to defame the Muslims and their religion for various motives, and with various means. These people have great influence and power over the American media, and the religious media in particular; people such as Steve Emerson, Daniel Pipes, Judith Miller, and Karl Thomas, who have started the campaign of misinformation more than a year and a half before the events of September 11. This is indeed a revealing fact about the campaign's true motives.

Jewish and Christian extremists view Islam as a historical challenge and a danger, and this stereotyping of Islam and Muslims was successful to a great extent, and has infiltrated - whether by design or not - the American mind. In his book "Silent No More," Senator Paul Findley writes: "Sometimes false images of Islam arise from malice, at other times, as William Shakespeare might write, from 'vaulting ambition'."[554] Salam al-Marayati, national director of the Los Angeles-based Muslim Public Affairs Council, said: "There are many hypocrites among Christian leaders, but unlike other religions, Islam is routinely linked with violence in news reports and articles. Religious identification rarely occurs when awful deeds occur at the hands of people of other faiths. News accounts never identified the slaughter of Kosovar Albanians as killings by Eastern Orthodox Serbs, of Burmese as killings by Buddhists, or of Palestinians as killings by Jews. Perpetrators are routinely identified by nationality, not religious affiliation –except when they are Muslims. Violent Christians are not seen as discrediting Christianity. But if any Muslim does wrong, it is invariably reported as an element in an 'Islamic threat' to America. When we pause and reflect on the venom of the 'Jewish' state that invades Lebanon and kills thousands, that bombs Palestinian homes and transfers Palestinians from their homeland, we resist the temptation of thinking that Judaism has any violent or intolerant underpinning. Definitely a double standard applies here, in which Islam is blamed for international conflicts."[555] Findley added: "This double standard reinforces the most widely held and virulent stereotype of Islam, the one that links Muslims with terrorism."[556]

Manufacturing Provocations:

Gene Bird, a former US Foreign Service officer who heads the Washington-based Council on the National Interest and closely follows Middle-East related activities at both ends of Pennsylvania Avenue in Washington, called the terrorist image of Islam a "hot button". He added: "It is used frequently, because it gets action. It plays on fears and stirs emotions. It is cultivated and propagated by lobbyists, because they know it wins support for multibillion dollar, unconditional grants to Israel year after year."[557] Bird noted that the stereotype prompts governmental decisions that are costly to the American people. "In the past decade, the bias has facilitated annual US grants to Israel that averaged $4.7 billion."[558] Paul Findley remarked: "By providing unconditional aid, despite Israel's abuse of Palestinian rights, succeeding US administrations have stained America's reputation as a champion of universal human rights."[559]

The author also mentioned that: "In 1994, the year after radicals bombed the World Trade building in New York City, public television stations across the nation broadcast Emerson's principal triumph, a television documentary called "Jihad in America: An Investigation of Islamic Extremists' Activities in the United States.' It was a patchwork of dark predictions, innuendoes, and disturbing glimpses of frenzied strange people chanting loudly in a foreign language. The film spread a cloud of fear across the nation and did more to create distrust of US Muslims than any other event in my memory."[560] Paul Findley further adds: "I doubt that the term 'Emersonism' will make its way into the dictionary, but through 'Jihad in America,' Emerson damaged American society more permanently than McCarthyism."[561]

6-Settling political scores:

The allegations against Islamic charities have pushed some parties and governments to settle political scores and mobilize public opinions for the benefit of some political and religious factions in the US and abroad. Reactions of Muslims and Arab nations are included in this framework. Some Arab states have increased their harassment and oppression of Islamic political activists and their organizations and parties, closing their affiliated charities even though they were not charged with any accusation. But they took the war on terror as an excuse to further violate the human rights of their populations. The specter of terrorism is raised by most states and political parties to eliminate the opposition, or to withhold the legitimate rights of the people. Terrorism allegations have become a mean of vengeance against individuals, groups, and organizations. In the Palestinian occupied territories, the Israeli Government has adopted the most atrocious type of terrorism, with the tacit support of the American media, to settle accounts with anyone - organization or state - who supports the Palestinian people. The war on terrorism has been exploited in Russia, China, India, Pakistan, Kashmir, the Philippines, Indonesia, the Balkan states, and many other states. States all over the globe rose in unison to settle old scores under the banner of the war on terror, to such extent that some human and civil rights organizations have warned against this aspect of "the war on terror."

The numerous drastic measures against the Islamic charities in the US and abroad, and the ongoing campaign against them that has started before the 9/11 events all point out that they were targeted, but the 9/11 events gave the US Government the chance to put them in the forefront of the war's agenda and, some may say, to settle the score with them.

Examples abound of actions that have been taken, and are still being taken, against Muslims to settle political scores in many countries. One example that exposes the extent of exploitation of the war on terrorism is what has been going on in India: Indian security apparatus has closed mosques and Muslims' schools in six provinces. "The Indian Government is adopting a new policy of closing mosques and schools that are classified by their intelligence agencies as centers of anti-nationalist activities," says *al-Hayat* newspaper of London.[562] Lal Krishna Advani, India's vice Prime

Minister and one of the extremist hawks in the governing Janata Party in New Delhi, is behind this project.

Advani confirmed in an interjection before the Indian Parliament's Internal Affairs Committee that the government was planning to present a bill to the parliament to "regulate the places of worship" and that the government was still studying the possible implementation of the bill. Right after the September 11 event, the Indian Government asked its intelligence agencies to prepare a list of what they described as "illegal mosques and schools." An official at the Indian Interior Ministry claimed that a large number of mosques and Islamic schools have spread along six provinces on the Indian borders. Advani said that the increase of schools and mosques falls in the grand scheme of penetrating the frontiers and inciting the inhabitants, and the secret agencies have already asked the Interior Ministry to move quickly to limit the spread of the "Illegal" mosques, relying on the new regulations, considering this a most prominent priority. Advani disclosed that the central government has asked the different regional governments to move against the religious organizations whose activities are in conflict with the 1988 rules concerning the misuse of religious organizations.[563]

In fact, terror allegations have become a strong bargaining chip in the political arena which put the whole Muslim world and the Muslim organizations at a great disadvantage. Is one of the objectives of the campaign to inflict such negative results on the Muslims and their organizations?

7-Destroying and weakening the sources of Muslim power

Mohammed al-Roken writes in the Daily Star: "There are many ways to judge how advanced a country is. Levels of education, culture, material prosperity and technological progress are all yardsticks used to compare between nations. Another important yardstick involves the number of nongovernmental civil institutions active in the country and how large a role they play in serving society."[564] The real power of a state resides in the power of its citizens' groups, of its independent organizations, including its humanitarian organizations. To target these organizations would result in weakening the state. Islamic charities in particular are a symbol of Muslim unity regardless of national borders and political delineations. They represent the pains of Muslims across the world and also their hopes; a substitute to the imperialistic hegemony of the powerful, and that is why they are targeted.

The perception of Islam and its organizations as competitors to the American hegemony might be one of the motives behind the campaign against Islamic charities. Islamic humanitarian organizations' comprehensive understanding of humanitarian aid includes mutual participation in development, and therefore holds the promise to be in the future a source of information and a strong competitor in the media and exchange of information. In spite of their young age and limited resources, Islamic charities, were successful in forming a strong tie between Muslim governments and also between Muslim populations around the globe, enriching the flow of information among the Muslims, and therefore they constitute a competing power from Washington to Palestine as expressed by Emerson. Thus, the ferocious campaign is not merely a matter of holding the Islamic charities accountable for certain mistakes they have committed, and it did not stop or even subsided for more than three years now, after targeting and effectively closing a score of charities, because it has marked certain Islamic charities to be gone, and prodded by hard-liners, has targeted countries as well, as stated in *Newsweek*, "The hard-liners want more…[They] are expected to ask the NSC to present the Saudis with an ultimatum: crack down on the suspected terrorist financiers or Washington will!"[565]

As recently as October 2004, the FBI has raided the office of the Islamic American Relief Agency, based in Columbia, Missouri, "hauling away boxes of records and computers. At the same time, federal agents also raided the home of the group's former executive director and interviewed as many as 90 others across the United States, people who had either been donors or had other suspected ties to the group."[566] This tactic of interrogating donors is meant to intimidate them and keep them away from the charities, thus cutting the charities' life blood, an effective way to destroy them.

Ahmad Yusuf, former President of the United Association for Research and Studies has pointed out to old motives and objectives even before the 9/11 events, where he wrote in an article titled *"Targeting reformation capabilities under the excuse of terrorism"* that what he saw as the openly hostile US policy toward the Muslim world and its aspirations is targeted at killing the factors of changes and reform in the Muslim nations, which are promoted by an Islamic and nationalist revival. This policy serves to preserve the US vital interests, and economic privileges in the Arab region. Therefore, the striking of the Islamic - and even nationalistic - activities under the pretext of fighting terrorism or extremism, will be Washington's and the West's plan for the foreseeable future.[567]

The goal of the campaigns of allegations against the Islamic charities might also be to exert political, military, or economic pressure on certain countries in order to get more concessions or privileges, such as in the Lockerbie case which lingered for years during which pressure was exerted and huge amounts of money were extracted.

Officials in Islamic charities noticed that some parties who have strong influence on the US administration regard the charities as factors of progress and change in their countries and communities, and that they are one of the centers of power that refuses cultural globalization, and Westernization, and which have a positive role in reinforcing the religious identity of the Muslim nation.

The charities' activities have greatly participated in uniting Muslims across the countries, and have achieved what many Arab and Muslim political entities could not achieve. Some Islamic charities constituted through their successful work a connectedness between the donor and the receiving countries especially where no diplomatic relation exists between the two. The unwarranted vilification of Islamic charitable organizations has resulted in preventing them from exercising their rights whether inside the US or outside, which in turn will serve the interests of the American extreme right that seeks to weaken Muslim countries and peoples.

Such campaigns in the US seek to silence all Muslim voices that are starting to demand their rights in many fields, and to close all Muslim institutions, including the ones that are mainly working in the research field such as the International Institute of Islamic Thought (IIIT) in Virginia, or organizations that concentrate only on civil rights and Muslims' relations with others in the US such as the Council on American Islamic Relations (CAIR). In reality the events of September 11 have marked the start of a multifaceted war, as openly stated by Colin Powell, former US Secretary of State: "We're asking all of the nations to join together to use political action, diplomatic action, economic action, legal action, law enforcement action, and, if necessary, join with us… in military action."[568] Thomas Friedman has explicitly said that the war was not only about terrorism; he wrote: "If 9/11 was indeed the onset of World War III, we have to understand what this war is about. We're not fighting to eradicate "terrorism." Terrorism is just a tool. We're fighting to defeat an ideology… World War II and the cold war were fought to defeat secular totalitarianism - Nazism and Communism - and World War III is a battle against religious totalitarianism, a view of the world that my faith must reign supreme and can be affirmed and held passionately only if all others are negated. That's Bin Ladenism. But unlike Nazism, religious totalitarianism can't be fought by armies alone. It has to be fought in schools, mosques, churches and synagogues, and can be defeated only with the help of imams, rabbis and priests."[569] Thus it can be said that America is on a crusade against Islam, veiled under the pretext of the war on terror or on religious totalitarianism, but indeed the real goal is to hit at the core of Islam, starting by its easy targets, Islamic charities, and striking at one of its pillars, Zakat, which forms a strong tie between the rich and the poor and a cooperation between the governments and their people, and which Muslims in America and elsewhere are finding great difficulty to give it to those it is due to. In fact Huntington revealed in his book, "The Clash of Civilizations,": "The underlying problem for the West is not Islamic fundamentalism. It is Islam!"[570]

8-Effects and consequences: Further evidence that exposes the truth

In his article "Under Suspicion," Gideon Burrows has highlighted the negative consequences incurred by the campaigns on the Islamic charities, saying: "A combination of police raids, media attacks and regulatory investigations - resulting in a draining away of public support and the loss of hundreds of thousands of pounds in donations - has made the past year probably the worst ever for the UK's Islamic charity sector."[571]

Fadi Itani, director of north London Muslim Welfare House, said to the *Guardian* that he expected a drastic reduction in donations to Islamic charities, especially from overseas. "Well intentioned individuals who wish to contribute to charitable projects like ours, which provide for the most deprived in society, have become hesitant," he said. Burrows added: "US prosecutors investigating charities have published whole lists of donors, and people are afraid the same might happen here."[572]

Studies point out to the catastrophic effects of terror allegations on Islamic charities which might see their charity income drop like stones. News of closing or freezing the assets of Islamic organizations amidst allegations of terrorism left Muslims with the feeling that if they donated to Islamic charities their names might appear on a list even though they were sure the charities have done nothing wrong. Even charities which have been cleared of any wrongdoing could not shake out the "stigma of being investigated" and have suffered financially as a consequence.

Speakers at the Pace Law Review Symposium on Anti-Terrorism Financing Guidelines, have widely criticized the US Treasury Department guidelines, and said that the "situation has lead to a decrease in international philanthropy."[573] Estimate of the decrease in fundraising has reached 50% for some charities.[574] Benjamin Duncan wrote at *al-Jazeera* website: "Groups set up to assist impoverished peoples…are struggling to hold on to their base support, according to several representatives of the Muslim American community. Attorney Ladale George, a Chicago-based attorney who advises more than 30 American Muslim charities, said there has been an estimated 40% reduction in financial support since September 11 for the groups he represents."[575]

Attorney Ladale George said "many of the groups he works with have complained that the post-9/11 drop-off in funding is only hurting the people who need help the most," wrote *al-Jazeera* news channel in its website.[576]

Of course the most damaging consequences were the closing of many Islamic organizations in the US and around the world. Global Relief Foundation and Holy Land Foundation were the victims in the US whereas al-Haramain Foundation based in

Saudi Arabia, a behemoth of charitable organization comparable in size and reach to the United Way of America, has been brought down. A score of Islamic organizations based in Europe have also been closed, organizations that provide aid to Palestinians were specifically targeted. It is left to the reader's to imagine the effect of these measures on the poor, orphans, and destitute around the world.

The unjust measures against the Islamic charities were multiple and varied from freezing the assets to closure, to seizing the charities' computers, to defamation and unfound allegations. Even when attempts to close or freeze the assets of an organization after allegation of terrorism support have failed, they were nevertheless closed for reasons other than terrorism. Closing is the goal and the reason will easily be fabricated for that purpose. For example, when attempts to close al-Haramain branch in Bosnia and Herzegovina under the allegation of terror support have failed, the branch was later closed because foreign workers were employed without permission.[577] Al-Haramain Oregon branch was closed without even being charged. And in Egypt, the US ambassador asked the government to close 25 local religious organizations at once in November 2002, under the allegations of ties to al-Qaeda, but in fact the real reason was the effective role the organizations had in boycotting US products![578]

The campaign has indiscriminately targeted organizations without differentiating between the local ones such as in Egypt and Yemen, and the ones that are active on the international level, such as the Saudi and Kuwaiti charities, taking both administrative and financial measures against them.

These results that this study has reached would not have been possible if there were not a concurrence of events, officials' statements, and the positions of some individuals who sought to find the truth. It is relevant to mention the opinion of Professor

Jonathan Benthall, anthropologist and fellow researcher, and co-author of "The Charitable Crescent" who personally told me, during our meeting in London on February 5, 2005, that he arrived at the same conclusion namely that he agreed that the allegations of terrorism against the Islamic charities were unfounded and lacked judicial finding of fact, though he disagreed on the motives and goals.

Finally, what has been mentioned here constitutes the most important evidence and proofs that expose the real objectives of the campaign that has targeted most, if not all, Islamic charities. The results of the campaign and the negative effects on the charities, the violation of many basic rights of organizations and individuals, the unjust accusations of the charities and the lopsided judicial procedures which left to the charities the burden to prove their innocence, doing away with the principle of "innocent until proven guilty", all this strongly indicates that the campaign's goals are beyond the war on terror financing. Were the neo-conservatives, the Zionists, and Christian Zionists, who were behind this campaign, successful in moving the Bush administration according to their visions and ideologies? Yes to a great extent. But does it serve the interests of the United States; does it promote the spread of democracy and freedom? No, but it does serve their Zionists' and neo-conservatives' interests. Needless to say that this campaign has violated the rights and curtailed the freedom of international and local non-governmental organizations, and has also violated the rights of many populations, and the sovereignty of many states

Islam and the West: Competition or Confrontation?

This question has come up many times: Is Islam a threat to the West? Is it part of the so-called "global gladiators?" The question has repeatedly been posed after the 9/11 events, and some answers have popped out in a score of articles and reports. The 9/11 Commission Report's answer to the question is clear:

"We're not in the middle of a war on terror" the commissioners say in the report. "We're not facing an axis of evil. Instead we are in the midst of an ideological conflict." Thomas Friedman echoed the same opinion: "We're fighting to defeat an ideology," he wrote. The report went even further to say: "We are facing a loose confederation of people who believe in a perverted stream of Islam that stretches from Ibn Taymiya to Sayyd Qutb." Thus, the large majority of Sunni Muslims who hold Ibn Taymiya as a respected scholar (who died almost 600 years ago) are targeted as enemies. David Brook wrote in the *New York Times*: "Our enemies are primarily an intellectual movement, not a terrorist army," suggesting to "set up a fund to build secondary schools across Muslim states" to correct their thinking. We are faced with a belief system that aims at "the restoration of the caliphate," he wrote. The message is: While the North American States were united centuries ago, and European countries are uniting now, as are many Asian countries, the Muslim countries have no right to even think about the possibility to unite, either economically, ideologically, or otherwise.

Perhaps Huntington has most clearly defined how the West sees Islam, when he wrote in his "clash of civilizations" book: "The Islamic Resurgence... [is] at least potentially threatening to the West."[579] He quoted a "very senior member of the Clinton administration pointing to Islam as the global rival of the West."[580]

While it is difficult to hastily answer this question, contrary to Huntington's convictions about the inevitable clash of civilizations, I believe that competition is a legitimate right shared by all religions and cultures, and that is for the good of humanity. Islam emphasizes the importance of competition, in doing good, high morality, and in work as stated in the Qur'an: "And for this let all those strive who want to strive."[581] Competition that enriches all civilizations is very different from a clash of civilizations. In the

1950s, Lester Pearson wrote that humans were moving into "an age when different civilizations will have to learn to live side by side in peaceful interchange, learning from each other, studying each other's history and ideals and art and culture, mutually enriching each others' lives. The alternative, in this overcrowded little world, is misunderstanding, tension, clash, and catastrophe."[582]

To the hidden forces that promote the clash of religions and civilizations, the war on so-called terrorism means a war on Islam, as some statements indicate - the "ideology of Islamic radicals is the great challenge of our new century...in many ways, this fight resembles the struggle against communism in the last century," declared President Bush.[583] They are confident that just as the West has triumphed against Nazism and communism, so it will prevail against Islam. Yet they do not realize that one of the major factors of the West's victories was that it was not against religious forces that possess a cultural and ideological alternative as in the case of Islam. The comparison is faulty because Islam and Islamic organizations - a global gladiator, as called by Toffler - spring from an ideology that has a long history and presents a political and cultural alternative. F. Gregory Gauss III writes in *Foreign Affairs* that Washington's Western democracy advocates "do not appreciate that in those [communist] regimes, liberalism prevailed because its great ideological competitor, communism, was thoroughly discredited, whereas the Arab world offers a real ideological alternative to liberal democracy: the movement that claims as its motto 'Islam is the solution.'"[584]

The West's perception of Islam as a threat stems mostly from a misunderstanding of what this religion stands for. This misunderstanding has been worsened by some extremist groups' defamation of Islam. Perhaps a clarification of some basic aspects of Islam, and comments from some Western thinkers, would help better understand Islam and Muslims - including their institutions and organizations - as maybe a competing religion and culture, but not as an enemy:

1-The Concept of God: Muslims believe that there is a God Who created this universe and all that is in it. He knows the needs of all creatures - those that are known to man and those that are not. All events and acts of His creatures are recorded and well-kept with Him. He has sent prophets and messengers with sacred books to enlighten and save humanity. He is the God of all human beings regardless of their languages, their races, and their ethnic backgrounds. God provides for all.[585]

2-Islam : Islam is the last of the heavenly messages to all humankind.[586] The message of Islam is a continuation of all messages before it and is a complement to them. The essence of the message is "to worship God alone and to follow the prophets' example in doing good." The same message is in the Bible where Jesus said: "Worship the Lord your God, and serve Him only."[587]

Religious belief is a necessary component in all human lives. Leopold Weiss, Austrian thinker and philosopher, wrote: "The cardinal task of every religion [is] to show man not merely how to feel but also how to live rightly. With an instinctive feeling of having been somehow let down by his religion, Western man had, over the centuries, lost all his real faith in Christianity; with the loss of this faith, he had lost the conviction that the universe was an expression of one Planning Mind and thus formed one organic whole; and because he had lost this conviction, he was now living in a spiritual and moral vacuum."[588] About the Western material life he wrote: "The current adoration of 'progress' was no more than a weak, shadowy substitute for an earlier faith in absolute values, a pseudo-faith devised by people who had lost all inner strength and were now deluding themselves with the belief that somehow, by mere evolutionary impulse, they would outgrow their present difficulties...I did not see how any of the new economic systems that stemmed from this illusionary faith could possibly constitute more than a palliative for Western society's misery; they could, at best, cure some of its symptoms, but never the cause."[589] After he discovered what distinguishes Islam from other religions, Weiss wrote: "Islam did not seem to be so much a religion in the popular sense of the word as, rather, a way of life; not so much a system of theology as a program of personal and social behavior based on the consciousness of God. Nowhere in the Koran could I find any reference to a need for 'salvation'. No original inherited sin stood between the individual and his destiny - for nothing shall be attributed to man but what he himself has striven for. No asceticism was required to open a hidden gate to purity: for purity was man's birthright, and sin meant no more than a lapse from the innate positive qualities with which God was said to have endowed every human being. There was no trace of any dualism in the consideration of man's nature: body and soul seemed to be taken as one integral whole."[590]

3-The Message and the Messenger: Prophet Muhammad was born in Makkah in 570 AD. His message came as a continuation, a completion, and a confirmation of the Books revealed to Moses and Jesus namely the Torah and the Bible. Prophet Muhammad was a man - not a deity - whose dates of birth and death are known and documented. His life, acts, ideas, and words were also recorded. God has sent him as a Messenger to all mankind, a Messenger of mercy to all humanity and not exclusively to the Arabs.

Muhammad was an exemplar husband, father, grandfather, and a caller and guide to the Truth, and he was a Messenger and Prophet. He was an open book for all to learn and has taught Muslims everything : the way they should clothe themselves, sleep, eat, and pray, even have marital intimacy. All details of his life are known, his life at home, in the mosque, with his friends, in the war fields, during prayer, and when he talks to the people of the Book. He is a source of knowledge for all Islamic laws, and a source of guidance for all mankind, and he is a brother of all the Prophets God has sent. He is a descendant of Ishmael, the son of Abraham. He and Prophets Isaac, Jacob, Joseph, Moses, and Jesus are brethren, and whoever believes in Muhammad must believe in them all. Muhammad's Message is in the Qur'an, which is the word of God revealed to Muhammad, and which is divinely guarded against alteration, a miracle from God: that not a single word or a single letter from the Qur'an has been added, removed, altered or even changed place for more than 1400 years. Leopold Weiss wrote about the Qur'an: "The Qur'an never left its followers forget that the life of this world was only one stage of man's way to a higher existence, and that his ultimate goal was of a spiritual nature. Material prosperity, it said, is desirable but not an end in itself."[591] And about the message of Islam, he wrote: "Its [Islam's] approach to the problems of the spirit seemed to be deeper than that of the Old Testament and had, moreover, none of the latter's predilection for one particular nation; and its approach to the problems of the flesh was, unlike the New Testament, strongly affirmative. Spirit and flesh stood each in its own right, as the twin aspects of man's God-created life. Was not perhaps this teaching, I asked myself, responsible for the emotional security I had so long sensed in the Arabs?" [592]

4-Historical Truth Regarding the Spread of Islam : At the dawn of Islam Arabs were very backward people, worshipping idols and believing in legends. When Islam started to spread, people from different tribes, cultures, and races came to embrace it. Islam has engendered one of the most prosperous civilizations in history, with clear principles and rules for all humanity. Among these are the rules stated by Prophet Muhammad during his farewell pilgrimage sermon addressing people in general, and not only Muslims, saying: "O people listen to me for I do not know whether I will be here next year in this august place. O people! Your blood and your wealth are as sacred as the sacredness of this day of yours, in this month of yours, until you meet your Lord. O people! Your Lord is One, and you are from the same father: you are all from Adam, and Adam is from dust, and the best among you is the most pious. There is no distinction between an Arab and a non-Arab except through piety. Everything pertaining to the days of ignorance is under my feet completely abolished. Abolished are also the blood revenges of the days of ignorance. And fear God concerning women!" Like any other civilization, the Arab-Islamic civilization had its days of prosperity, its days of supremacy when the principles on which it was built were spread far and wide in all corners of the globe. Then it passed by a phase of weakness and backwardness when its followers departed from these principles. Leopold Weiss has described this rise and decline of the Islamic civilization, writing: "The most important feature of that new civilization – a feature which set it entirely apart from all other movements in human history – was the fact that it had been conceived in terms of, and across from, a voluntary agreement of the people concerned. Here, social progress was not, as in all other communities and civilizations known to history, a result of pressure and counter pressure of conflicting interests, but part and parcel of an original 'constitution.' In other words, a genuine social contract lay at the root of things: not as a figure of speech formulated by later generations of power-holders in defense of their privileges, but as the real historic source of Islamic civilization."[593] In his book "Islam at the Crossroads," after analysis and comparison, Weiss came out with the strong conviction that "Islam as a spiritual and social phenomenon is sill, in spite of all the drawbacks caused by the deficiencies of the Muslims, by far the greatest driving force mankind has ever experienced."[594]

A reading in the history of Islam and how quickly it has spread, and it's just dealing with other civilizations help answer the question.[595]

5-Life and Death : Life and death are undeniable facts, and so are, to the believers, resurrection and the hereafter. Muslims believe that all people will one day face this truth, and that life is a mere passage, a stage, a bridge to the hereafter, and death is a gate by which all must pass; it will lead them to either heaven or to hellfire, according to their deeds in this world. This life is a field for the Muslim where he strives to make others happy and where he participates to bring greater benefits not only for Muslims but also for non-Muslims and even for animals, and plants.[596]

6-The Hereafter, Heaven and Hell : Is there life after death? Will people, nations, rulers, and governments, be held accountable for their actions? If we have given ourselves the right to question, assess, direct, punish, and reward our own fellow humans, shouldn't we accept to be judged, punished or rewarded by the One Who created us?

Some people have posed themselves as gods and have already decided who will go to heaven and who will abide in hell, but Muslims believe that God has the exclusive right to judge His creatures, and He, the Infinitely Just, will do it according to their deeds, the good ones and the evil ones, and on the Day of Judgment, He is the Most Merciful, more merciful than a mother towards her newborn. Heaven is the eternal abode for those who worshipped God Alone and did good and furthered justice and peace in this world, and hellfire will be the eternal abode of those who denied God, brought evil and misery to others.

7-Islamic Fundamentalism : Adherence or return to the fundamentals is not a characteristic exclusive to Islam, it is a global phenomenon. Just as Jews and Christians seek to give religion a greater role in their life so do many Muslims. But adherence to the fundamentals of the religion does not mean recurring to violence. Anyone in his right mind would not compare fundamentalism in

Islam with extremism and violence, or compare it to violent sects in other religions.

Christian fundamentalism is thriving in the US and has infiltrated all aspects of life. It has great weight on the political level. Born-Again Christians have seen their numbers increase to reach more than 50 million in the US alone, as Senator Paul Findley has remarked[597]. Israel, a Jewish state built on religious fundamental principles, and built on the Palestinian land, is unconditionally supported by the US, especially fundamentalist Christians. It is therefore unacceptable to revile Islamic fundamentalism, especially that Islam, contrary to Christianity and Judaism, does not deny or defame Jesus and Moses or any prophet before them, but on the contrary, Muslims love and respect them, as this is part of their religion. Islamic fundamentalism is not driven by the concept of the "Decisive Battle" or "Armageddon," and is not founded on the marginalization of others.

8-The Concept of Jihad in Islam : The concept of Jihad has been wrongly equated with terrorism and thus jihad has been vilified by the Western media. Jihad does not mean terrorism; it is a concept shared by most nations of the world if one tries to understand it in an objective rational way.

When people are oppressed, subjugated by others, and when truth purposely gets hidden, then Jihad is legitimate to liberate them and to let peace and justice prevail. The concept of jihad has a lofty goal to liberate mankind from subjugation and tyranny. Jihad is only against those who deny others the freedom to spread justice, self-determination, and the propagation of moral principles. Even in case of victory, Islam prohibits forcing the victors' faith on others, as stated in the Qur'an: "Let there be no compulsion in religion, Truth stands out clear from error."[598]

At the same time when Islam encourages its adherents to protect themselves, their properties and their honors from any aggression, their behavior even during their struggle is bound by detailed rules in Islam which prohibit them from attacking civilians, bringing harm to animals and the environment, destroying places of worship, or harming children and the elderly who are not raising arms against them.

Most importantly, Muslims prefer peace, and whenever possible are required to avoid war. Islamic laws favor peaceful resolutions to war in solving problems among nations and peoples. But this unfortunately is sometimes impossible.[599]

Jihad in Islam is not in contradiction with international laws, and is not a foreign concept to the notion of national defense shared by all other nations. The obligation on a nation to defend itself, the properties, honor, and religious freedom of its inhabitants against foreign occupation, and aggression is a shared concept with all religions and human laws.

Thus Jihad has the lofty goal, and uses the legitimate honest means, both to deter the oppressor and to free the populations from oppression and tyranny. If understood rightly, jihad would be accepted and included in the charter of the United Nations.

9-The Palestinian Question : The Palestinian issue is a global Islamic issue, where the interests of some conflict with those of others. It is one of the most important issues facing the world today. Muslim populations around the world, Muslim scholars, and Islamic organizations are all keenly interested in this issue, because they know the important position the Holy Land holds in the Muslim faith: Jerusalem (al-Quds) is the third holiest place in Islam after Makkah and Madinah. Using extremist views in solving the political problem and marginalizing the Palestinian people and their organizations is bound to kindle the religious and civilizational tensions among the followers of the religions involved.

It is the right of the Muslim peoples to preserve their Islamic identity, and they do seek to overcome the tensions that characterize their current situation. Muslims, and their religious leadership in particular, are going forward toward the reform and development of their societies, and do not wish to start or be part of a fourth world war[600]; they refuse to enter in a clash of civilizations, but they seek to peacefully coexist and to compete for the spread of moral principles, through mutual cooperation and exchange of benefits between Muslim nations and others. This alone will enable the world to build a better future where mutual understanding, trust and equal participation in the stewardship of the world toward true peace and freedom.

This brief exposition of the fundamentals of Islam makes it clear that Muslims do not seek confrontations but rather honest competition. Unfortunately, some forces are seeking to marginalize them and are escalating the conflict to deprive them from the chances to compete.

Islam and the West: Competition and Conflict

There is one truth that no one can deny: that Islam existed before the birth of the United States, and thus is not geared toward the enmity of the US. Gary Leupp, "Islam has been around for approximately 1400 years. Established on the West coast of Arabia 900 years before European settlement in America…it was not designed as an anti-US movement!"[601] Commenting on the ignorance of the people about Islam, he said: "I am painfully aware of this ignorance. But I realize it serves a purpose. It is highly useful to a power structure that banks on knee-jerk popular support whenever it embarks on a new military venture."[602]

But why is the West in conflict with the Muslim world? The answer to this question perhaps lies in understanding the causes of the poor relations between the West and the Islamic world. These causes have been studied by Fred Haliday who sees them as a reaction to the West's behavior toward the Muslim world; in brief: that the West has for a long time dominated the Muslim world and directly ruled it, and is still dominating it albeit indirectly, interfering in the affairs of the Muslim states, against the benefits of the Muslim and Arab populations; that the West seeks to divide the Muslim world, and kill any initiative to unite it. The Muslim world sees the West as indifferent to the issues that are dear to Muslims, such as the occupation of Palestine, Kashmir, Chechnya, Iraq, Bosnia, and others. There is one cause that Haliday considers even more important than the rest, which is the double standard the West uses in human rights issues, especially in the case of the Israeli behavior toward the Palestinian people. Another cause equally important is the attempt to impose by force, through the technology of communication and economic power, Western values on the Muslim and Arab world, especially in the fields concerning the particularities of the Muslim and Arab cultures. Haliday has also mentioned another cause which is the US support of dictatorial regimes in the Muslim world which in turn have engendered extremism, violence, and terrorism.[603]

The Muslim world, its peoples and governments, its civilization, values, and moral principles, its religion and its just laws, all these are an important component of the international equation, an essential partner in the leadership of the world, its security, and stability. To marginalize or ignore its rights and issues will jeopardize the international peace. It is important to know here that Islam as a religion and a way of life is different from the Muslims' state of affairs, their mistakes, and transgressions toward this religion, which has caused them to become backward. Leopold Weiss has eloquently expressed this, saying:

"These popular Western views could be summarized thus: the downfall of the Muslims is mainly due to Islam…the sooner the Muslim peoples are freed from their subservience to Islamic beliefs and social practices and induced to adopt the Western way of life, the better for them and for the rest of the world. My own observations had by now convinced me that the mind of the average Westerner held an utterly distorted image of Islam…It was obvious to me that the decline of the Muslims was not due to any short-comings in Islam but rather to their own failure to live up to it. For, indeed, it was Islam that had carried the early Muslims to tremendous cultural heights."[604]

Paul Findley has also emphasized the West's misunderstanding of Islam, saying: "When they [the American people] learn the truth about Islam - the many common beliefs and commitments that link it with Christianity and Judaism - they will offer the hand of friendship and cooperation. After all, Muslims find in the U.S. Constitution the same basic protections and opportunities that are envisioned in the ideal Islamic state as set forth in the Qur'an, namely religious freedom, the absence of compulsion in religion, tolerance for people of other faiths, and the protection of civil liberties for all people, including minorities."[605]

Prince Charles, Heir to the British monarchy in a recent public speech at Oxford University stated: "If there is much misunderstanding in the West about the nature of Islam, there is also much ignorance about the debt our own culture and civilization owe to the Islamic world. It is a failure, which stems, I think, from the straight-jacket of history, which we have inherited. The medieval Islamic world, from Central Asia to the shores of the Atlantic, was a world where scholars and men of learning flourished. But because we have tended to see Islam as the enemy of the West, as an alien culture, society, and system of belief, we have tended to ignore or erase its great relevance to our own history."[606]

In spite of these clear facts, the statements of many officials in the US Government, the huge amount of literature in the media, and the many new laws and regulations, the violations of human rights and freedoms, indicate that the real concern of this campaign against Islamic organizations is not to stop terror financing, and not even to stop extremism or Islamic fundamentalism, but in fact it is to stop the spread of Islam itself.

The best example to prove this is Wolfowitz's statement concerning the goals of the Iraq war: that it was to conquer the hearts and minds of the people, and to generalize the Turkish secularist model on all Middle Eastern countries. The logical question that follows is: what are the chances that the US Government will succeed in reversing, or at least stopping, the tide of Islam? In his book "Beyond Peace," former President Richard Nixon has recognized that both secularism of the West and secularism in the Muslim world could not triumph over Islam. Huntington has also emphasized this by saying: "In the long run, however, Mohammed wins out. Christianity spreads primarily by conversion, Islam by conversion and reproduction."[607]

This inevitable outcome is also due to the authenticity of the source of Islam: the Qur'an, Islam's holy book, has not been altered since it was revealed to the Prophet Muhammad. It is still recited by all Muslims in Arabic exactly the same way it was revealed to Muhammad, and thus has been preserved as God has decreed: "We have without doubt, sent down the Message (the Qur'an); and We will assuredly guard it (from corruption)."[608] Moreover, Islam is the only religion where, by agreement of numerous scholars from East and West, its book does not contain a fact that contradicts any scientific fact from the time of its revelation to this time.[609]

Because we are talking here about civilizations that have the capabilities to compete in bringing happiness to humankind, to guide people to moral principles they believe in and ultimately to success, it is obvious that the civilization that is more beneficial to mankind would be the winner. The concept of civilizational clash, as theorized by Huntington, and as brought to fruition as a by-product of certain US policies, to take away any opportunity for Islam to compete, will at the end harm only the one who practices it. History abounds with lessons; one has only to consider the defunct Soviet Union that practiced a prominent role in this clash, using all means of oppression, but although it possessed all means of material survival, it collapsed almost overnight.

"The total failure of Marxism…and the dramatic breakup of the Soviet Union," the Japanese philosopher Takeshi Umehara has suggested, "are only the precursors to the collapse of Western liberalism, the main current of modernity. Far from being the alternative to Marxism and the reigning ideology at the end of history, liberalism will be the next domino to fall."[610]

Huntington has emphasized the concept of conflict that is rooted in the West and America in particular, far from being a competition of ideas, he said: "The West won the world not by the superiority of its ideas or values or religion (to which few members of other civilizations were converted) but rather by its superiority in applying organized violence. Westerners often forget this fact; non-Westerners never do."[611] In spite of the West's practice of violence against the rest of the world, Huntington warned that: "In the emerging era, clashes of civilizations are the greatest threat to world peace, and an international order based on civilizations is the surest safeguard against world war."[612]

Hopefully, what has been presented here has helped the reader decide who is the competitor and who can be said to be the aggressor. It hopefully also has clarified the true objectives of the global American campaign, or perhaps more appropriate to some, the global American war against the Islamic organizations.

Conclusion

The world is experiencing great changes since 9/11. These changes have the effect – or the objective - of shrinking the role of the people, nations, societies, and their organizations, curtailing their rights to freedom and dignity, and their freedom of expression. This is done by few extremist cliques among the political and religious men and war merchants in the US having at their hands many new tools. Most of the allegations and excuses they relied on in this war are far from the truth. Into the wall of the CIA building's central lobby in Langley, Virginia, is written the following verse from the Bible: "And ye shall know the truth and the truth shall set you free"[613]. The conclusion at which we have arrived after studying this issue is summarized in the following points:

The most important issue of our time is **global security, which is everyone's responsibility**. The primary latent source of instability in our world today is the loss of hope and the despair brought on by the poverty of many of the world's peoples. Attempting to turn the world's attention away from its primary concerns is a danger to world security. Sensing this danger, French President Jacques Chirac has called for the formation of an international coalition to fight poverty, similar to the coalition to fight terrorism, saying: "What can be done for terrorism can be done for poverty."[614] The President of the World Bank has spelled out what should be done: "Improving stability in countries emerging from conflict, and in poor countries racked by hopelessness, is as important now as it was 60 years ago when the world was struggling to restore peace and rebuild the lives of millions. Stronger support globally for the fight against poverty is the best investment that can be made in building a more peaceful world and a safer future for our children."[615] "Investing in development is the safe thing to do," he said. "It makes America and the world more secure to increase global economic and social stability and decrease frustrations that can lead to violence."[616]

The need for non-governmental humanitarian organizations is greater than ever in a world where even more people are born in poverty, as attested by the World Bank President. "Over the next three decades, more than two billion people will be added to the planet's population, 97 percent of them in the poorer nations," he said, "and all too many will be born with the prospect of growing up into poverty and disillusioned with a world that they will view as inequitable and unjust. Instability is often bred in places where a rapidly increasing youth population sees hope as more of a taunt than a promise."[617]

Marginalizing and closing humanitarian organizations that participate in the development of these poor countries does not help global security. Islamic charities are part of the global charity sector and are active.

Participants in the fight against poverty.

America's actions in the so-called War on Terror in the name of security have become a cause for the loss of security. Those actions have become fuel for war and nourishment for violence. They are being employed as a justification for the continued presence of terrorism perpetrated by individuals and organizations. Indeed, from this perspective, it would seem that such terrorist acts are desired, since American policy, military influence and international actions presuppose this situation. America's conduct has become a strong indicator that it is operating under a theory of a clash of civilizations and a clash of religions.

A quick look at the US State Department report on terrorist attacks - from an official American viewpoint - released in April 2004 gives a clear indication that the number of victims due to terror attacks is insignificant compared to the victims of the US war on Iraq and Afghanistan to name a few. The report assessed that in 2003 there were 190 "global terrorist attacks", resulting in 307 deaths, eight attacks less than the previous year which resulted in 725 deaths. *Al-Majallah* magazine commented on these statistics, saying: "If we compared the number of victims of global terror, as assessed by the US State Department Report, to the number of innocent civilian victims of the US aggression on Iraq and Afghanistan, it becomes clear that terrorism is not a threat to global security as much as it is an incident which the US administration is trying to globalize to realize its own covetous goals."[618]

French author Emmanuel Todd, who anticipated the fall of the Soviet Union in his best seller book *After the Empire: The Breakdown of the American Order*, wrote: "The United States would have to become just one liberal democracy among others, scale back its military machine, retire from its geo-strategic activities and humbly accept the gratitude of the rest of the planet for its long years of exemplary service. This page is unlikely to be written. We do not yet know if the universalization of liberal democracy and peace is an inevitable historical process. We do know, however, that such a world poses a threat to the United States. Economically dependent, America requires a minimum level of global disorder in order to justify its politico-military presence in the Old World."[619]

3. What some people see as an American military, political, and economic Crusade is precisely what has sewn the seeds of hatred and animosity against America. This feeling is prevalent in most countries, organizations and people throughout the world, so much so that fixing the matter has become extremely difficult if not impossible.[620] This hatred was fostered by America's new principles of "preemptive war" and the "War on Terror," and not by the Islamic charities activities, nor by the Islamic curricula in the Arab world, as alleged by the US. These allegations served only as pretext for closing the charities and changing the curricula. The hopes of thinkers and scholars in America and abroad for a new century of better stability, more freedom, for civilizational dialogue and better cultural and political communication with the Muslim world have been greatly diminished by the US military actions.

4. The majority of the American people have become yet another victim of the War on Terror. They woke up from the September 11 attacks to find that the event has to some extent overturned the American Constitution and other constitutions around the globe. Civil liberties have been diminished; democracy has been confined to a political routine between two parties. The American people have found that demonstrations, protests, and the voicing of public opinion have fallen on deaf ears. The wars in Afghanistan and Iraq have taken place among this atmosphere of protests, inflicting a chronic economic hemorrhage upon the American people in the tens of billions of dollars. A study performed by Columbia University economist Joseph E. Stiglitz and Harvard lecturer Linda Bilmes revealed that the cost of the Iraq war could top $2 trillion.[621] The official conservative statistics published by the Pentagon in January 2006 - 2210 killed and 16,420 wounded[622] since the start of the Iraq war - are a strong indicator that the American people's resources, their comfort, their soldiers and their families are victims of this war where there is no winner and no light at the end of the tunnel. The US military actions have only increased the US isolation from the world.

Commenting on the preemptive war, Andrew Bacevich told the *Los Angeles Times*: "Indeed, today the Bush administration's aim is not to win but to relieve itself of responsibility for waging a war that it began but cannot finish. Debate in national security circles focuses not on deploying war-winning technologies or fielding innovative tactics that might turn the tide, but on how we can extricate ourselves before our overstretched forces suffer irreparable damage."[623] American soldiers are indeed becoming victims of this war on terror.

5. We believe that **Muslim humanitarian organizations** are the best contributors to moderating individuals and their actions. America knows this very well. Such organizations are the best way for guiding people's contributions to legitimate and conspicuous channels. They also instill people with a sense of the importance of the human right to security in both their lives and their wealth. They work under the Islamic principle to give each his due (Zakat is a due to the poor) and encourage kindness of heart. Mistakes committed by some Islamic charities have been given disproportionate attention in American statements and actions and the campaign waged against them has been spurred by the perception that they are a religious and an ideological competitor to the Western civilization, especially in the area of propagating Islam and Islamic principles and morals and Islamic culture.

The NGOs - including the global charities - are facing politicization and weakening of their independence; they are forced to follow certain governments' agenda. Islamic charities in particular are facing oppression and a war of smearing and defamation under the allegation of supporting terror. Scrutiny of the facts however reveals a different reality: there are American organizations which are benefiting from this environment and which are profiting from the donations of Americans and tax benefits to support rebellions, separatist factions, terrorism, and even kindle revolutions in all corners of the globe. Organizations which were working under the guise of promoting democracy were in fact fomenting revolts in the previous soviet republics from Ukraine and Kyrgyzstan to Georgia and Kazakhstan. American-based Zionist organizations are unconditionally supporting Israeli state terrorism and Israeli terrorist organizations which are terrorizing the Palestinian people. This dire situation requires the establishment of an independent international committee, or committees, to investigate all elements of the issue, including Islamic and non-Islamic organizations, to arrive at the truth. The United Nations might be the first contender because of its independence and authority, but it is not the only possibility, as long as the issue is studied by an international entity and not monopolized by one superpower. Only this would close the door to allegations by confirming or dismissing them.

6. All of the commotion being stirred up against Muslim charities throughout the world and Saudi charities in particular has resulted in a frenzy of blind generalization that is supported by one particular event: two branches of one of these charities were closed by political decrees without evidence or a judicial decision. The only explanation given was that two or three non-Saudi employees working at these branches had engaged in some undesirable activity. Just as the war in Iraq was partially based on the alleged existence of weapons of mass destruction, the actions taken against the Islamic charities were based on evidence that turned out to be just newspaper clippings, another hoax. Is this a pattern of things to come?

It has become clear throughout the previous chapters and especially in the third chapter in which the 9/11 commission was shown to have brought no substantial evidence, the fourth and fifth chapters where other cases were presented, and the seventh chapter that further attempted to demonstrate, using public American and Western statements, the underlying objectives of the campaign against terrorism. The Friends of Charities Association (FOCA) in the US has reached a similar conclusion regarding the allegations linking the charitable organizations to the support of terrorism. They subsequently issued two open letters to the US Congress voicing their opinion.[624] We have included the text of both letters in the appendix.

Reasonable people in the American administration, and representatives of the American people, should be alerted to the consequences of this new McCarthyism that has generalized the allegations of terrorism on most Islamic entities, and should not follow the extreme right and the Zionist lobby, which is seen by some as guiding the world into a clash of religions and civilizations. Generalizations extend the circle of fire and lead to dire consequences. Jerrold Post, a George Washington University professor, said at the Madrid Conference: "In this struggle, the moral high ground needs to be maintained…To depart from these standards is to lower ourselves to the level of the terrorists and to damage liberal democracy."

7. This study, to the extent that it appears to defend Muslim charities and condemn those allegations and expose the extreme right-wing centers of power in America that are instigating the American people and the world towards a clash of civilizations, has a nobler purpose. This purpose is to give a strong warning against what could be the outcome if these reckless policies continue unabated. Humanity is threatened in its development, progress, and security and indeed in its continued existence. We hope to hear more voices from around the world join in declaring the truth, conveying this concern and this fear for humanity's future, working for the freedom to compete, and working to prevent conflict and war.

The number of victims in the global war on terror is increasing daily at an alarming rate. This war has transgressed all customs and principles, has violated the human rights of the American people and peoples in other countries around the world, has brought death and destruction, and has increased poverty and ignorance. While I was contemplating this, I remembered the words of President Bush in his speech to the American public on September 11 2001: "We're the brightest beacon for freedom"[625]. But reality says otherwise. This reality reminds me of God's words in the Qur'an: "Their intention is to extinguish Allah's Light with their mouths, but Allah will complete His Light, even though the unbelievers may detest."[626] And He said: "For the scum disappears like froth cast out; while that which is for the good of mankind remains on the earth."[627] The light of the Truth will shine bright and can not be extinguished by power, because Truth is stronger than power. Truth is power.

Appendix

<u>1-Letters to the U.S. Congress</u>

January 2, 2004

The Honorable Richard Shelby
Chairman, Senate Banking Committee
534 Dirksen Senate Office Building,Washington, DC 20510

Dear Senator Shelby:

In response to your hearing on terrorism funding held on September 25, 2003, entitled "Prevention of Terrorism Financing," I would like to take this opportunity to respond. We represent the religious leaders for the Two Holy Mosques in Saudi Arabia. Our duties are to ensure a tranquil haven of worship in the holy cities of Makkah and Madinah for over one billion Muslim men and women around the world. God says in the Qur'an: "So cooperate in righteousness and piety and do not cooperate in sin and aggression" (Chapter 5: Verse 2). Righteousness is based upon searching for the truth and reaching it. The worst type of aggression is the aggression against truth by hiding it or by distorting it.

In this spirit, we seek to cooperate with you by examining the evidence that was presented to the Committee and offering our feedback. Any reader of this testimony will notice that most of it is based upon rhetoric that seeks to incite the emotions. Mr. Wayne's testimony, however, concentrates on speaking to people's intellect rather than to their emotions. This is not the case with the testimony of then-Treasury General Counsel David Aufhauser who fills two pages with emotive speech and rhetoric. So we will concentrate more on what Mr. Wayne says. Mr. Wayne's testimony on page 3 states:

It is more important to note that many of the changes implemented by Saudi Arabia go beyond what we would have legal authority to do....Saudi Arabia is working with us closely in the context of the new task force on terrorist financing...Saudi Arabia submitted, jointly with the US, the names of two branches of a major Saudi NGO, as well as that of a major Saudi financier, for worldwide asset-freezing because of their links to al-Qaida....Saudi Arabia's new banking regulations place strict controls on accounts held by charities. Charities cannot deposit or withdraw cash from their bank account, nor can they make wire transfers abroad via their bank account. And Saudi Arabia has banned the collection of donations at mosques and instructed retail establishments to remove charity collection boxes from their premises, something that is undoubtedly extremely challenging for Saudi Arabia....

Later, it seems that Mr. Wayne still thinks that all these issues are not enough:

We believe the Saudi government is implementing its new charity regulations but there too we will need to see results.

The other testimonies all claimed that the Saudi government has not taken enough action to deal with the issue of financing terrorism. They repeat the claim that the Saudi government has taken many steps to put limits on the charities but they must do more. The questions which these testimonies raise and which must be answered are the following:

a- Can anyone imagine the European or United States governments taking the actions that the Saudi government has taken against their charities?

b-   All of the actions taken by the Saudi government in putting limitations on their charities were carried out as a result of pressure from the US government. How can these things be reconciled with American values? Many have given their lives to bring the values upon which the United Sates prides itself; the same values that the US has repeatedly asked the Saudi government to violate. The charities of Saudi Arabia adopt tens of thousands of orphans around the world, operate hospitals that cure the sick, build and operate schools that enable thousands of students to educate themselves. America is now demanding that restrictions be put in place to handicap these charities and minimize these activities. If America looks at this from a humanitarian point of view, how can she possibly feel satisfied with this?

c-   From a political point of view, how does taking these actions benefit the national interest of the United States? Is the United States prepared to face the consequences of handicapping charities and preventing them from undertaking their humanitarian activities? Is it this type of behavior that explains why so much of the world hates the United States? Is it not true that the Saudis are on the same side as the US, fighting the same scourge of unabated evil terror and victimizing innocent civilians of both our nations?

Some parts of the testimony concentrate on raising conspiracy theories about the leading Saudi charity, World Assembly of Muslim Youth (WAMY), casting doubts upon its activities, and insinuating links to terrorism while encouraging efforts to harm or oppose them. The testimony of Mr. Aufhauser claims that this charity has a strong relation with 500 student and youth organizations worldwide. If that is true, how does it benefit the national interest of the US to create enemies amongst 500 student and youth organizations around the world? Is it in America's interests to proceed with these actions without reasonable justification, based only on rumors and baseless claims? The office of WAMY in the US is still open. Is that because the US government understands that closing it without legal reason will breach the constitution and American justice system?

All the accusations raised against Saudi charities are based upon only one case: that two branches of Al Haramain Islamic Foundation were closed based on mere accusations that two or three employees (non-Saudi) had become involved, on a personal level, with activities that the charities did not endorse. Based just upon this one incident, those testifying before the Committee raise doubts about the head office and all the branches of the charity. Some went even further and raised doubts about every other charity operating out of Saudi Arabia. This gives us a clear indication as to the spirit from which this testimony comes.

It is very beneficial to end this letter with the wise statement from Georgetown University Law Professor David Cole Which was published in the *Law and Religion Journal*, Volume XV No. 12. Cole writes: "[W]hen the fear of terrorism leads our government to sacrifice the principles on which it is founded, we have already lost."

In closing, we urge you to consider to invite testimony representing other, more well-informed viewpoints, and to encourage your Senate colleagues on other Committees to do the same. We look forward to hearing from you and continuing a dialogue to reach our mutual goals of peace and understanding among all people.

Best regards,
Friends of Charities Association (FOCA) Members

2-Open Letter to the Members of the US Congress April 4, 2006

American Non-Governmental Organizations (NGO's) are truly an unparalleled model of success worldwide and a backbone of the success of American democratic values. This model is the best expression of American freedom and we hope it will find its way beyond the North American frontiers to the countries of the southern hemisphere, and that it will not end with the end of the cold war. The practical way of spreading freedom and democracy requires more free and independent NGO's in the third world and not the opposite. The members of the US congress are the guardians of the American values, they keep them from being hijacked inside America or transgressed upon outside, and they bear a great responsibility in protecting these values especially with regard to the rights of individuals and organizations.

The Islamic charitable organizations are part of the international NGO's, and thus their scope goes beyond narrow national interests to work for the welfare of all humankind. Islamic NGO's participated in the areas of international relief and development and their contributions were recognized worldwide especially by the beneficiaries and the supporters of humanitarian work. It is one of the requirements of the American values of freedom and democracy for the American government to work at increasing the number of these organizations and to condone their relief work aimed at solving the problem of poverty, their educational work aimed at removing ignorance and their efforts in the upbringing of younger generations that support security, the real pillar of world stability.

We believe that the Islamic charities are best able to regulate individuals and curb their transgressions. They are the best to ensure that money is transparently distributed to its legitimate recipients. They are building the schools that teach the warding off of turmoil and corruption, and protect those who seek security and tranquility in a turbulent world. They teach to give each one their due by building a watchful conscience and a merciful heart. The Islamic charities and the religion they sprang from are not a marginal factor in the international arena to be ignored or their programs and goals to be fought.

The Islamic charities with their programs and works constitute a real fulfillment of human rights in speech and in deeds and not mere slogans or political weapons or tools of diplomatic pressure. They help the oppressed and the destitute, they treat the sick, teach the illiterate, and guide to the true religion of Allah. The principles of freedom and democracy consider such organizations as the safety valve and the guardians of societies, peoples, and nations. Besides these works, the Islamic charities are consolidating the rule of law with the religious principles of self-control before enforcement, moral principles before desires, to bring in benefits and ward off mischief through their legal rights and freedoms gained during the cold war. Beyond that, the world at large is benefiting from the programs and works of these organizations that greatly contribute to world stability.

Where would the people's conscience in the world and in America in particular stand with the regard to the following statement of Former Secretary of State Colin Powell about the increase of poverty worldwide: "Half the people on this planet, about 3 billion human beings, live in destitute poverty. More than a billion people lack clean water. Two billion lack adequate sanitation and electrical power?"[628]

Where are the justice and the human rights when we know that eleven million people in the horn of Africa are threatened to die because they are under the poverty line according to a statement of the Food and Agriculture Organization (FAO) on January 7, 2005. And how does the practice of freedom and democracy in the 21st century stand when the international Islamic organizations are discriminated against because of their religion and as a result many places stricken by disasters are deprived of their participation in spite of the great need for extra governmental and popular resources. Countries such as Afghanistan, Pakistan, Kashmir, Iraq, Palestine, Indonesia and Bangladesh that were stricken by wars, earthquakes and Tsunamis have been deprived of the relief that the Islamic charities could have offered because of the measures that were taken against them, including arrests, freezing of accounts, and administrative and financial bureaucratic measures that burden the charities preventing them from offering clothing to the poor, shelter to the refugees, medical help to the sick, food to the hungry, and education to the illiterates. People in need of relief are cursing these freedoms and democracies that are not standing at their side and that are preventing them from getting relief. Who will be responsible for the three million victims of the 2005 famine in Niger, and who are actually dying now?

Poverty, sickness, and illiteracy are increasing in the world, while the US Administration is preventing numerous relief and development organizations from playing their role, increasing hatred toward the US. US discrimination against Islamic organizations is practiced even inside the Muslim countries where they are based. This discrimination has resulted in a sharp increase in hatred among the poor, the orphans, and the rich and poor populations alike toward the US. What is the benefit of the US administration from this bitter harvest?

The policy of the US administration seems to be at the hands of people blinded by arrogance and hubris from seeing the damages incurred to the US, and who lack the foresight to assess the outcomes of this policy. This trend confirms that there is a hidden power working to isolate the United States and prevent it from fulfilling the global humanitarian benefits, and goes even further to exploit the international organization for its interests at the expense of the international law, the United Nations and its organizations, and other peoples' rights. It is a power that has no concern for your interests and the interest of your people, but is only concerned in kindling the war so that freedoms are curtailed and democracies weakened. It seeks to reduce tolerance and encourage a clash of civilizations.

The major factors that contributed to the fall of the former US foe – the Soviet Union – are being espoused now by the US, which has become a single pole of hegemony, arrogance, and terror. Your previous success of enduring power against the Soviet Union was due to the slogans you raised championing justice, freedom, and democracy during the Cold War.

We realize that the extent of errors and transgressions is increasing and spreading inside the US and out, and this necessitates a revision of your government's policy. Christopher Patten, the European Commissioner for External Affairs said: "The US gains more by working with the grain of international opinion than she loses in freedom of action by accepting external disciplines." He also mentioned former US President Kennedy as saying: "My fellow citizens of the world: ask not what America will do for you, but what together we can do for the freedom of man."[629]

Two thousand American intellectuals, academics, and artists have appealed to you through a communiqué entitled *Not in Our Name*, and released on September 11, 2003, in commemoration of the 9/11 attacks, condemning the so-called "War on Terror," and where they say: "We believe that people of conscience must take responsibility for what their own governments do – we must first of all oppose the injustice that is done in our name. Thus we call on all Americans to RESIST the war and repression that has been loosed on the world by the Bush administration. It is unjust, immoral, and illegitimate. We choose to make common cause with the people of the world." And they asked: "What kind of world will this become if the U.S. government has a blank check to drop commandos, assassins, and bombs wherever it wants?"[630]

It seems that peace and stability are not a goal of some people in your administration who have hidden interests. What would happen if the US administration allocated the budget of one year of the expenditures on the war in Iraq for the eradication of poverty, famine, and diseases such as AIDS in Africa? How big would the material and moral gain be? How much respect would the world's nations have toward the US power and moral legitimacy to the leadership of the world?

We have no explanation for the motives of the campaign against the Islamic charities, especially that analyses and studies of the issue of the alleged Islamic organizations terror-support have arrived at the opposite, to the point that the culprits are in fact the victims, and are now entitled to sue for moral and material damages they have incurred. The book *Innocent Victims in The Global War on Terror* presents examples and results of the positive contributions of these Islamic organizations. A reading of the seventh chapter of the famous 9/11 commission report reveals the explicit emphasis that accusations against the Islamic charities are not only false but inexistent. Judging by this report, it becomes apparent that the US administration has no evidence whatsoever for these accusations; the report being devoid of any facts or events that inculpate them. The case study that was used to prove the culpability of the Islamic charities has on the contrary proven their innocence, according to the rule: "innocent until proven guilty."

The practice of religious freedoms requires that no pressure be applied, whether directly or indirectly, on the Islamic humanitarian organizations, and that discrimination against Islamic charities because of their religious affiliation be abandoned. For these organizations are major representatives of religious freedom for the Muslims (both donors and recipients).

It is only the repetition of these false accusations in the mass media that has conveyed the understanding that they were proven facts. As a result, a large number of Islamic organizations have been destroyed, marginalized, or weakened. The field of competition has been diminished because of the quantitative, qualitative poor presence of the Islamic organizations. For their human and financial resources have been dwindled, and thus the goal of the war on these organizations has been realized and is apparent in the suffering of the recipients among the poor, the refugees, the sick, and the victims of earthquakes and other disasters, and the hatred toward America has increased, and the likelihood of revenge has multiplied.

The world is witnessing a political and administrative revival, thanks to the US administration which has contributed to this before the 9/11 events. There is no more monopoly of knowledge and information, and everyone has a better understanding of what is good and what is evil, and can distinguish between truth and falsehood. Everyone knows what the world has reaped through the unwise policies adopted after September 11, 2001. Wise people in America and around the world are seeking an end to this new craziness, and end to the one-polar vision of the world; a vision that destroys the wide space shared by diverse religions, cultures, and civilizations which seek competition - not conflict -, peace, justice, and freedom. Wise people of the world are seeking a new beginning that will put an end to the wars that contribute to the increase of poverty, disease, and illiteracy. They seek to stop all political pressures exerted on governments so that the Islamic relief and humanitarian organizations can freely and democratically play their role, and participate with the other humanitarian organizations in bringing a better world.

Finally, we call all sensible people in the US administration, and the representatives of the American people to realize that the first people who are victimized are the American people and the

United States in general because of the new McCarthyism and generalization. Therefore they should not be misled by the extreme right and the Zionist lobby, for the generalization engenders an extension of the circle of hatred towards America, and a fall of the principles of freedom and democracy, upon which it was built and to which it calls. The renouncement of these American principles will lead to adverse consequences as mentioned by Jerrold Post, a Georges Washington University professor, who said at the Madrid Conference: "In this struggle, the moral high ground needs to be maintained...To depart from these standards is to lower ourselves to the level of the terrorists and to damage liberal democracy."[631]

Friends of Charities Association (FOCA) Members

3-The list of the first group of persons and Institutions quitted by the Federal Court.

Akida bank limited
Akida Investment Co.Ltd,
Al Baraka
Al Baraka Bancorp.Inc
Al Baraka Investment and development corporation
Al Barakati Exchange LIC
AlBarakati Exchange Group
Al Barakati Financial Company
AlBarakati Group
AlBarakati Group of Companies
AlBarakati International
AlBarakati Wiring Services
Al Haramain
Al Haramain Foundation
Al Haramain Foundation Inc
Al Rajhi Banking & Investment Corporation
Al Shamal Bank
Al Taqwa Trade property & Industry Company Limited
Asat Trust Reg
Bank Al Taqwa.Ltd
Barakati
Barakati International
Barakati International Foundation
Barakati International Companies
Barakati International Inc
Barakati North America Inc
Barakati Adminstrative Services S.A
DMI Trust
Dallah Al AlBaraka Group
Dar Al Maal Al Islami
Faisal Islamic Bank
Gulf Center S.R.L

Human Concern International
Ibrahim Afandi
International Releif Organization
Islamic Investment Company of The Gulf EC
Islamic Releif Organization
Khalid Bin Mahfouz
Kingdom Of Saudi Arabia
Mercy International Releif Agency
Mercy International
Miga Malaysia Organization SA Gulf & African Chamber
Nada International Anstalt
Nada International Organization SA
Nasco Sas Di Ahmed Idris Nasdrreddin EC
Nscoservice S.R.L
Nascotex SA
Nasreddin Company
Nasreddin Foundation
Nasreddin Group International Holding Limited
Nasreddin Group International Limited holding
National Commercial Bank
Sultan Bin Abdulaziz al Saud
Mohammed al Fiasal al Saud
Naif Bin Abdulaziz al Saud
Salman Bin Abdulaziz al Saud
Turki al Fiasal al Saud
Salleh Abdulla Kamel
Sanabel Al – Kheer Inc
Saudi High Commission for Releif
Shaykh Adil Abul Galil Betargy
Success Foundation
Sulaiman Abulaziz Al-Rajhi
Tadamon Bank
Vazir
Youssef M.Nada & Co. Gesellschaft

Index

Symbols

700 Club 201

A

Abacha, Sani 145
AbdelKerim, Riad 85
Abdil Wahhab, Shaikh Muhammad
     Bin 114
Abu Ghraib prison, Iraq 36, 127, 192
Abu Heen 166
Aceh 24
a-Dhari, Harith 187
Advani, Lal Krishna 256
Afghanistan 4, 23, 27, 36, 43, 53, 61,
     62, 65, 74, 75, 77, 81, 87, 102,
     105, 108, 133, 145, 152, 154,
     161, 162, 173, 174, 175, 176,
     177, 180, 191, 192, 193, 208,
     209, 211, 281, 282, 293, 330
AID 23, 24, 73, 169
Akash, Munir 327
Al-Ahram 316
Al-Aqsa Charitable Foundation 78
Albania 55, 59, 105
Al-Barakah 77
Al-Bayan 319
Albright, Madeleine 217
Alewa, Jaber 167
Algeria 133
al-Haramain Islamic Foundation (HIF)
     59, 60, 61, 76, 96, 97, 98, 101,
     102, 103, 105, 106, 107, 108,
     109, 110, 111, 112, 113, 114,
     123, 128, 131, 132, 133, 134,
     136, 155, 156, 158, 196, 197,
     198, 199, 262, 263, 319, 320,
     323, 325, 329
Al-Hayat 90, 169, 174, 315, 317, 318,
     326, 334

al-Ihsan al-Khayri Center 85
Al-Jazeera 65, 168, 186
Al-Kawthar 331
Allawi, Iyad 31
Al-Majallah 281, 314, 319
al-Moayad, Mohammed Ali 84
Al-Mujtama 314, 327, 331, 336
Al-Muntada al-Islami 57
Al Mustansiriya University 192
Al-Qaeda 75, 77, 81, 93, 94, 103, 104,
     105, 106, 107, 108, 109, 114,
     133, 165, 173, 177, 263, 319
Al-Riyadh 331
Al-Roken, Mohammed 251
Al-Saadi, Abdel Kader 186
Al-Shaikh, Saleh, Saudi Arabia
     Minister of Islamic Affairs 196,
     198, 199
Al-Watan 317, 318, 332
American Friends Service Committee
     129
American Hegemony 161, 178
American Lausanne Committee 233
American research center, SEAT 95
Amnesty International 36, 190, 328
Andalousia 41
Annan, Kofi 30, 31, 32, 174
Annan, Kojo 31
Anti Ballistic Missile Treaty 178
Anti Defamation League (ADL) 171
Arab Commission for Human Rights
     85
Arab Committee for Human Rights
     227
Arafat, Yasser 171, 249
Armageddon 122, 182, 252, 253, 272
Arnaout, Enaam 156, 157
Ashcroft, John 92, 113, 129, 318
Associated Press 62, 186, 218, 323, 331
Aufhauser, David 91, 98, 154

301

Itani, Fadi 154, 261

J

Jamaah Islamiyah 81
Janata Party 257
Japan 179, 335
J. Carter Company 168
Jewish Monthly, The 333
Jewish PACs 249
Johns Hopkins University 192, 212
Johnson, Lyndon, US President 250
Jordan 73, 80, 104, 171, 180
Jourdan, Jérôme Bellion 21, 48, 64,
     158, 195, 205, 206, 209, 216,
     235, 314, 315, 316, 325, 329,
     330, 331, 332
Joynt, Scott 144, 324, 325

K

Kaag, Dr. Mayke 54, 316
Kalla, Jusuf 22
Kaplan, David 156, 325
Karadzic, Radovan 157
Kashmir 4, 25, 44, 75, 102, 256, 275
Kazakhstan 59, 217, 218, 283
Kenya 58, 81, 105, 133, 320
Kermode, Franklin 250
Khales, Yunes 208
KindHearts 134
Klein, Naomi 184, 186, 328
Kobilica, Anela 158
Kosovo 4, 23, 55, 59, 62, 102, 164,
     221
Kurlantzick, Joshua 140, 173, 324, 326
Kuwait, -Central Bank of 76
Kuwaiti Government 76, 86, 90
Kuwait International Islamic Charity
     60
Kyl, Jon 102, 115, 116, 199, 204, 319,
     321, 329
Kyoto accords 20
Kyrgyzstan 217, 218, 283

L

Lancet 184
Lebanon 43, 77, 96, 164, 171, 247, 254
LeBaron, Richard 76
Le Bon, Gustave 237, 332
Lefkowitz, Josh 196, 329, 330
Left Hook 187
Leupp, Gary 274, 335
Levin, Jonathan 196, 329, 330
Levitt, Matthew 116, 137, 138, 139,
     153, 198, 210, 318, 319, 321,
     323, 324, 325, 329, 331
Libération 176, 327
Libi Fund 172
London Conference on Partnership
     for Peace and Development in
     Palestine 68
Los Angeles Times 185, 282, 336
Love, Rick 232
Luque, Nancy 140

M

Maariv 55
Macpherson, Robert 233
Madrid Conference 285
Makkah Charitable Foundation 58
Malawi 79
Manna, Haytham 22, 167, 239, 314,
     326, 332
Margarethe II, Queen of Denmark
     236
Martel, Charles 238
Masleša, Ramo 156
Massachusetts Institute of Technology
     192
Mauritania 79, 115, 313, 315
McCarthy 242
McCarthyism 255, 285
McDonald Restaurant Chains 228
McMahon, Martin 243, 244
Medact 191, 328
Médecins Sans Frontières (MSF) 206
Mercy International Relief
     Organization 81

References

Introduction

[1] **Colin L. Powell**, "U.S. Has Moral Obligation to Help Develop Poor Nations: By 2006, U.S. Aid Will Be As Great As Marshall Plan," *Global Viewpoint/ Foreign Policy* (Dist. Tribune Media Services, 1/3/05)

[2] **"Somalia**: Two Million Facing Food Crisis, FAO Says," December 22, 2005, *IRN*, available from: http://www.irinnews.org

[3] *West Africa: Despite Food Crisis in Mali, Mauritania, Niger, 2004-2005 Sahel Harvest Better than Expected*, UN Office for the Coordination of Humanitarian Affairs, April 3, 2006, available from www.IRINnews.org

[4] **"Starvation** Looms in African Horn," *BBC News*, January 6, 2006

[5] *Report of the High Level Panel on Threats, Challenges, and Changes*, United Nations General Assembly, fifty ninth session, Agenda Item 55 Findings and recommendations, December 2, 2005, p.2.

[6] **Ibid. p.45.**

[7] *BBC News* on January 10, 2005, *New York Times* during the first week of January 2005, *Newsweek* on January 25, 2005.

[8] **Alvin Toffler**, *Power Shift*, Bantam Books, (1990), p.450.

Chapter I

[9] **Rana Foroohar**, "Wary of Aid", *Newsweek international, Atlantic edition*, January 24, 2005, p.24.

[10] **Ibid.**

[11] **"The non-governmental order"** *The Economist*, Vol.353 Issue 8149, p20.

[12] **Adeeb Dimitry**, *"Dictatorship of Capital"* أديب ديميتري "دكتاتورية رأس المال"، P. 490. (translated from Arabic)

[13] **Ibid.**

[14] **"The non-governmental order"** *The Economist*, Vol.353 Issue 8149, p20.

[15] **Ibid.**

[16] **"Looking at the Future** with Alvin Toffler," *USA Today*, February 7, 2000.

[17] **Ibid.**

[18] **Ibid**

[19] **Alvin Toffler**, *Power Shif*, Bantam edition, 1990, p. 458.

[20] **"Al-Harb al-Khafiyah** Lissaytara Alal'Aalam," (Hidden War for Global Domination), a*l-Ittihad*, February 26, 2002.

[21] **Ibid.**

[22] **Ibid.**

[23] **Ibid.**

[24] **Ibid.**

[25] **Ibid.**

[26] **Dominique Moïsi**, "Early winners and losers at a time of war", *Financial Times*, November 19, 2001, p15.

[27] **"Al-Harb al-Khafiyah Lissaytara Alal'Aalam**," (Hidden War for Global Domination), a*l-Ittihad*, February 26, 2002.

[28] *L'année Stratégique 2003*, sous la direction de Pascal Boniface, Institut de Relations Internationales et Stratégiques,

[29] **Interview** with Sen. Paul Findley, a*l-Bayan Magazine*, September, 2003.

[30] **Jonathan Benthall** & Jerome Bellion Jourdan, *The Charitable Crescent* (1992)

[31] **Dr. Haytham Manna**, *A Scream before the Kill, the future of humanitarian and charitable associations in the Saudi Arabian Kingdom*, International Bureau for Humanitarian NGOs.

[32] **Rana Faroohar**, "Wary of Aid", *Newsweek International, Atlantic Edition*, January 24, 2005.

[33] **Ibid.**

[34] **Ibid.**

[35] **Ibid.**

[36] **Ibid.**

[37] **Ibid.**

[38] **Ibid.**

[39] **Ibid.**

[40] **Ibid.**

[41] **Ibid.**

[42] **Jesse Helms**, *Journal of the US Department of State*, , available from: www.state.gov/s/Archive/

[43] *Al-Mujtama magazine*, January 1, 2005.

[44] **Ibid.** In reality not all Arab charities have been stopped but some have been stopped and others have had their activities decreased. Also it seems that the number of Western charities is closer to 300, rather than 3000.

[45] *Al-Mujtama Magazine* of Kuwait mentioned that there are around 40 Christian missionary organizations and only two Islamic organizations. a*l-Mujtama*, June 11, 2005.

[46] **Richard Perle** is a research fellow at the American Enterprise Institute, a member of the Board of Advisors of the Foundation for Defense of Democracy – a right wing pro-Israel group-. He is also a board member of the Jewish Institute of National Security Affairs (JINSA), and a former director of Jerusalem Post

[47] **David Frum** and Richard Perle, *An End to Evil*, p. 233 (Balantine Books, 2004).

[48] http://news.bbc.co.uk/go/pr/fr

[49] *Statement to the Security Council by the secretary –General on the closure of the Oil-for-Food Programme*, November 20, 2003. Available from: www.un.org/Depts/oip/background/latest/sgstatement031119.html

[50] *Al-Majallah* February 13, 2005

[51] www.bbcarabic.com , November 21, 2004, and *al-Majallah* February 13, 2005

[52] *Al-Hayat* (London) 15/11/2004 quoting *New York Times.*

[53] *Al-Hayat* (London) December 18, 2004

[54] **"UN Geneva** office bugged, latest reported case of spying on world body", *UN News service*, December 17, 2004, available from: www.un.org/apps/news/

[55] **U.S. President** Harry S. Truman's address at the laying of the Cornerstone of the United Nations Building, New York City, October 24, 1949.

[56] **Toffler**, *al-Ittihad* newspaper, February 26, 2002.

[57] *Surveillance Under the USA PATRIOT Act*, April 3, 2003, available from : www.aclu.org/safefree/general/17326res20030403.html

[58] **Jessica** Williams, *50 Facts that Should Change the World,* (Icon Books, 2004)

[59] **Ibid.**

[60] **Ibid.**

[61] **Anup** Shah, Poverty Facts and Stats, April 3, 2006, available from: www.globalissues.org/TradeRelated/Facts.asp.

[62] **Japanese** military reported 93 suicide cases from among 230,000 individuals in the army from March 2003 to March 2004, and 64 suicide cases (from among 147,000) from March 2004 to March 2005. www.alalam.ir/site/search/details.asp?arch=O&id

[63] *Giving USA 2001*, a publication of Giving USA Foundation, Center of Philanthropy at Indiana University. See also Giving USA 2002, Giving USA 2003, and Giving USA 2004.

[64] **Jonathan** Benthall & Jerome Bellion Jourdan, *The Charitable Crescent* (1992), pp. 17, 18.

[65] **Peter F.** Drucker, "Managing for the Future," p. 204 (Plume/Penguin, 1993).

[66] **Peter F.** Drucker, *Managing for the Future, the 1990s and Beyond*, Truman Talley Books / Plume, New York, November 1993, p. 203.

[67] www.ombwatch.org

[68] **For** a comprehensive list of these organizations see: www.interenvironment.org/wd/

[69] **David Watson**, "Indian Summer," *Oryx*, February 2006.

[70] *Bill and Melinda Gates Foundation,* Wikipedia, available from: http://en.wikipedia.org/wiki/Bill_%26_Melinda_Gates_Foundation

[71] **Tony** Allen-Mills, "'Pizza Pope' builds a Catholic Heaven," *The Sunday Times*, February 26, 2006.

[72] **Neil Clark**, "George Soros", *New Statesman*, June 2, 2003.

[73] **Jessica Williams**, *50 Facts that Should Change the World,* (Icon Books, 2004).

[74] **Ibid.**

[75] *West Africa: Despite Food Crisis in Mali, Mauritania, Niger, 2004-2005 Sahel Harvest Better than Expected,* UN Office for the Coordination of Humanitarian Affairs, April 3, 2006, available from www.IRINnews.org

[76] **"Starvation** Looms in African Horn," *BBC News,*January 6, 2006

[77] James D. Wolfensohn, "World Bank Meeting: Ending Poverty is the Key to Stability," *International Herald Tribune*, September 30, 2004.

[78] **Jessica** Williams, *50 Facts that Should Change the World,* (Icon Books, 2004)

[79] **Available** from: www.who.int/en/ and www.albasar.com

80 **World** *Development Report 2006: Equity and Development*, available from: www.econ.worldbank.org

81 **David** Fickling, "Pinter Demands War Crime Trial for Blair," *The Guardian*, December 7, 2005.

82 **"When** Noble Verdicts Are not Enough," *Al-Ahram Weekly*, Issue No. 781, February 9-15, 2006.

83 **"Q&A**: The Muhammad's Cartoons Row," *BBC News*, February 7, 2006, available from: http://news.bbc.co.uk see also : www.icsfp.com

84 **Qur'an, Surah 22, Verse 77**

85 **Qur'an, Surah 74, Verses 42-44**

86 **Qur'an, Surah 107, Verses 1-3**

87 **Jamie** Wilson, "The Culture of Charitable Work", *The Guardian*, June 21, 2002

88 **Ibid.**

89 **Jonathan** Benthall and Jerome Bellion, *The Charitable Crescent*, (1992), p. 85

90 **Qur'an, Surah 9, Verse 60**

91 *Sahih al-Bukhari*

92 **Qur'an, Surah 2, Verse 177**

93 *Sahih al-Bukhari*

94 **Al-Albani**, *Silsilah al-Ahadith al-Sahihah*

95 **Wasseem** ad-Dandashee, "بعد تشكيل هيئة عامة في السعودية تشرف على الأعمال الخيرية"*al-Watan* Arabic Newspaper, March30, 2004.

96 **Unpublished** field research by Dr. Mayke Kaag, Leiden University, Holland, 2004.

97 **Ibid.**

98 **Past** Senior Policy Analyst at the Institute for Research: Middle Eastern Policy (IRmep), Tanya C. Hsu is the author of a revealing book (as of print, soon-to-be published) entitled *Target: Saudi Arabia*. Her articles are widely published throughout the Middle East, Europe and the United States.

99 **Personal** communication.

100 **Statements** of the Saudi Interior Minister, a*l-Watan*, November 27, 2002

101 **Graham** Hancock, *Lords of Poverty*, (The Atlantic Monthly Press, 1989).p8.

102 **For** more information about the Paris and Geneva conventions see: www.IBH.fr

103 **Jonathan** Benthall & Jerome Bellion Jourdan, *The Charitable Crescent* (1992)

104 **James** D. Wolfensohn, "World Bank meeting: Ending poverty is the key to stability", *International Herald Tribune*, September 30, 2004. Available from: www.iht.com/articles/2004/09/30/edwolf

105 **Ibid.**

106 **Ibid**.

107 **"Taysir** Alluni: A Reporter Behind Bars," January 12, 2005, available from: http://english.aljazeera.net

108 **"US** Accused Over Jailing Reporters," *BBC News*, December 14, 2005, available from: http://news.bbc.co.uk/go/pr/fr/~/2/hi/americas/4527652.stm

Chapter II

[109] **Thom** Shanker and Eric Schmitt, "The Reach of War: Hearts and Minds; Pentagon Weighs Use of Deception in a Broad Arena", *New York Times*, 13/12/2004

[110] **Ibid.**

[111] **Noam** Chomsky, *Media Control*, p.14

[112] **Ibid.**

[113] **Ibid.**

[114] **Chomsky**, *Media Control* p. 42

[115] **Wendell** Belew Jr. "Remarks of M. Wendell Belew, Jr. prepared for Delivery at the Conference on Partnership for Peace and Development in Palestine" *The British Library*, London, 16 December, 2004.

[116] **David** B. Ottaway, "Groups US Battle Over Global Terrorist Label", *The Washington Post*, November 14, 2004.

[117] **Ibid.**

[118] **Edward** Said, "A Devil Theory of Islam," *The Nation*, August 12, 1996.

[119] **"The Non**-Governmental Order", *The Economist*, Vol.353, Issue 8149, 12 November, 1999, p20.

[120] **Judith** Miller, "Some Charities Suspected of Terrorist Role", *New York Times*, February 19, 2000.

[121] **Ibid.**

[122] *Newsweek*, September 2, 2004.

[123] *Quds* Press, February 12, 2000.

[124] *IslamOnLine*, September 14, 2003.

[125] **Speech** of an official at the Treasury Department before a branch committee at the US Senate; available from: www.Islamdaily.net

[126] **Ibid.**

[127] *Afaq* Arabyiah, August 21, 2003.

[128] *Afaq* Arabyiah, August 21, 2003.

[129] **Speech** given by an official at the Treasury Department before a branch committee at the US Senate.

[130] *Al-Watan* August 2, 2003.

[131] *Al-Watan*, March 1, 2004. American reaction to this decision is discussed in chapter seven.

[132] *Al-Hayat*, March 2005.

[133] *Al-Watan*, December 5, 2002.

[134] **Ibid**

[135] www.Islamtoday.net, December 12, 2002

[136] *As-Sunnah* magazine, April 2003.

[137] www.Islamonline.net

[138] *Ash-Sharq* al-Awsat, May 2, 2002.

[139] **Ibid.**

[140] *Ash-Sharq* al-Awsat, May 2, 2002.

[141] www.Islamtoday.net, [cited December 12, 2002].

[142] *Ash-Sharq al-Awsat*, July, 2003.

[143] *Al-Hayat*, January 3, 2003.

[144] *Ash Sharq Al Awsat*, August, 2003.

[145] *Afaq Arabiyah* August 21, 2003.

[146] *Al Quds Al Arabi*, August 7, 2002.

[147] *Afaq Arabyiah*, August 21, 2003.

[148] *Ash Sharq Al Awsat*, August, 2003.

[149] *Islam Today*, May 31, 2003.

[150] *Ash-Sharq al-Awsat*, July 2003.

[151] *Afaq Arabiyah* August 21, 2003, and a*l-Bayan*, September 28, 2001.

[152] *Ash-Sharq al-Awsat*, July 2003

[153] **Ibid.**

[154] **Ibid.**

[155] **Ibid.**

[156] **Matthew** Levitt, *Washington Institute for Near East Policy*, September 10, 2003.

[157] *Al Watan* August 12, 2001.

[158] *Attajdid*, issue 727, available from: www.attajdid.press.ma/

[159] **Matthew** Levitt, Charitable and Humanitarian Organizations in the Network of International Terrorist Financing, *Washington Institute for Near East Policy*, August 1, 2002.

[160] **Matthew** Levitt, "Subversion from Within: Saudi funding of Islamic Extremist Groups Undermining U.S. Interests and the War on Terror from within the United States", *Washington Institute for Near East Policy*, September 10, 2002.

[161] *Al-Hayat*, June 22, 2002.

[162] *Okaz*, January 18, 2002.

[163] www.islammemo.com , November 18, 2002.

[164] **Ibid**.

[165] **William** Galberson, "Focus Changes in Terror Case Against Sheik," *The New York Time*s, January 20, 2005.

[166] **William** Glaberson, "Terror Case Hinges on a Wobbly Key Player," *The New York Times*, November 27, 2004.

[167] **Caryle** Murphy and Del Quentin Wilber, "Terror Informant Ignites Himself Near White House," *The Washington Post*, November 16, 2004.

[168] **Jeralyn**, Ashcroft: "Another Terror Case Bites the Dust", January 20, 2005, at: www.Talkleft.com

[169] www.aljazeera.net , December 2003.

[170] **Ibid.**

[171] **The text** of the American demands was published in Arabic by a*l-Hayat* newspaper on January 14, 2002. The English copy was provided by a*l-Hayat* offices in London.

[172] *Al-Hayat* January 14, 2002.

[173] *Al-Watan*, August 8, 2002; and a*l-Madinah*, March 22, 2002.

[174] **Attorney** General Ashcroft Briefing on New Anti-Terrorism Immigration Policies, available from: http://usinfo.state.gov

[175] **Douglas Farah**, "U.S. Pinpoint Top Al-Qaeda Financiers; Treasury Official Heads to Europe to Seek Help in Freezing Backers' Assets", *The Washington Post*, October 18, 2002.

[176] *Al-Bayan*, United Arab Emirates newspaper, December 9, 2001.

[177] **Matthew Levitt**, "Charitable and Humanitarian Organizations in the Network of International Terrorist Financing", *Washington Institute for Near East Policy*, August 1, 2002.

[178] **Ibid**.

[179] **Benjamin Duncan**, "American Islamic Charities in Crisis", December 2003. available from: www.english.aljazeera.net

[180] **Ibid.**

[181] **Ibid.**

[182] *Afaq Arabiyah*, August 21, 2003.

[183] **Ayesha** Ahmad and Neveen A. Salem, "Exclusive: Federal Agents Target Muslims, Raid Organizations and Homes" www.islam-online.net/English/News/2002-03/21/article03.shtml , March 21, 2003.

[184] **Marwa** El-Naggar, " 'Operation Green Quest' Singles Out Muslims" www.Islam-online.net/English/News/2002-03/21/article10.shtml, March 21, 2003.

[185] *Ash-Sharq al-Awsat*, May 2, 2002.

[186] www.Islamtoday.net, June 7, 2003.

[187] *Al-Majallah magazine*, issue 1255, February 29, 2004.

Chapter III:

[188] *National Commission on Terrorist Attacks Upon the United States, Ch. 7, Al-Haramain Case Study*, p.120. Available from: http://www.9-11commission.gov/staff_statement/911_TerrFin_Ch7 [25/09/2003].

[189] **Debra** Morris, "Charities and Terrorism: The Charity Commission Response", *The International Journal of Not-for-Profit Law*, April 10, 2002

[190] **E. Anthony** Wayne, Assistant Secretary for Economic and Business Affairs Testimony Before the Senate Banking Committee, Washington, DC, September 25, 2003.

[191] **Ibid.**

[192] **Jon** Kyl, "Terrorism and the spread of Wahhabi power in the United States", *Front Page*, July 3,, 2003.

[193] **David** Rennie, "Bible Belt Missionaries Set Out on a 'War for Souls' in Iraq", *The Telegraph*, UK, December 28, 2003.

[194] **Janice** D'Arcy, "Some Organizations Mix Missionary Work with Aid," *The Baltimore Sun*, January 8, 2005.

[195] ***National*** *Commission on Terrorist Attacks Upon the United States, Ch. 7, Al-Haramain Case Study*, p.114. Available from: http://www.9-11commission.gov/staff_statement/911_TerrFin_Ch7 [25/09/2003].

[196] **Ibid.**

[197] ***Ash Sharq*** *al Awsat*, Arabic newspaper, 6/10/2004.

[198] ***National*** *Commission on Terrorist Attacks Upon the United States, Ch. 7, Al-Haramain Case Study*, p.122. Available from: http://www.9-11commission.gov/staff_statement/911_TerrFin_Ch7 [25/09/2003].

[199] **Ibid. p.123**

[200] **Ibid. p.124**

[201] **Ibid. p125**

[202] **Ibid. p.125**

[203] **Ibid. p.126**

[204] **Ibid. p.127**

[205] **Ibid.**

[206] **Ibid.**

[207] **Ibid.**

[208] **Ibid.**

[209] **Ibid. p.129**

[210] **Ibid. p.115**

[211] **Ibid. p.114**

[212] **Ibid. p.114, see also footnote.**

[213] **Ibid. p. 114.**

[214] **Ibid.**

[215] **Ibid. p. 115.**

[216] **Ibid. p. 116.**

[217] **Ibid. p.118.**

[218] **Ibid. p. 116, 117**

[219] **Ibid. p. 118.**

[220] **Ibid. p. 120.**

[221] **Ibid. p. 120.**

[222] **Ibid. p. 128.**

[223] **See** previous excerpts from the 9/11 Commission Report.

[224] **In fact** all countries bear the responsibility for this closure, which is a result of political decisions. The closure should have been based on separate judicial rulings in the US, Saudi Arabia, Bosnia, Pakistan, Somalia, Indonesia, Kenya, and other countries. See at the end of this chapter how Holland judicial system dealt with al-Haramain Amsterdam branch.

[225] **Wasseem** ad-Dandashee, "بعد تشكيل هيئة عامة في السعودية تشرف على الأعمال الخيرية"*al-Watan*, Arabic Newspaper, March30, 2004.

[226] ***National Commission*** *on Terrorist Attacks Upon the United States, Ch. 7, Al-Haramain Case Study*, p.118

[227] **Lynne Bernabei** and David Cole, "Stereotyping hurts the war", *The Washington Times*, November 24, 2003, p. A23.

[228] **Ibid.**

[229] **Ibid.**

[230] **Ibid.**

[231] **Ibid.**

[232] **Ibid**.

[233] *Front Page*, December 30, 2002.

[234] **Jon Kyl,** "Terrorism and the spread of Wahhabi power in the United States", *Front Page*, July 3, 2003.

[235] **Ibid**.

[236] **Matthew Levitt** is a former FBI analyst at the Counterterrorism Operations Office of Anti-Terrorism. His bachelor degree was from Yeshiva University, a private Orthodox Jewish university. He is a senior fellow at the Washington Institute for Near East Policy.

[237] **One** of the most important Zionist pro-Israel institutes in the US; it is very hostile to Islamic organizations and movements. Most of its experts are among the right conservative Zionist Jews. It plays an influential role in the adopted policies towards Iraq, and the Middle East.

[238] **Matthew Levitt**, *Washington Institute for Near East Policy*, September 10, 2003.

[239] **M. A. Salloomi**, *the Charity Sector and Allegations of Terrorism*, (in Arabic) 3rd edition, p. 81.

[240] **Sahih Bukhari** (a collection of authentic sayings of the Prophet Muhammad)

[241] **Qur'an, Surah 2, verse 256**

[242] **Qur'an, Surah 10, Verse 99**

[243] **Qur'an, Surah 50 Verse 45**

[244] **Qur'an, Surah 34 Verse 25**

[245] *International Religious Freedom Report,* released by the Bureau of Democracy, Human Rights and Labor, U.S. Department of State, September 15, 2004.

[246] **Available** from: www.usa.gov/fsearch/index

[247] **Saudi Arabia**, International Religious Freedom Report 2005, Released by the Bureau of Democracy, Human Rights, and Labor on November 8, 2005, available from: www.state.gov/g//drl/rls/irf/2005/51609.htm

[248] **"Summary of Presentations** at Pace Law Review Symposium on Anti-Terrorist Financing Guidelines," published on December 12, 2004, *OMB Watch*, available from: www.ombwatch.org

[249] **Grace Halsell**, *Forcing God's Hand: Why Millions Pray for a Quick Rapture-And Destruction of Planet Earth,* comments from back cover, Amana publications, 2003 edition.

[250] **Ibid. p. 18.**

[251] **"Survey** Shows Intolerance among Christian Activists", *Institute of First Amendment Studies*, September/ October 1997 survey. Available from: www.publiceye.org/ifas/fw/97oc/survey.html

252 **Protocol** *I, Additional to the Geneva Conventions of August 12, 1949, and relating to the Protection of Victims of International Armed Conflicts*, June 8, 1977.

253 **Protocol** *II, Additional to the Geneva Conventions of August 12, 1949, and relating to the Protection of Victims of Non-International Armed Conflicts, June 8, 1977.* Available from: www.globalissuesgroup.com/geneva/protocol2.html

254 **David** B. Ottaway, "Groups US Battle Over Global Terrorist Label", *The Washington Post*, November 14, 2004.

255 **Ibid.**

256 **Ibid.**

257 **Wendell** Belew Jr. *Remarks of M. Wendell Belew, Jr. prepared for Delivery at the Conference on Partnership for Peace and Development in Palestine,* The British Library, London, 16 December, 2004.

258 **Ibid.**

259 **Ibid.**

260 **Ibid.**

261 **Ibid.**

262 **Ibid.**

263 **David** B. Ottaway, "Groups US Battle Over Global Terrorist Label", *The Washington Post*, November 14, 2004.

264 **Ibid.**

265 **David** B. Ottaway, "Groups US Battle Over Global Terrorist Label", *The Washington Post*, November 14, 2004.

266 **Katherine** Hughes, "Crime of Compassion," January, 22, 2006, available from: www.dhafirtrial.net.

267 **Ibid.**

268 **Jennifer** Van Bergen, "The case of Dr. Dhafir," *CounterPunch.*

269 **Michael** Powell, "High-Profile N.Y. Suspect Goes on Trial", *Washington Post,* Oct 19 2004.

270 **Etgar** Lefkovits, "Carter calls for funding Palestinians," *Jerusalem Post,* January 26, 2006.

271 **William** fisher, "Sentence First, Verdict Afterward?" *Inter Press Service News Agency.*

272 **Jennifer Van Bergen**, "The case of Dr. Dhafir," *CounterPunch.*

273 **Michael Powell**, "High-Profile N.Y. Suspect Goes on Trial", *Washington Post,* Oct 19 2004.

274 **Jennifer Van Bergen**, "The case of Dr. Dhafir," *CounterPunch.*

275 **Michael Powell**, "High-Profile N.Y. Suspect Goes on Trial", *Washington Post,* Oct 19 2004.

276 **From** statement of Dr. Rafil Dhafir at his sentencing.

277 **Jennifer Van Bergen**, "The case of Dr. Dhafir," *CounterPunch.*

278 **A considerable** number of staff workers and managers worldwide have been designated, their assets seized or frozen, without court orders.

[279] **Amsterdam** court refused a request to continue to ban al-Haramain Dutch branch, registered as a charity in Holland. The ban was removed on March 31, 2005 when the judges found no evidence against the charity, in spite of the US and UN designations. The Dutch thorough investigations yielded no inculpating information against the charity. Justice is served when the judicial system is evenhanded.

[280] **Among** them are: The Saudi government, Prince Sultan Bin Abdil Aziz, Prince Turki al Faisal, Prince Muhammad al Faisal, Professor Salah Kamel, Dalla al Baraka Group, the late Shaikh Muhammad Abdallah al Jumeih, Shaikh Hamad al-Husaini, Professor Abdul Rahman Bin Mahfoodh, Tarak, Umar and Bikr AAl Laden, Ar-Rajhi Bank, the Saudi-American Bank, Arabi Bank.

[281] **For more** information on the issue, see most newspapers dated January 19, 2005.

[282] **Mark Freeman**, "The Seda-Saudi Connection", *Mail Tribune*, August 21, 2005.

[283] **"Charges** dismissed in al-Haramain Islamic charity case", *The Associated Press*, September 11, 2005.

[284] **"Charges** dismissed in al-Haramain Islamic charity case", *The Associated Press*, September 11, 2005.

[285] **Javid Hassan**, "Political Motive Seen in Closure of al-Haramain," *Arab News*, April 8, 2005.

[286] **Graig Smith** and Souad Mkhennet, "Algerian tells of Dark Odyssey in U.S. Hands," *The New York Times*, July 7, 2006.

[287] **Ibid.**

[288] **Ibid.**

[289] **Mary Beth Sheridan**, "U.S. Muslim Groups Cleared," *The Washington Post*, November 19, 2005.

[290] **David Yonke**, "Leaders Vigorously Rebut US Allegations; Board Members Deny Hamas Ties," *The Blade,* February 21, 2006, available from: http://toledoblade.com

Chapter IV

[291] **Jennifer Barrett**, "Q&A: 'We Have Barely Scraped the Surface'." *Newsweek,* September 30, 2003.

[292] **Matthew Levitt**, *Washington Institute for Near East Policy,* September 10, 2003

[293] **Matthew Levitt**, "Political Economy for Middle East Terrorism" *Washington Institute for Near East Policy,* January 15, 2003

[294]

Matthew Levitt, "Stemming the Flow of Terrorist Financing: Practical and Conceptual Challenges" *Washington Institute for Near East Policy,* spring 2003

[295] **Ibid.**

[296] **Jeremy Scott***, BBC Online*, available from: http://news.bbc.co.uk.go/pr/fr/-h/arabic/world_news/newsid_3194000.3194324.html, March 18, 2002.

[297] **Matthew Levitt**, "Political Economy for Middle East Terrorism" *Washington Institute for Near East Policy*, January 15, 2003

[298] **Matthew Levitt**, "Stemming the Flow of Terrorist Financing: Practical and Conceptual Challenges", *Washington Institute for Near East Policy*, spring 2003

[299] **Ibid.**

[300] **David E. Kaplan**, "The Saudi Connection", *US News and World Report*, December 15, 2003.

[301] **Christopher H. Schmitt** and Joshua Kurlantzick, "When Charity Goes Awry", *US News & World Report*, October 29, 2001.

[302] **Ibrahim Warde**, "Clean money, just a little soiled," *Le Monde Diplomatique*, November 2001.

[303] **Ibid.**

[304] **"Safeguarding** Charities in the War on Terror", OMB Watch, October 2005. Available from: http://www.ombwatch.org

[305] **Ibid.**

[306] **Ibid.**

[307] **Ibrahim Warde**, "Clean money, just a little soiled," *Le Monde Diplomatique*, November 2001.

[308] **Ibid.**

[309] **Ibid.**

[310] **Ibid.**

[311] **Ibid.**

[312] **Hassan Barise**, "War on terror hits Somali orphans", *BBC News*, May 20, 2003. Available from: http://news.bbc.co.uk/go/pr/fr/-/2/hi/africa/3044485.stm

[313] **Sarah Toyne** and Jeremy Scott-Joynt, "Following the money trail", *BBC News Online*, November 7, 2001. Available from: http://news.bbc.co.uk/2/hi/business/1553153.stm

[314] **Ibid.**

[315] **Ibid.**

[316] **Sarah Toyne** and Jeremy Scott-Joynt, "Following the money trail", *BBC News Online*, November 7, 2001. Available from: http://news.bbc.co.uk/2/hi/business/1553153.stm

[317] **Ibid.**

[318] **Ibid**

[319] ***Safeguarding*** Charities in the War on Terror, OMB Watch, October 2005. Available from: http://www.ombwatch.org

[320] **Ibid**

[321] **Debra Morris**, "Charities and Terrorism: The Charity Commission Response", *The International Journal of Not-for-Profit Law*, April 10, 2002

[322] **Sean O'Neill**, "Britain rejects Bush's charges against charity", *The Telegraph*, September 25, 2003.

[323] **Jeevan Vasagar**, "Palestinian relief funds frozen", *The Guardian*, August 28, 2003.

[324] **"Charity Commission** policy on charities and their alleged links to terrorism", available from: www.charity-commission.gov.uk/tcc/terrorism.asp

[325] **Debra Morris**, "Charities and Terrorism: The Charity Commission Response", *The International Journal of Not-for-Profit Law*, April 10, 2002

[326] **Ibid.**

[327] **See letter** from BOND to British foreign minister at: www.interpal.org

[328] **Debra Morris**, "Charities and Terrorism: The Charity Commission Response", *The International Journal of Not-for-Profit Law*, April 10, 2002.

[329] **Debra Morris**, "Charities and Terrorism: The Charity Commission Response", *The International Journal of Not-for-Profit Law*, April 10, 2002

[330] **Jamie Wilson**, "The Culture of Charitable Work", *The Guardian*, June 21, 2002

[331] **For more** information, visit the charity's website, www.islamic-relief.com

[332] **Jamie Wilson**, "The Culture of Charitable Work", *The Guardian*, June 21, 2002

[333] **Matthew Levitt**, "Political Economy for Middle East Terrorism" *Washington Institute for Near East Policy*, January 15, 2003

[334] **Gideon Burrows**, "Under suspicion," *The Guardian*, February 28, 2002.

[335] **Ibid.**

[336] **Ibid.**

[337] **Jeremy Scott-Joynt**, "Interpal under the microscope", *BBC News Online*, October 16, 2003.

[338] **Ibid.**

[339] **Andrew Purvis**, "Money Trouble," *Time Europe Magazine*, July 1, 2002.

[340] *Al Mujtama Magazine*, Kuwait, issue 1602, May 22, 2004.

[341] **David Kaplan**, "The Saudi Connection", *US News and World Report*, December 15, 2003.

[342] **The readers** remarks here many contradictory measures taken toward al-Haramain, and the apology that followed afterward, then the closing of one of its offices for reasons other than terrorism. Chapter seven will discuss this aspect in detail.

[343] **Andrew Purvis**, "Money Trouble," *Time Europe Magazine*, July 1, 2002.

[344] **Ibid.**

[345] **Ibid.**

[346] **Ibid.**

[347] **Ibrahim Satti** has resigned after all attempts to open the schools have failed due to US pressure. The buildings were put under the charge of the Islamic Shaikhdom, which is itself under financial duress.

[348] **Ibid.**

[349] **Jonathan Benthall** and Jérôme Bellion-Jourdan, *The Charitable Crescent*, Ch. 6.

[350] **Field investigation.**

Chapter V:

[351] **Zbigniew Brzezinski**, *The Great Chessboard*, Basic Books, 1997.

[352] **Samuel P. Huntington**, *The Clash of Civilizations and the Remaking of World Order*, Simon & Shuster, 1998.

[353] **Palestine** was part of the Muslim land for 14 centuries, where Muslims coexisted peacefully with Christian minorities, except at intermittent times during the Crusade Wars. Palestine was under the British mandate from 1914 to1938, and it was then that Britain opened the door for Jews around the world to migrate to Palestine. Immediately after Britain left Palestine, the Jews announced the establishment of their state on Palestinian land except the West Bank and Gaza, which were occupied later on in 1967. Palestinians endured dispossessions, forced migrations with no right to return, and genocide.

[354] **For** more information see www.arabji.com/palestine/govt.htm

[355] **United States** State Department, Historic Background Office of the Historian, Bureau of Public Affairs, *The United States and the Global Coalition Against Terrorism, September 2001-December 2003*, available from: www.state.gov/r/pa/ho/pubs/fs/5889.htm

[356] **Delinda C. Hanley**, "Islamic Charities Frozen Before Eid as Jewish Charities Support Settlers, Soldiers," *The Washington Report on Middle East Affairs*, January, February, 2002.

[357] ***Ash-Sharq** al-Awsat*, August 29, 2003.

[358] **Delinda C. Hanley**, "Islamic Charities Frozen Before Eid as Jewish Charities Support Settlers, Soldiers," *The Washington Report on Middle East Affairs*, January, February, 2002.

[359] **Ibid.**

[360] **Ibid.**

[361] ***Al-Hayat**, London, (Safar 6 1425 H), 2004

[362] www.Islamonline.net , November 4, 2003.

[363] **Dr. Haytham Manna**, "A Scream Before the Kill, the future of humanitarian and charitable associations in the Saudi Arabian Kingdom", *International Bureau for Humanitarian NGOs*.

[364] www.aljazeera.net (29/6/1435)

[365] ***Al-Hayat**, London, issue 14904, January 16, 2004.

[366] ***Ar Riyadh Daily** news*, issue 13309, December 1, 2004.

[367] **Delinda C. Hanley**, "Islamic Charities Frozen Before Eid as Jewish Charities Support Settlers, Soldiers," *The Washington Report on Middle East Affairs*, January, February, 2002.

[368] **Ibid.**

[369] **Ibid.**

[370] **For more** details on donations and grants to Israel see: www.us-israel.org/jsource and www.usaid.gov

[371] **Christopher H. Schmitt** and Joshua Kurlantzick, "When charity goes awry", *US News and World Report*, October 29, 2001.

[372] **Ibid.**

[373] **Dr. Haytham Manna**, a*l-Hayat* February 1, 2002.

374 **Zainab Hafni**, زينب حفني "التسقط الحرية و لتحايا العبودية" ash-*Sharq al-Awsat*, issue 8509, March 16, 2002.

375 **Brittany Jarvis**, "Physical, spiritual death threatens 26.7 million Afghans," *International Mission Board, Southern Baptist Convention*, October 23, 2001.

376 **Ibid.**

377 **Janice D'Arcy**, "Some organizations mix missionary work with aid," *The Baltimore Sun*, January 8, 2005.

378 *Al-Qabas* Kuwaiti newspaper, March 12, 2002.

379 **Pierre Hazan**, "Washington, chauffard du droit international", *Libération*, February 15, 2002.

380 **Dexter Filkins**, "Flaws in U.S. Air War Left Hundreds of Civilians Dead," *New York Times*, July 21, 2002.

381 **Thomas L. Friedman**, "Yes, a war partly over oil," *The international Herald Tribune*, January 6, 2003.

382 **Patrick J. Buchanan**, "Neocons Setting Up Rumsfeld as Iraq Fall Guy," *Washington Report On Middle East Affairs*, March 2005, p26.

383 **See** www.newamericancentury.org/statementofprinciple.htm.

384 **Paul Findley**, "What is Bush's Real Goal in Iraq?" *Washington Report On Middle East Affairs*, March 2005, p 27.

385 **Available** from: www.eia.doe.gov

386 *Al-Mujtama* Magazine, October 22, 2004.

387 **Timna Rosenheimer**, "'This War is Genocide', an interview with former Us Attorney General Ramsey Clark", *Ha'aretz*, January 3, 2003.

388 **"Letter on Iraq** by Former Attorney General Ramsey Clark to UN Security Council", available from: www.progressiveaustin.org/iraqlark.htm

389 **Munir Akash**, *The Right to Sacrifice the Other: The American Genocides*, Beirut: Riad El-Rayyes Books, June 2002.

390 **Christopher Hitchens**, "Songs Fit for Heroes," *The Nation*, February 1989.

391 **David Rennie**, "Bible Belt Missionaries Set Out on a 'War for Souls' in Iraq", *The Telegraph*, UK, December 28, 2003.

392 **Shawn Hendricks**, "Disaster relief teams ready to serve in Iraq," *International Mission Board*, March 25, 2003.

393 **Ibid.**

394 **David Rennie**, "Bible Belt Missionaries Set Out on a 'War for Souls' in Iraq," *The Telegraph*, UK, December 28,2003.

395 **Ibid.**

396 **Ibid.**

397 **Fahmi Huwaydi**, مجلة المجلة، فهمي هويدي "حرب الأرواح في العراق", *al-Majallah Magazine*, issue 1250, January 31, 2004.

398 www.cair-net.org

399 **David Rennie**, "Bible Belt Missionaries Set Out on a 'War for Souls' in Iraq," *The Telegraph*, UK, December 28,2003.

400 **Janice D'Arcy**, "Some organizations mix missionary work with aid," *The Baltimore Sun*, January 8, 2005.

[401] **Jackson Lears**, "How a War Became a Crusade," *New York Times*, March 11, 2003.

[402] **"Evangelist Bush**," available from: http://bushwatch.org/evangelist.htm

[403] http://elosboa.masrawy.com/13042003/132212news.htm

[404] **Rod Nordland** and BabakDehghanpisheh, "Rules of Engagement," *Newsweek*, November 29, 2004.

[405] **Edward Wong**, "The Reach of War: Prisoners; American jails in Iraq Bursting With Detainees," *New York Times*, March 4, 2005.

[406] **Naomi Klein**, "In Iraq, the US does eliminate those who dare to count the dead," *The Guardian*, December 4, 2004.

[407] **Ibid.**

[408] **Ibid**. More information could be found in Basel An-Nairab's book *Killing of the Witnesses* where he documented the crimes committed against the news reporters and journalists.

[409] **The term** "Sunni minority" appeared after the fall of Baghdad under the American attack. In reality Sunnis are the majority in Iraq.

[410] www.iraqirabita.org

[411] **M. Junaid Alam**,"Civilization versus Barbarism?" Interview with Noam Chomsky, available from www.lefthook.org/Interviews/AlamChomsky122304.html.

[412] **Ibid.**

[413] **Ibid.**

[414] **Ibid.**

[415] **Ibid.**

[416] **Opinion around** the World: Nine-Country AP/Ipsos Poll, *Buy American? Global Publics Question U.S. Export Of Consumer Goods And Democracy*, February 23, 2005. See also: *ash-Sharq al-Awsat*, زين العبادين الركابي, "الجهاد على الديمقراطية: من ضهدا ينقبل ضهدا ما بنقبل امب الكيرم علو", March 3, 2005.

[417] **Helena Cobban**, "Unintended consequences of war," *The Christian Science Monitor*, January 9, 2003.

[418] **Human Rights Watch**, *Off Target, The Conduct of the War and Civilian Casualties in Iraq*, summary and recommendations

[419] **Amnesty International**, *Iraq: Looting, lawlessness and humanitarian consequences*, Report number MDE14/085/2003, April 11, 2003.

[420] **Amnesty International**, *Iraq, One year on the human rights: situation remains dire*, report number MDE !4/006/2004, March 18, 2004.

[421] **Karl Vick**, "Children Pay Cost of Iraq's Chaos; Malnutrition Nearly double what it was Before Invasion," *The Washington Post*, November 21, 2004 p A01.

[422] **Medact**, *Enduring Effects of War, Health in Iraq 2004*, Published in London, UK, 2004, by Medact.

[423] **Gilbert Burnham**, Shannon Doocy, Elizabeth Dzeng, Riyadh Lafta, and Les Roberts, *The Human Cost of the War in Iraq A Mortality Study, 2002-2006* available: http://web.mit.edu/CIS/pdf/Human_Cost_of_War.pdf

[424] ***Apdated Iraq Survey** Affirms Earlier Mortality Estimates*, Johns Hopkins, Bloomberg School of Public Health, Public Health News Center, October 11, 2006.

[425] **Paul Reynolds**, "Huge Gaps Between Iraq death Estimates," *BBC news website*, 20, 10, 2006. Available at:
http://news.bbc.co.uk/go/pr/fr/-/2/hi/middle_east/6045112.stm

Chapter VI:

[426] **Jonathan Benthall** & Jerome Bellion Jourdan, *The Charitable Crescent* (1992), p. 36.
[427] **Jonathan Benthall** & Jerome Bellion Jourdan, *The Charitable Crescent* (1992), p. 4.
[428] **Kenneth R. Timmerman**, "Documents detail Saudi Terror Links," *Insight on the New* magazine, May 20, 2002.
[429] **Michael Scott Doran**, "The Saudi Paradox", *Foreign Affairs*, January/February, 2004.
[430] **David B. Ottaway**, "US Eyes Money Trails of Saudi-Backed Charities", *The Washington Post*, August 19, 2004.
[431] **Ibid.**
[432] **Ibid.**
[433] **Josh Lefkowitz** and Jonathan Levin, "Kingdom Cover," *National Review Online*, February 11, 2004.
[434] **David B**. Ottaway, "US Eyes Money Trails of Saudi-Backed Charities", *The Washington Post*, August 19, 2004.
[435] **Ibid.**
[436] *National Commission* on Terrorist Attacks Upon the United States, Ch. 7, Al-Haramain Case Study, p 115. Available from:
http://www.9-11commission.gov/staff_statement/911_TerrFin_Ch7 [25/09/2003].
[437] *National Commission* on Terrorist Attacks Upon the United States, Ch. 7, Al-Haramain Case Study, p 115. Available from:
http://www.9-11commission.gov/staff_statement/911_TerrFin_Ch7 [25/09/2003].
[438] **Ibid.**
[439] **Jennifer Barrett**, "Q&A: 'We Have Barely Scraped the Surface'." *Newsweek*, September 30, 2003.
[440] **Matthew Levitt**, "Charity Begins in Riyadh," *Weekly Standard*, February 2, 2004.
[441] **Josh Lefkowitz** & Jonathan Levin, "Kingdom Cover", *National Review Online* February 11, 2004.
[442] **Ibid.**
[443] *New York Post* April 6, 2003.
[444] **Jon Kyl**, "Terrorism and the spread of Wahhabi power in the United States," *Front Page*, July 3,, 2003.
[445] **Simon Henderson** testimony before the Senate Judicial Committee Subcommittee of Terrorism September 10, 2003.
[446] **Ibid.**

[447] **Ibid.**

[448] **Bill Berkowitz**, "Pat Robertson Counts His Federal Blessings," *Tom Paine*, available at: http://liberalslikechrist.org/about/robertsonblessings.html

[449] *Giving USA 2002*, p. 98.

[450] **White House Office** of Faith-Base and Community Initiatives, *Regulatory Changes*, available from: www.whitehouse.gov/governemnt/fbci/reg-changes.html

[451] **White House Office** of Faith-Based and Community Initiatives, *Guidance to Faith-Based and Community Organizations on Partnering with the Federal Government*, available from www.fbci.gov

[452] **Ibid.**

[453] **Ibid.**

[454] **Ibid.**

[455] **Ibid.**

[456] **Ibid.**

[457] **Ibid.**

[458] **Ibid.**

[459] **"In honor of Bill of Rights Day**: A Look at the First Amendment," *OMB Watch*, December 15, 2003. www.ombwatch.org

[460] "Bush Ends 'Discrimination' Against Faith-Based Charities", *Agence France Press*, January 15, 2004.

[461] **Josh Lefkowitz** & Jonathan Levin, "Kingdom Cover", *National Review Online*, February 11, 2004.

[462] **Dore Gold**, "Reining in Riyadh", *New York Post*, April 6, 2003.

[463] **Jonathan Benthall** & Jerome Bellion Jourdan, *The Charitable Crescent* (1992), pp. 17, 18.

[464] **Ibid. p. 30**.

[465] **Ibid. p. 31.**

[466] **Ibid. p. 92**

[467] **Jonathan Benthall**, *Humanitarianism and Islam After 11 September*, Humanitarian Policy Group report 14, (London: ODI 2003).

[468] **Ibid.**

[469] **Jonathan Benthall** & Jerome Bellion Jourdan, *The Charitable Crescent* (1992), p. 111.

[470] **Karin Von Hippel**, *The Roots of Religious Extremist Terrorism*, Center for Defense Studies at King's College London.

[471] **Robert Fisk**, "How can the US bomb this tragic people?" *The Independent*, September 23, 2001.

[472] *Afghanistan: The Making of US Policy, 1973-1990*, introductory essay to the National Security Archive microfiche collection, published in 1990.

[473] **James A. Phillips**, "The US and Pakistan at the Crossroads," *The Heritage Foundation*, December 7, 1982.

[474] **Jonathan Benthall** & Jerome Bellion Jourdan, *The Charitable Crescent* (1992), p. 71.

[475] **Jonathan Benthall** & Jerome Bellion Jourdan, *The Charitable Crescent* (1992), p. 111.

[476] **Matthew Levitt**, "The Two Faces of Saudi Arabia", *Weekly Standard*, June 30, 2003.

[477] **David E. Kaplan**, "The Saudi Connection", *US News & World Report*, December15, 2003.

[478] *New York Times*, July 7 2002.

[479] **Graham Hancock**, *Lords of Poverty*

[480] **Dr. Ghazi al Qasibi**, د. غازي القصيبي "أمريكي والسعودية، حملة إعلامية أم مواجهة سياسية؟" ص115

[481] **Robert Fisk**, "A Strange Kind of Freedom," *The Independent*, July 9, 2002.

[482] **Mohammed Abdullah al-Roken**, "The West Has Political Motives for Targeting Islamic Charities," *The Daily Star*, July 27, 2002.

[483] *Gulf Affairs Magazine* No. 31, 2002, and *al-Ray al-Aam* (Sudan), June 7, 2002.

[484] **Karin Von Hippel**, *The Roots of Religious Extremist Terrorism*, Center for Defense Studies at King's College, University of London.

[485] *Al-Kawthar* **magazine**, issue 26, 2004.

[486] **"Hindu Swayamsevak** Sangh, Registered Charity No. 267309", UK Charity Commission investigation, available from: www.charity-commission.gov.uk/investigations/inquiryreports/hss.asp

[487] *Al-Riyadh* **Saudi newspaper**, December 16, 2002.

[488] **Angana Chatterji**, "Unholy Alliance, The India Development Relief Fund and Hindutva", *Dissident Voice*, December 5, 2002.

[489] **Jonathan Benthall** & Jerome Bellion Jourdan, *The Charitable Crescent* (1992), pp. 154, 155.

[490] **Jonathan Benthall** & Jerome Bellion Jourdan, *The Charitable Crescent* (1992), p. 155.

[491] **Jonathan Benthall** & Jerome Bellion Jourdan, *The Charitable Crescent* (1992), p. 156.

[492] **"Who is Victor Yushenko?"**, article translated from the Russian and is available from: http://informacia.ru/facts/ushenko-facts.htm

[493] *Al-Mujtama Magazine* (Kuwait), issue 1644, March 26, 2005.

[494] **Steve Gutterman**, "Russian Official: US using Non-Governmental Groups to Spy", *The Associated Press*, May 12, 2005.

[495] **Steve Gutterman**, "Russian Official: US using Non-Governmental Groups to Spy", *The Associated Press*, May 12, 2005.

[496] **Delinda C. Hanley**, "Islamic Charities Frozen Before Eid as Jewish Charities Support Settlers, Soldiers," *Washington Report on Middle East Affairs*, January, February, 2002.

[497] **Ibid.**

[498] **Delinda C. Hanley**, "Islamic Charities Frozen Before Eid as Jewish Charities Support Settlers, Soldiers," *Washington Report on Middle East Affairs*, January, February, 2002.

[499] **Peter F. Drucker**, *Managing for the Future, the 1990s and Beyond*, Truman Talley Books / Plume, New York, November 1993, p. 203.

[500] See *Giving USA 2004*. pages iii and 10, See also Dr. M. A. al-Salloomi, (Charity Sector and Terror Allegations), p.338, د. السلومي، القطاع الخيري و قواعد إلى راهب. See also Judith Miller, "Some Charities Suspected of Terrorist Role", *New York Times*, February 19, 2000.

[501] **Kenneth R. Timmerman**, "Documents detail Saudi Terror Links," *Insight on the News* magazine, May 20, 2002.

[502] **Ibid**

[503] *Al-Watan* **newspaper**, July 1, 2002.

[504] *Al-Watan,* **July** 1, 2002. See also, Okaz, July 11, 2002.

[505] **Neil Clark**, "George Soros", *New Statesman*, June 2, 2003.

[506] *Al-Orobiyah* **magazine** September 2001.

[507] **Graham Hancock**, *Lords of Poverty*, p. 9 (The Atlantic Monthly Press, 1989).

[508] **Graham Hancock**, *Lords of Poverty*, p. 9 (The Atlantic Monthly Press, 1989).

[509] **Graham Hancock**, *Lords of Poverty*, p. 8 (The Atlantic Monthly Press, 1989).

[510] **Graham Hancock**, *Lords of Poverty*, p. 22 (The Atlantic Monthly Press, 1989).

[511] **Barry Yeoman**, "The Stealth Crusade", *Mother Jones*, May/June 2002.

[512] **Ibid.**

[513] **Ibid.**

[514] **Ibid.**

[515] **Ibid.**

[516] *North American Conference* on *Muslim Evangelization*, Glen Eyrie, Colorado Springs, Colorado (October 15-21, 1978), available from: www.lausanne.org/Brix?pageID=14390

Chapter VII:

[517] **Some of these motives** and objectives have been presented in the Paris Conference for Humanitarian NGOs, in January 9-10, 2003, organized by the International Bureau for Humanitarian NGOs, www.ibh.fr

[518] **Jonathan Benthall** & Jerome Bellion Jourdan, *The Charitable Crescent*, (1992).p 2

[519] **Ibid. p. 5.**

[520] **Ibid. p. 74.**

[521] **Hannah Cleaver**, "We Need a Counter-Balance to Islam, Says Danish Queen," *The Telegraph*, April 15, 2005.

[522] **"Danish Queen** Raps Radical Islam," *BBC News*, April 14, 2005.

[523] **Leopold Weiss**, *The Road to Mecca*.

[524] **Gustave Le Bon**, *La Civilisation Des Arabes*, livre V (translated).

[525] **Dr. Haytham Manna**, *A Scream before the Kill, the future of humanitarian and charitable associations in the Saudi Arabian Kingdom*, International Bureau for Humanitarian NGOs.

[526] *Islamic Charities and their Relation with Terror*, al-Jazeera TV Channel Symposium, October 21, 2000.

[527] **Glenn Kessler**, "Terrorists' Funding Targeted: Tracing Flow Has Been Hard in Past", *The Washington Post*, September 15, 2001.

[528] *Al-Quds al-Arabiyah*, April 29, 2002.

[529] **Ash-Sharq al-Awsat**, October 26, 2002.

[530] **Glenn Kessler**, "Terrorists' Funding Targeted: Tracing Flow Has Been Hard in Past", *The Washington Post*, September 15, 2001.

[531] **Jeff Cohen** and Norman Solomon, *Knee-jerk Coverage of Bombing Should Not Be Forgotten*, available from http://www.fair.org/media-beat/950426.html

[532] **John F. Sugg** "Steve Emerson's Crusade," *Fairness & Accuracy In Reporting*, February 199, http://www.fair.org

[533] **Ibid.**

[534] *The Jewish Monthly*, March 1995.

[535] **Senate Judiciary** Committee Report, April 27, 1995.

[536] **Az-Zaitouna**, Arabic newspaper, July 16, 2002.

[537] **"The War on Islamic Charities** is going on in Palestine on the Global and Local Levels," a*l-Asr Electronic Magazine*, September 21, 2002. www.asr.com. و ايلود ةلصاوتم نيطسلف ي ةيمالسإلا ةيريخلا تاسسؤملا ىلع برحلا" محلحايا"، جلم لعلا رصعلا ةيمويلا ةيكتلكالا، 21/9/2002.م.

[538] **"Dangers Facing Middle** East, Perils of Inaction Should Not Be Neglected, Special Coordinator Tells Securiy Council", *United Nations Press Release*, SC/7603, December, 16, 2002.

[539] **Pual Findley**, *Silent no more*, Amana Publications, Fourth edition 2003, p. 85

[540] **Fahmi Huwaydi**, *al-Majallah Magazine*, April 19, 2002.

[541] **Timna Rosenheimer**, "'This War is Genocide', an interview with former Us Attorney General Ramsey Clark", *Ha'aretz*, January 3, 2003.

[542] **Abdus Sattar Ghazali**, "Iraq and Palestine are Two Sides of the Same Coin," *American Muslims Perspective online magazine*, available from: www.ampesrpective.com

[543] **M. Shahid Alam**, "Israel's Proxy War?", *Media Monitors*, available at: www.mediamonitors.net/mshahidalam1.html

[544] **Grace Halsell**, Israeli Extremists and Christian Fundamentalists: The Alliance," *Washington Report on Middle East Affairs*, December, 1988.

[545] **Grace Halsell**, *Forcing God's Hand*, Amana publications, 2003 edition, p 102.

[546] **Ibid. p 111**.

[547] *The 50 Most Influential Christians in America*, published by The Church Report Magazine, available from: http://www.thechurchreport.com.

[548] **Mohammed Abdullah al-Roken**, "The West Has Political Motives for Targeting Islamic Charities," *The Daily Star*, July 27, 2002.

[549] **Ibid.**

[550] **Grace Halsell**, "Israeli Extremists and Christian Fundamentalists: The Alliance", *Washington Report on Middle East Affairs*, December 1988.

[551] **Grace Halsell**, "Israeli Extremists and Christian Fundamentalists: The Alliance", *Washington Report on Middle East Affairs*, December 1988.

[552] **Grace Halsell**, "Militant Coalition of Christian Fundamentalist and Jewish Orthodox Cults Plots Destruction of al-Aqsa Mosque", *Washington Report On Middle East Affairs*, March, 2000.

[553] **Ibid.**

[554] **Paul Findley**, *Silent no more*, Amana Publication, 2003 edition, p. 68.

555 *Los Angeles Herald-Examiner*, February 26 1989, p. G-1.
556 **Paul Findley**, *Silent no more*, Amana Publication, 2003 edition, p. 67.
557 **Ibid. p. 85.**
558 **Ibid.**
559 **Ibid. p. 86**
560 **Ibid, p. 68.**
561 **Ibid, p. 69.**
562 *Al-Hayat,* October 14, 2003.
563 *Al-Hayat*, October 14, 2003.
564 **Mohammed Abdullah al-Roken**, "The West Has Political Motives for Targeting Islamic Charities," *The Daily Star*, July 27, 2002.
565 **Michael Isikoff** and Mark Hosenball, "Charity and Terror", *Newsweek*, December 9, 2002.
566 **Michael Isikoff** and Mark Hosenball, "Terror Watch: The Money Trail", *Newsweek,* October 20, 2004.
567 **Ahmad Yusuf,** a*l-Siratul-Mustaqim*, October 1999.
568 **Colin Powell** interview with Jin Lehrer, *Online News Hour, PBS*, September 13, 2001, available from:
www.pbs.org/newshour/bb/military/july-dec01/powell_9-13.html
569 **Thomas Friedman**, "Foreign Affairs; The Real War", *New York Times*, November 27, 2001.
570 **Samuel Huntington**, *The Clash of Civilizations and the Remaking of World Order*, (Simon and Shuster, 1996), p. 217.
571 **Gideon Burrows**, "Under Suspicion", *The Guardian*, November 28, 2002.
572 **Gideon Burrows**, "Under Suspicion", *The Guardian*, November 28, 2002.
573 **"Summary of Presentations** at Pace Law Review Symposium on Anti-Terrorist Financing Guidelines," published on December 12, 2004, *OMB Watch*, available from: www.ombwatch.org
574 **"Market Watch**: Government scrutiny, Heightened publicity Leads to varying results for Muslim Charities," *Arab American Business Magazine*.
575 **Benjamin Duncan**, "US Islamic Charities in Trouble", *al-Jazeera*, November 23, 2003, available from: www.english.aljazeera.net
576 **Ibid**.
577 *Ash-Sharq al-Awsat*, November 23, 2002.
578 **See** www.islammemo.cc
579 **Samuel Huntington**, *The Clash of Civilizations and the Remaking of World Order,* (Simon and Shuster, 1996), p. 302.
580 **Ibid, p. 215**
581 **Qur'an, 83:26.**
582 **Lester Pearson**, *Democracy in World Politics*, (Princeton University Press, 1955), pp.83-84.
583 **"President Discusses** War on Terror at National Endowment for Democracy," available from: www.whitehouse.gov/news/releases/2005/10/20051006-3.html
584 **F. Gregory Gauss** III, "Can Democracy Stop Terrorism?" *Foreign Affairs*, September, October, 2005.

[585] **For more** on Islam and life see:
www.religionofislam.com and www.islam-guide.com

[586] **Islam is not for the Arabs only**. At the beginning of the 21ˢᵗ century, about 1.3 billion, 22% of the world population, were Muslims; only 25% of them are Arab.

[587] **Matthew** 4:10 Deut. 6:13

[588] **Leopold Weiss**, *The Road to Mecca*, p. 107, 108.

[589] **Ibid. p. 108.**

[590] **Ibid. p. 101.**

[591] **Ibid. p. 101.**

[592] **Ibid. p. 101, 102.**

[593] **Ibid. p.176.**

[594] **Leopold Weiss**, *Islam at the Crossroads*, from the foreword page.

[595] **For more** information on the history of Islam, see: www.lajna.net

[596] **For more** information, visit: www.todayislam.com.

[597] **Senator Paul Findley**'s interview with *al-Bayan Magazine*, September, 2003.

[598] **Qur'an, S.2, A.256.**

[599] **It is expressly explained in the Qur'an: "Allah forbids you not, with regard to those who fight you not for (your) Faith, nor drive you out of your homes from dealing kindly and justly with them, for Allah loves those who are just." (S. 60, A. 8), and it says: "But if they fight you, slay them." (S.2, A 191).**

[600] **On April 2002**, James Woolsey, former CIA director, said that the US has entered a fourth world war that will go on for years to come.

[601] **Gary Leupp**, *Challenging ignorance on Islam: a Ten-Point Primer for Americans*, July 24, 2002, available from www.counterpunch.org

[602] **Ibid.**

[603] **Fred Haliday**, *The Third World War*.

[604] **Leopold Weiss**, *The Road to Mecca*,p.121.

[605] **Senator Paul Findley**'s interview with *al-Bayan Magazine*, September, 2003.

[606] **Prince Charles** speech available from: www.muslimheritage.com

[607] **Samuel Huntington**, *The Clash of Civilizations and the Remaking of World Order*, (Simon and Shuster, 1996), p. 65.

[608] **Qur'an, S. 15, A. 9**

[609] **Maurice Bucailles**, *The Bible, the Qur'an, and Science*.

[610] **Takeshi Umehara**, "Ancient Japan Shows Post-Modernism the Way," *New Perspectives Quarterly*, No. 9, Spring 92.

[611] **Samuel Hunti**ngton, *The Clash of Civilizations*, p. 51.

[612] **Ibid. p. 321**.

Conclusion:

[613] **Book of John** 8:32.

[614] **French President** Jack Chirac's Speech at *The International Conference on Financing for Development*, Monterrey, Mexico, March 22, 2002.

[615] **James D. Wolfensohn**, "World Bank Meeting: Ending Poverty is the Key to Stability," *International Herald Tribune*, September 30, 2004.

[616] **Ibid.**

[617] **Ibid.**

[618] *Al-Mujtama Magazine*, February 12, 2005.

[619] **Emmanuel T**odd, *After the Empire: the Breakdown of the American Order*, Columbia University Press, (November 12, 2003), pp. 56-57.

[620] **Bush** has even appointed *Karen Hughes* to lead a campaign to ameliorate the US image abroad. See *ash-Sharq al-Awsat*, March 14, 2005.

[621] **Jason Szep**, "Cost of Iraq War Could Top $2 Trillion-Study", *Reuters*, January 9, 2006.

[622] **US casualty** status, available at the US Department of Defense website: www.defenselink.mil/news/casualty.pdf

[623] **Andrew Bacevich**, "We Aren't Fighting to Win Anymore," *Los Angeles Times*, February 20, 2005.

[624] **See** http://www.friendsofcharities.com/Default.stm

[625] **President George W. Bush** Statement in his Address to the Nation, September 11, 2001.

[626] **Qur'an, S. 61, A. 8**

[627] **Qur'an, S. 13, A. 17**

[628] **Colin L. Powell**, "U.S. Has Moral Obligation to Help Develop Poor Nations: By 2006, U.S. Aid Will Be As Great As Marshall Plan," *Global Viewpoint/ Foreign Policy* (Dist. Tribune Media Services, 1/3/05)

[629] **Christopher Patten**, *America and Europe: an Essential Partnership*, speech delivered at Chicago Council on Foreign Relations, Chicago, October 3, 2002.

[630] *A Statement of Conscience: Not In Our Name*, available from: www.notinourname.org

[631] **Jerrold Post**, *Psychology, Addressing the Case of Terrorism*, p. 7, Volume 1, The International Summit on Democracy, Terrorism and Security, March 8-11, 2005, Club de Madrid.